Reimagining Race
in Psychology

This important book brings together race, mental health and applied psychology, unpacking these areas from differing perspectives and offering new insights in support of training and development of practice.

The ability to work with issues of race and intersectionality within psychology is vital. Contributors with experience in counselling psychology and applied psychology from across varied social contexts and professional settings reframe and challenge familiar concepts such as movements to decolonise the curriculum, psychology and therapy. The chapters offer clinical vignettes, lived experiences and reflective questions to provoke the reader's thinking and engage with curiosity and sensitivity around cultural bias, discrimination, language, and the evolution of terminologies. This book captures the relationship between the ethos of counselling psychology and race, offering a much-needed guide for how to encompass race and racialised experiences in the training and practice of psychology. Rooted in the United Kingdom context but applicable more widely, contributions cover training, supervision, ethical practice, racial trauma, bias and diagnosis, and politics, as well as perspectives and approaches in practice at the intersection of race and gender, age, neurodiversity, sexuality, and spirituality.

This is a key resource for the continued development of in-training and experienced psychologists and psychotherapists, as well as other practitioners within the mental health and allied professions. It will also be of use to students in clinical training programmes and courses such as applied psychology, counselling, and psychotherapy.

Yetunde Ade-Serrano is a chartered and registered Practitioner Counselling Psychologist who works primarily in independent practice. She also works as an Expert Witness in Family Courts and as a Domestic Violence Risk Assessor. Dr Ade-Serrano is a UK-based practitioner.

Ohemaa Nkansa-Dwamena is a registered and chartered Counselling Psychologist and an Associate Professor in Counselling Psychology at City, University of London, UK. She works primarily in private practice with former clinical positions in NHS, forensic, higher education, and third sector settings.

BPS Professional Practice and Development Series
British Psychological Society

In partnership with the British Psychological Society (BPS), Routledge is pleased to present *BPS Professional Practice and Development*, a series of inspiring books designed to support continuing professional development. Offering accessible, evidence-based guides to deepen understanding, develop expertise and improve techniques and strategies, books in this series address key topics and challenges faced by psychologists in their research and practice, and include case studies and real-life examples in relevant contexts.

Each book strikes a careful balance between research and practical strategies, as well as resources for implementation and opportunities for reflection. Covering a broad range of subject areas for practitioners in a range of roles, titles may also be accompanied by digital resources to support professionals in employing new strategies and practices in their work.

Reimagining Race in Psychology
Challenging Narratives and Widening Perspectives in Training and Practice
Edited by Yetunde Ade-Serrano and Ohemaa Nkansa-Dwamena

For more information about this series, please visit: BPS Professional Practice and Development Series - Book Series - Routledge & CRC Press

Reimagining Race in Psychology

Challenging Narratives and Widening
Perspectives in Training and Practice

EDITED BY YETUNDE ADE-SERRANO AND
OHEMAA NKANSA-DWAMENA

Routledge
Taylor & Francis Group

LONDON AND NEW YORK

Designed cover image: Abstract Aerial Art/Getty Images

First published 2025
by Routledge
4 Park Square, Milton Park, Abingdon, Oxon OX14 4RN

and by Routledge
605 Third Avenue, New York, NY 10158

Routledge is an imprint of the Taylor & Francis Group, an informa business

© 2025 selection and editorial matter, Yetunde Ade-Serrano and
Ohemaa Nkansa-Dwamena; individual chapters, the contributors

British Library Cataloguing-in-Publication Data
A catalogue record for this book is available from the British Library

ISBN: 978-1-032-54119-8 (hbk)
ISBN: 978-1-032-54115-0 (pbk)
ISBN: 978-1-003-41524-4 (ebk)

DOI: 10.4324/9781003415244

Typeset in Dante and Avenir
by KnowledgeWorks Global Ltd.

Contents

List of figures and tables

Figures

Tables

About the editors

Yetunde Ade-Serrano, a chartered and registered Practitioner Counselling Psychologist works primarily in independent practice. She also works as an Expert Witness in Family Courts and as a Domestic Violence Risk Assessor. Dr Ade-Serrano is the co-founder of the Black and Asian Counselling Psychologists' Group established 13 years ago in the service of nurturing the identities of Black and Asian Counselling Psychologists as researchers and practitioners. Dr Ade-Serrano is a mentor and clinical supervisor with special interests in self-exploration and growth, Black women's identity, African Psychology and Spirituality, and meaning-making processes of individuals as it pertains to their survival in the world. Dr Ade-Serrano is an advocate for racial and cultural awareness, its implications for personal and professional growth.

Ohemaa Nkansa-Dwamena, is an Associate Professor of Counselling Psychology. She is a charted Counselling Psychologist and registered with the Health Care Professions Council in England. Ohemaa is also an advanced certified schema therapist and supervisor. As a practitioner psychologist and researcher, Ohemaa's work focuses on multiple identity negotiation, minority identities, and intersectionality and issues related to race, culture and mental health. Ohemaa works primarily in academia at City, University of London, and in private practice with former clinical positions in NHS, forensic, higher education, and third-sector settings. She is the co-founder of the Black and Asian Counselling Psychologists' Group established 13 years ago in the service of nurturing the identities of Black and Asian Counselling Psychologists as researchers and practitioners.

Contributors

Byron Al-Murri is an HCPC registered and BPS chartered Counselling Psychologist, clinical and research supervisor, and lecturer in Counselling Psychology at the undergraduate and doctoral level, at York St John University. Byron's research interests are in difference and diversity in psychotherapy, multicultural competence, and social justice, having recently published a chapter in the Handbook of Social Justice in Psychological Therapies. Power, politics, change (co-authored with Dr Jasmine Childs-Fegredo, 2023). He has worked as a clinician in the third sector, with clients from across the lifespan. He is a pluralistic practitioner, integrating CBT, psychodynamic psychotherapy, and humanistic philosophy.

Natalie V. Bailey, embodies a multifaceted role as a Counselling Psychologist, published author, lecturer, speaker, and trainer, alongside being the visionary founder of Well Minds Together. Beyond her impactful work within the NHS and private sectors, she specialises in addressing the nuanced needs of hard-to-reach communities, particularly focussing on the UK's Black Caribbean community to enhance access to psychological services. She is Black British of Black Caribbean decent. Through her roles in clinical practice, academia, and community engagement, she champions inclusivity and resilience, striving to cultivate a more accessible and compassionate psychological care landscape for all.

Amelia Baldwin is a Chartered Counselling Psychologist. She is currently a senior lecturer in Counselling Psychology at the University of West Of England and a practitioner psychologist in private practice. Amelia is an Associate Fellow with the British Psychological Society and is a member of the Division of Counselling Psychology. Over the past two decades, Amelia has gained experience as a therapist, advocate, researcher, leader, and supervisor in various settings, including the voluntary sector, NHS services, and academia. She is an intersectional feminist who leads on varied aspects of anti-racist, decolonial, systemic thinking, and feminist approaches to therapy, research, and supervision.

Ranjot Bhogal is an award-winning Counselling Psychologist renowned for her ground-breaking research. She is the creator of the Punjabi Depression Inventory, which has revolutionised our comprehension of the cultural symptoms of depression symptoms within Punjabi-speaking communities. In addition to her academic contributions, Dr Bhogal excels in her role as a clinician, running a thriving independent practice. She is also highly sought-after as a speaker and advocate for mental health awareness, leveraging her expertise to inspire change and promote destigmatisation.

Melissa Butler is a consultant Counselling Psychologist with over 15 years' of experience working in the mental health field. She has held various appointments in settings including the NHS, local authority, non-profit, and with international clients. She is passionate about supporting people from marginalised communities and spent the majority of her career and research specialising in this area. Currently, Dr Butler works for a national health and social care charity where she leads the psychology service in a multicultural London borough. Alongside this role, Dr Butler runs a thriving private practice, where she offers therapy, bespoke training and consultancy services.

Neha Cattra is a Principal Chartered Counselling Psychologist with leadership roles in education and training, with a remit for increasing access to trainings. A passionate educator, Neha inspires Trainee Clinical Psychologists through teaching, managing, and supervising doctoral level equality, diversity and inclusion research at The University of Surrey. Her post-doctoral BABCP accredited Masters in CBT at OCTC, allows her to bring her expertise to the development and evaluation of the Specialised CBT Pathway at Surrey. In her work with The Division of Counselling Psychology, she served a crucial role in the governance and development of Counselling Psychology at a national level.

Divine Charura is a Professor of Counselling Psychology. Divine is a Coaching Psychologist and a Counselling Psychologist. Divine is also a psychotherapist and an Honorary Fellow of the United Kingdom Council for Psychotherapy (UKCP). Divine has co-authored numerous books. These include Love and Therapy: In relationship [with Stephen Paul] and with Colin Lago co-edited Black Identities + White therapies: Race respect and diversity (2021). His latest book is the Handbook of Social Justice in Psychological Therapies. Power, politics, change (co-edited with Dr Laura Winter, 2023).

Juan Du is an award-winning bilingual psychotherapist, researcher and mindfulness teacher. She holds an MA in Cross-Culture Communication and an MSc in Experimental Psychology and has completed her doctorate in Counselling Psychology and Psychotherapy at Metanoia Institute. Juan is passionate about promoting culturally sensitive therapy and race equality in mental healthcare services in the United Kingdom. She developed Mindfulness Calligraphy Enhanced Therapy (MCET®) as a culturally sensitive psychological approach to bridging the underrepresented Chinese clients. Her work and research have won her the UKCP members research funding in 2020 and the BPS Division of Counselling Psychology Diversity Award in 2022.

Andre Etchebarne is a Lecturer in Counselling Psychology at the University of Manchester. He teaches on the Counselling Psychology Professional Doctorate and works for a community pain management service in the NHS. Andre is passionate about improving Counselling Psychology training and addressing health inequities related to racism.

Dominique Fray-Aitken is a BPS chartered Counselling Psychologist and HCPC registered practitioner psychologist. By birth, she is American and by cultural upbringing, she is Black British Caribbean. She identifies as deaf and relies on lip reading and cochlear implant for communication. She is currently learning level three British Sign Language. She has been working in private practice for about seven years. Her clinical interests include identity(-ies), disabilities/differences, relationships, trauma, race and culture.

Cerisse Gunasinghe is a Lecturer and Research and Impact Lead in the Psychology Department (City, University of London) as well as an accredited Counselling Psychologist. Previously while a Post-Doctoral Research Associate at King's College London, Cerisse was one of the lead coordinators of the Tackling Inequalities and Discrimination Experiences in health Services (TIDES) Study, the HYPE (improving the Health of Young People) Project and the Health Inequalities Research Network (HERON). As a member of the HERON leadership team, Cerisse was Lead Coordinator for UP&RUNNING and the Biomedical Research Centre (BRC) Youth Awards as well as supporting the RISE (Research methods in School Education) programme.

Hayat Hussein is a Counselling Psychologist who is passionate about considering how social, cultural, and political contexts can influence individuals and how clinicians need to be more culturally competent, flexible and understanding towards this. Furthermore, she has experience working within the NHS and charitable organisations such as 'Midaye Somali Development Network' and Freedom From Torture. Hayat particularly has extensive experience working with people presenting with histories of severe and multiple traumas, including those with refugee and asylum seekers status. She has a keen interest in community psychology and narrative approaches that focus on storytelling.

Adebayo Idowu is a Principal Counselling Psychologist with over 12 years' of clinical experience working in the NHS and private practice. He completed a Doctorate in Counselling Psychology at City University London. His clinical interests include work with adults with complex mental health problems, such as personality disorders, paranoid schizophrenia, bipolar disorder, post-traumatic stress disorder, complex trauma, severe depression and anxiety. He uses a broad range of psychological models, including CBT, DBT, EMDR, CFT and ACT. He has developed an interest in community psychology with the vision to promote the voices of excluded groups. He is passionate about cross-cultural anti-discriminatory practice.

Raisa Kumaga is a senior Counselling Psychologist with a background in mental health social work, having received her training at The Hague University in the Netherlands. She furthered her education by completing a Master of Philosophy (MPhil) at Cambridge University in the United Kingdom. Drawing from both her clinical expertise and personal experiences in the Netherlands, she developed a keen interest in addressing the challenges faced in accessing psychological interventions for racialised communities and decolonising psychological practice. Her commitment to understanding the psychological experiences of second-generation Somalis, whose families were displaced during the Somali Civil War in the 1990s, is evident in her doctoral research in Counselling Psychology.

Jaspreet Tehara is a Senior Counselling Psychologist in the NHS working in Older Persons services currently. He is presently developing a care pathway for older persons with mood disorders and psychosis experiences for his Trust, as well as engaging in developing further professional support for ethnic community staff. Jaspreet teaches at various universities as an associate lecturer. His research interests include sexuality, gender, and racialised experiences. He is also Clinical Director at Metarelational Psychological Services, working with patients in private practice.

Tumi Sotire is a British-born Nigerian with Dyspraxia, founded The Black Dyspraxic to highlight intersectionality in neurodiversity. Awarded the Mary Colley Award from the Dyspraxia Foundation for advocacy, he advises the Centre for Neurodiversity at Work at Birkbeck University and the Co-Production Board for Neurodiversity in Business. Tumi, a judge for the Genius Within Neurodiversity Awards, also contributes to The Diverse Creative CIC Future Leader's Advisory Board and Noetic's Community Advisory Board. Through his diverse roles, Tumi actively promotes inclusion and empowerment within neurodiverse communities, driven by his personal experiences and dedication to fostering understanding and support.

Andrew Stockhausen at the time of writing is in the final stages of completing his doctoral thesis to become a Counselling Psychologist. He works in private practice as a psychotherapist where his therapeutic approach is integrative, combining psychodynamic and schema therapy to meet his client's needs. Andrew has worked for several NHS mental health services, specialising in trauma-focussed approaches. His clinical areas of interest include addressing the unique psycho-emotional stressors that LGBTQ+ people experience as a result of belonging to stigmatised minority groups; and working with adults who have experienced adverse childhood events like neglect, physical, and emotional trauma.

Mou Sultana is a Counselling Psychologist (CPsychol, BPS; M.Ps.S.I; APA) with Vhi and Psychotherapist (UKCP; ICP) in private practice. She specialises in trauma, sexuality, perinatal mental health and domestic violence. Mou chairs the Ethnic Minority Special Interest Group at the Psychological Society of Ireland. She is a lecturer and supervisor at the Irish College of Humanities and Applied Sciences, Ireland. She is also the author of '*What's so natural about sexuality?*' published by Routledge in 2018 and '*The Becoming Model: Integrative Perinatal Counselling*' published by Routledge in 2024.

Asuka Yamashina is a Japanese Counselling Psychologist who is BPS chartered and an HCPC registered practitioner psychologist, supervisor and trainer based in London, practising privately with adults and couples. She often works with clients of multiple or minority cultural, racial and spiritual identities and incorporates embodied and transpersonal approaches for trauma treatment such as energy psychotherapy.

Preface

Predating the parturition of this book are numerous literary discoveries highlighting the necessity for the explicit consideration of racial experiences within Applied Psychology – at a minimum, in the training of psychologists or indeed in their practice. There are exemplars of publications meeting such a brief in the United States (US) but sparsely in the United Kingdom (UK) in spite of the wealth of expertise. Of course, we do not minimise the transportation of psychologically shared knowledge across the globe.

In this book, the aim is to contest the familiar narratives in a way that allows for new perspectives to be reimagined. We have heard most of it before! How many more ways can it be retold? We critique traditional and contemporary definitions of what people of colour are or what they likely represent.

All the chapters are authored by people of colour disporting the ethos of the Counselling Psychology profession whilst speaking more broadly to racial issues in Applied Psychology. Our current racialised environment in the UK has permanency we are ethically bound to challenge, dispelling myths about its nature, history and culture of origin.

What goes up must come down! What is of today is only a re-membered story of the past! The "woke" culture has enabled the manifestation of expectations and recommendations around awareness processes (e.g., decolonisation). We would suggest that this consciousness rising does not negate what has always been required nor the work that has and continues to take place. Decolonising psychology and therapy, cultural curiosity and sensitivity, cultural bias, language, and uncontested concepts in the understanding of people of colour, evolution of terminologies (e.g.,

BME, BAME, minoritised, racialised, marginalised etc.) and people's unique engagement with this are still all vital.

When you read this book, you will notice that authors adopt a myriad of terminologies for people of colour, reflective of the notion that individuals may or may not choose to identify in different ways, and it is not for us to prescribe what this might be.

The chapters that follow implicate the limited use of techniques and literature that is not an adoption of Eurocentric modes. In fact, the commonality of individually constructed chapters denotes the rejection of single narratives, opting for the intentional positioning of individual and collective schemas, the unique set of environments people of colour have had to and continue to survive in.

As people and professionals of colour, must we reimagine the science of psychology or critique it? Who does it serve particularly with the endeavour of reimagining the intersection of race and psychology?

Whether you come to this book as a person of colour or otherwise, as a student or qualified professional – new or seasoned, "still you rise" (Maya Angelou)[1] and still you learn. We hope your journey with the book, provides opportunities to inquiry, to shape and to re-learn. Or perhaps the book confirms that which you know and gives you the courage to RISE, REAPPRAISE, and DECONSTRUCT.

Note

1. Angelou, M. (2013). And Still I Rise. United Kingdom: Little, Brown Book Group.

Acknowledgements

We dedicate this book to the Black and Racialised Lives lost in the UK and globally.

We pay homage to all of the authors for their bravery, courage and voices in journeying with the editors and birthing a vision long held.

Thank you to all who have crossed our paths in teaching us the value of connectedness, the value of separation, and justice.

That which is ours will come to us without passing us by – thank you readers.

PART 1
AT THE PERCEIVED INCIPIENT

Frameworks

1

Cerisse Gunasinghe

Overview

I invite you to consider frameworks for research that have transformative and translational implications for evidence-based practice. I highlight philosophy, theory, and research from other disciplines (e.g., cross-cultural psychology, sociology, and law) that you might consider useful in developing your own knowledge and understanding as well as integrating into aspects of your work.

In this chapter, critical race theory and intersectional theory (as they pertain to psychology) are proposed as useful frameworks when conceptualising research with racialised and ethnic minoritised groups. Following on from this, coproduction and community-based participatory research (CBPR) methodological approaches are highlighted as potential ways to address existing racial inequity and underrepresentation in research and knowledge dissemination together with the importance of reflexivity when working with diverse populations – to ensure the psychological safety of researchers and participants, its use as a space to monitor cultural biases or assumptions, and where the power is located when working to advocate for, and promote empowerment for marginalised groups. Finally, the chapter ends with recognising the importance of cultural sensitivity and empathy in both research and clinical practice.

DOI: 10.4324/9781003415244-2

Evidence-based practice

> You can hear other people's wisdom, but you've got to re-evaluate the world for yourself.
>
> (Mae Jemison)

The British Psychological Society (2017) asserts that the integration of research is crucial to and should be embedded in the practice of psychologists and therefore underlies the five core competencies (Figure 1.1). The following diagram illustrates what these areas of skills and knowledge are, how they connect and the role of research.

> Research provides the evidence base for the practice of psychology. Research methods in psychology vary from qualitative observation to quantitative scientific method, so it is important to distinguish the nature and quality of the evidence underpinning any knowledge or techniques being applied. In general, basic research develops theories, models and data to describe and explain psychological processes and structures, while primary research develops and evaluates

Figure 1.1 Core competencies of psychologists as outlined by the British Psychological Society (image adapted from British Psychological Society, 2017)

ways of using psychological knowledge to intervene with people, organisations, processes or technologies to achieve desired effects. Secondary research consolidates other research to identify higher order trends and directions.

(Extract taken from British Psychological Society, 2017)

Given that the scientist-practitioner model has been maintained as integral to the training and practice of counselling psychologists since the 1950s (Howard, 1986), it is crucial that we adopt practices both in clinical practice and research that reflect the evolving needs of the populations we intend to serve. Roberts et al. (2020) proposed reasons for what they suggested as embedded racial inequality in the production and publication of empirical research across developmental, social, and cognitive psychological sciences. The authors identified that over a period of 40 years, there were very few studies where research focussed on race and ethnicity (Roberts et al., 2020).

Similarly, within Counselling Psychology research, while there has been an increase in applied research, racialised and ethnic minoritised individuals remain underrepresented in study populations as well as in publication authorship (Hawkins et al., 2022; Roberts et al., 2020). Furthermore, Hawkins et al. (2022) identified in their evaluation of the representation of people of colour in counselling and Counselling Psychology peer-review literature and found a number of underexamined areas, for example studies involving sexual minorities or on adult trauma and violence, just to name a few. If we really are to help reduce racial inequity and disparities in mental health care, then there has to be recognition of the need, and substantial effort to diversify and decolonise the frameworks that guide research and evidence-based practice. Like seen in the words of Mae Jemison, who defied the status quo around her to become the first African-American woman to travel into space, there needs to be a close look into changing frameworks that have an impact on so many. With this in mind, methodological frameworks for widening participation and inclusivity of racialised and ethnic minoritised individuals will be presented and explored in more detail later in this chapter.

Critical race theory and intersectionality as theoretical frameworks

The arena of Counselling Psychology research has continued to expand over time with the application of a wide range of theoretical and methodological frameworks. Traditionally, as with other disciplines of psychology, much of the research conducted was through a positivist or post-positivist lens and was regarded as the 'received view' (Ponterotto, 2005). However, James and Prilleltensky (2002) argued that we need to be critical about the way in which we apply theory to practice when working with individuals from diverse ethnic backgrounds.

The author proposes that our existing diagnostic categories and psychotherapy interventions are socially constructed, and there are erroneous assumptions that symptom clusters and prognosis are universal. As a result, this reduces their validity across all cultures. James and Prilleltensky (2002) propose that 'the social course of illness is shaped by the local world of the afflicted'. Therefore, the individual's context, which includes relationships, what is morally at risk, adverse life events and social support, all affect the way symptoms are experienced and the extent to which they are problematic.

Criticalists would suggest that 'injustice and subjugation shape the lived world' (Ponterotto, 2005). The main objectives of criticalists are to bring about change and empowerment for those involved in the research, from restrictive social conditions to challenging dominant social structures. The researcher takes on an interactive and proactive role in the research and their beliefs are an obvious and integrated component of the research process. The critical-ideological epistemology underpins qualitative, multicultural, feminist, and social justice research (Haverkamp & Young, 2007; Morrow & Smith, 2000; Ponterotto, 2005). For this reason, it might be considered that qualitative research is the best fit for Counselling Psychology research. That's not to say that some phenomena relevant to Counselling Psychology cannot be observed using quantitative methods. It is important to hold in mind the type, specifically the wording of the research question and the philosophical, ontological, and epistemological lens that the researcher takes up given the phenomena under investigation or exploration.

In my view, combining multiple methods would help facilitate both the breadth and depth of the research and the acquisition of knowledge. With this in mind, it is important to consider to what extent existing theory and knowledge reflect the diverse experiences of racialised and ethnic minoritised groups given historical racial inequalities and injustice. Critical race and intersectional theories propose ways to reduce biases and inform anti-racist practices. These will be outlined in turn together with exploration of how they might be useful in psychological research that informs practice.

Critical race theory

One critical approach that can be drawn upon within Counselling Psychology practice and research is Critical Race Theory (Delgado, Stefancic, & Harris, 2012; Salter and Adams, 2013). Early activists and scholars in the field have been concerned with the discourses of civil rights and ethnic studies, yet locates them in a wider lens to include:

> … economics, history, context, group- and self-interest, and even feelings and the unconscious … critical race theory questions the very foundations of the liberal order, including equality theory, legal reasoning, enlightenment rationalism, and neutral principles of constitutional law.
>
> (Delgado, Stefancic & Harris, 2012)

Since the origins of Critical Race Theory in the 1970s, many scholars have contributed to evolving underpinning knowledge and international dissemination of work related to racial justice and equity across a range of disciplines, in particular law, education and social sciences.

Critical race theory in psychology

As reported by Salter and Adams (2013), Critical Race Psychology is a recommended framework for appraising and evaluating psychological theory and research with the aim of achieving social justice and equity in research and practice.

Critical Race Psychology seeks to address five key areas (Figure 1.2):

1. To approach racism as a systemic force embedded in everyday society (rather than a problem of individual bias)
2. Illuminate how ideologies of neoliberal individualism (e.g., merit, choice) often reflect and reproduce racial domination
3. Identify interest convergence as the typical source of broad-based support for reparative action
4. Emphasise possessive investment in privileged identities and identity-infused realities that reproduce racial domination
5. Propose practices of counter-storytelling to reveal and contest identity-infused bases of everyday society.

(Taken from Salter and Adams, 2013)

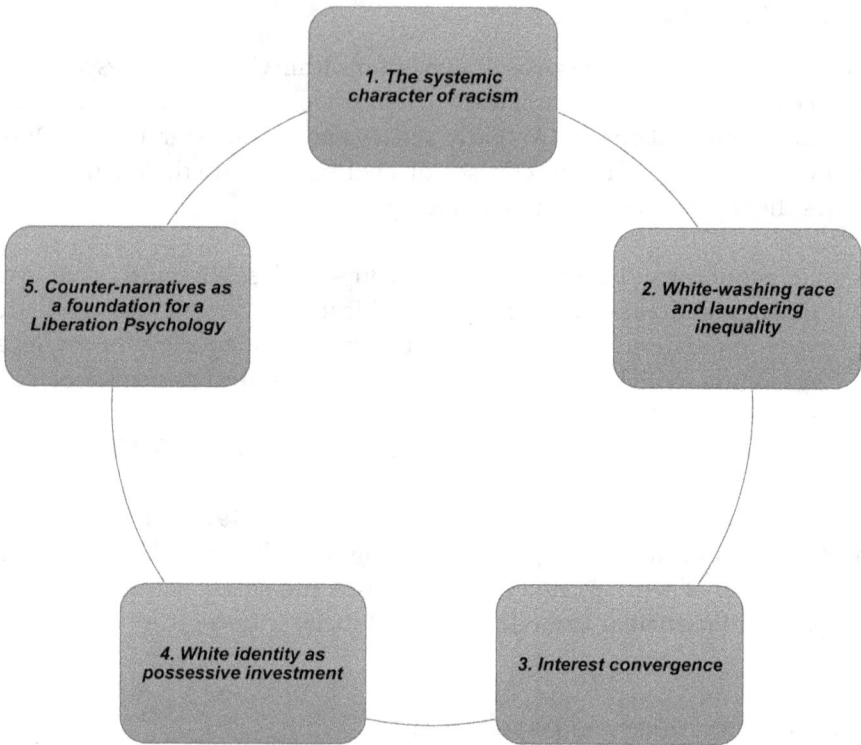

Figure 1.2 Five main pillars of critical race psychology (adapted from Salter and Adams, 2013)

How can critical race psychology guide research?

Critical Race Psychology research predominately seeks to explore questions and produce knowledge relating to race and racism with the aim of advancing social justice and equity (Salter & Haugen, 2017). With an orientation towards social justice, researchers, and practitioners would endeavour to go beyond illustrating health and social inequalities. Therefore, confronting and tackling discrimination embedded in systems as well as advocating for policy changes.

Those undertaking work within this framework must critique dominant narratives, established norms, theories, and frameworks that may preserve racial biases or give support to oppressive structures. Critical Race Psychology encourages community engagement (which will be discussed in more detail later in this chapter) and for researchers to prioritise the perspectives and experiences of marginalised groups, ensuring that their voices are heard and acknowledged. Research should actively engage with the narratives of individuals who have been historically oppressed or marginalised, giving them agency in shaping the research questions and outcomes.

Critical Race Psychology often advocates for interdisciplinary collaboration, bringing together scholars from psychology, sociology, law, and other fields to provide a more comprehensive representation and understanding of the areas of interest. Partnership with scholars from different disciplines can enrich research by incorporating a broader range of perspectives and methodologies. Researchers should critically examine their research methods, ensuring that they are culturally sensitive and inclusive. This involves questioning the appropriateness of existing methods and developing new ones that better capture the experiences of marginalised groups. Regarding research ethics, one should ensure that research questions and associated methodological approaches do not cause harm and replicate and/or perpetuate existing inequalities (for example, study findings should be disseminated with caution if they are to further disadvantage marginalised groups or promote prejudice and discrimination).

Critical Race Psychology emphasises the importance of intersectionality, recognising that individuals experience multiple forms of oppression or privilege simultaneously (e.g., race, gender, class). Research should reflect this complexity and avoid oversimplification.

Intersectionality

A prominent scholar within critical race theory literature is Professor Kimberlé Williams Crenshaw. Renowned for her work in civil rights, one of Professor Crenshaw's most significant contributions to the field was the concept of intersectionality. The framework of intersectionality illustrates how multiple personal, political, and social identities such as race, gender, class, sexual orientation, and other forms of identity do not sit in a single axis but are often being negotiated at any given time, intersecting with discrimination and systems of oppression and privilege (Crenshaw, 1989; Walker et al., 2024; Woodhead et al., 2022a, 2022b). Similarly to critical race theory, an intersectional position seeks social justice and equity with the intention of addressing systemic inequalities and promoting equity for individuals with intersecting identities. Intersectional thinking has been widely applied in various disciplines, including sociology, gender studies, and psychology. For example, understanding how the intersection of race, age, and socioeconomic status influences access to health care and health outcomes (Gunasinghe et al., 2018).

Figure 1.3 Wheel of Power/Privilege (adapted from Sylvia Duckworth, 2020)

An example is shown above of how the intersection of personal and social identities may place individuals at risk of marginalisation, the complexity of human experience, and where power and privilege are located (Figure 1.3).

It is possible to apply intersectionality across various stages of the research process, from conceptualisation to analysis and interpretation. Intersectionality encourages researchers to scrutinise and critically appraise specific social, cultural, and historical contexts that shape the experiences of individuals in addition to existing theories and frameworks to ensure they account for the complexities of intersecting identities. This may involve revising or expanding established models to better capture diverse experiences. Furthermore, to ensure that we are truly representing populations within our society, it is necessary to include individuals characterised across these personal, political, and social identities that intersect with race and ethnicity if we are to better understand and address disparities in health and social care research and evidence-based practice. Last but not least, researchers have a responsibility to inform and educate through the exchange of knowledge between themselves and others about the principles of intersectionality, with the aim of facilitating a more inclusive and nuanced understanding of social identities across all sectors including academic, healthcare, legal, and social welfare organisations.

Both Critical Race Psychology and Intersectional approaches recognise the importance of reflexive practice as this includes acknowledging and addressing power dynamics between researchers and participants. This is discussed in more detail in the next section of this chapter.

Reflexivity when conducting research on emotive topics

> For to be free is not merely to cast off one's chains, but to live in a way that respects and enhances the freedom of others.
>
> (Nelson Mandela)

Reflexivity is a crucial part of any research process, and I would encourage researchers to engage in self-reflection or within a reflective group regardless of the methodological design of a study, especially when conducting research in sensitive and/or emotive areas and when conducting research which focuses on the experiences of those not often included in research. This is a process whereby the researcher is transparent about the study or area under investigation, the role the researcher has played in conducting the research together with any biases that they may hold, how the data is analysed and motives underlying the application of its findings. Researchers should be aware of how their own identities and experiences influence the research process and outcomes.

There are two types of reflexivity, as outlined by Willig (2001). The first is identified as personal reflexivity, where the researcher reflects on the possible impact their own experience and its entirety can have on shaping the research and how it is reported. The second form of reflexivity is epistemological which encourages the researcher to engage with the theoretical assumptions that are being formulated and the implications this has for the project and the research conclusions.

Furthermore, reflective practice can help to acknowledge and address power dynamics between researchers and participants. Often, working alongside peer researchers can facilitate a fairer distribution of power.

Can research participation be therapeutic?

Similar to humanistic therapeutic approaches, one tries to connect with participants with empathy and compassion. At times, research participant narratives can connect with the lived (felt) experience of researchers, and the challenge might be for one to hold professional boundaries within the research context while conveying empathy and sustaining rapport. During my time of conducting clinical and research interviews, many participants have reported these as 'therapeutic' and for some, it being the first space that they were given to reflect on and voice their experiences.

Methodological frameworks for widening participation and inclusivity

A possible way to address inequity and underrepresentation in applied psychological research, that aligns with Critical Race Psychology and Intersectionality lens as well as the relational and humanistic positioning of Counselling Psychology, is through co-production, collaboration with, and involvement of marginalised communities and service-users. Hence, allowing for the voices and experiences of these individuals to inform and shape work addressing racism and oppression in health and social care.

Co-production and service-user involvement

The National Institute for Clinical Excellence (NICE) and the Social Care Institute for Excellence (SCIE) both provide guidance and recommendations for community engagement and co-production with people who access health and social care services either for their own care or for the care of others. Community engagement or public and patient engagement and involvement are processes where researchers, practitioners, and service users work in partnership, exchanging knowledge and expertise in the creation and implementation of research and clinical programmes. Therefore, distributing the power amongst all and ensuring that research findings are disseminated in ways that benefit the communities involved.

Community-based participatory research

Another methodological framework that can be adopted within research programmes which promote equity between researchers and research participants is CBPR. CBPR has social justice as its theoretical underpinning (Wilson, 2019) and suggests establishing long-term collaboration between researchers and community members to address issues relevant to the community. Improving community well-being is central to the approach.

CBPR emphasises the active involvement of community members in all aspects of the research process, from the identification of research questions to the dissemination of results. This ensures that the research is contextually relevant and addresses community needs, focusing on addressing real-world problems and promoting positive change. CBPR has been applied in various fields, including public health, education, environmental justice, and social sciences. An advantage is its ability to produce research that is not only scientifically rigorous but also relevant and meaningful to the communities involved. CBPR aims to empower community members by building their research skills and capacity. This enhances the community's ability to engage in research but also contributes to sustainable improvements in community well-being beyond the specific research project. Ethical considerations warranties that the research process is conducted in a manner that respects the rights, well-being, and privacy of community members.

Examples of community-based participatory research programmes that implemented co-production with service-users and community members are:

1. Improving the Health of Young People – The HYPE Project.

    At the time of writing this chapter, the paper describing and reporting findings of the HYPE Project was being peer-reviewed for publication. The HYPE Project was a research and resource platform co-designed and co-produced with young people aged 16 years and over. This was part of the work I undertook during my time as a Post-Doctoral Research Associate at King's College London under the supervision of Professor Stephani Hatch.

    Young people from diverse communities worked alongside the research team, stakeholders, clinicians, and academics throughout all stages of the project to develop a web-based platform that would (1) help improve young people's access to health and social services, (2) increase the provision of information of online resources, and (3) deliver complementary community-based events/activities to promote mental health and to ultimately support mental health difficulties for young people in the community.

2. Tackling Inequalities and Discrimination Experiences in Health Services (TIDES) study.

    As a co-investigator during phase two of the Tackling Inequalities and Discrimination Experiences in Health Services (TIDES) study (www.tidesstudy.com), I supported the team to engage with community members and conduct mixed-methods research. Phase two of the TIDES study was a UK-based project investigating inequalities in health service use and exploring discrimination experienced by healthcare staff and service-users (Rhead et al., 2020). Phase two was initiated in July 2020 to examine the national impact of COVID-19 on inequalities experienced by racial and ethnic minority health and social care staff groups. This was developed with and guided by a modified Delphi consensus process (Linstone and Turoff, 1975) with peer researchers and an expert panel (advisory group) comprising clinical academics, health and social care staff, senior leaders, and a wider stakeholder opinion group of health and social care staff across England.

Similarly, work by a colleague, Dr Juliana Onwumere and co-authors highlighted the continued vital need for evidence-based health and social care modernisation and that priority should be given to guaranteeing that marginalised individuals from Black racial communities have 'meaningfully and equitably supported' positions in guiding and informing such research (Onwumere et al., 2023). Consequently, is it important that when consulting and involving racial and ethnic minoritised individuals and groups that one is culturally aware of the similarities and differences that exist?

Cultural sensitivity and empathy

The practice of counselling psychologists includes the development and provision of interventions that facilitate a collaborative 'helping' relationship between clients and practitioners in the therapeutic encounter, and which is grounded in the humanistic model. Therefore, with less focus on sickness and pathologising people's lived experiences (Woolfe et al., 2003). As counselling psychologists, we strive to work effectively and appropriately with ethnic communities, resulting in a need for this profession to adopt a culturally sensitive approach or as Johnson and Nadirshaw (1993) asserted, a 'transcultural' approach, to their work which is also relevant to other disciplines. To achieve this, it has been suggested that we should think critically about existing conceptualisations and social construction of mental health (James & Prilleltensky, 2002) while being mindful of 'subjectivity and intersubjectivity, values and beliefs' (Division of Counselling Psychology, 2005), and validating individual experience.

Existing research has made significant efforts to inform clinical practice with a growing focus on documenting the personal meanings or individual narratives of lived experiences. One might consider a limitation of the literature is that the authors, many of whom acknowledge the diversity within racialised and ethnic minoritised groups, often make generalisations which can lead to an inadequate knowledge-base and misrepresentation.

According to the American Psychological Association (APA), cultural sensitivity is defined as an 'awareness and appreciation of the values, norms, and beliefs characteristic of a cultural, ethnic, racial, or other group that is not one's own, accompanied by a willingness to adapt one's behaviour accordingly' (American Psychological Association, 2024). The work of Professor Khatidja Chantler has shone a light on the complexity of culture in the context of counselling and psychotherapy and calls for an intersectional approach when working with marginalised and minoritised groups (Chantler, 2005).

In addition to the personal and social identities highlighted by APA, Chantler (2005) asserts that it is important to include assessment of the wider range of protected characteristics and how lived experience of these can influence outcomes. Furthermore, as James and Prilleltensky (2002) discussed, healthcare professionals need to be aware of what is morally at risk for the person who is experiencing psychological distress, in that, a 'good person' or 'good families' do not disclose family conflict to outsiders (e.g., mental health professionals).

With this in mind, my own doctoral research explored how six Pakistani Muslim women interpret cultural concepts of izzat (what was described as honour and self-respect); what role, if any, it has in their lives; and whether there is interplay between upholding izzat and the participants' help-seeking strategies for mental health and well-being. Through semi-structured interviews and analysis using an interpretative phenomenological analytic framework, this study highlighted new insights into the understanding of izzat and the implications cultural concepts have for strategies in managing or silencing psychological distress. Interviews illustrated tensions the participants experience when considering izzat, how these are negotiated to enable them to self-manage or seek help, and possible life experiences that might lead to self-harm and attempted suicide. Notably, cultural codes, in particular izzat, appear to vary over the life course and are influenced by migration (Gunasinghe et al., 2019).

To conclude, Counselling Psychologists and other allied professionals have training and skills that enable them to advance knowledge, understanding and application of cross-cultural and anti-racist theoretical frameworks and research evidence. I have presented some examples of existing literature and guidance that offer insights into promoting equity and addressing disparities in both clinical and research practice in the hope that readers can better serve the interests and needs of marginalised and underrepresented individuals and communities.

Chapter questions to provoke thoughts:

1. To what extent are your clinical practice and research activities informed by cross-cultural and anti-racist theoretical frameworks and research evidence?
2. How do you perceive potential barriers and what are the potential solutions to race and ethnicity equity in your day-to-day roles at work?
3. What might be your own biases and knowledge gaps relating to race and ethnic inequity in health, health services, and health-related research?
4. What action/change might you consider taking to promote equity in health and social care services and service use for racialised and ethnic minoritised groups?

References

American Psychological Association. (2024). APA Dictionary of Psychology. Retrieved January 22, 2024, from https://dictionary.apa.org/cultural-sensitivity

British Psychological Society. (2017). *Practice Guidelines: Third Edition.* https://doi.org/10.53841/bpsrep.2017.inf115

Chantler, K. (2005). From disconnection to connection: 'Race', gender and the politics of therapy. *British Journal of Guidance & Counselling, 33*(2), 239–256. https://doi.org/10.1080/03069880500132813

Crenshaw, K. (1989). Demarginalizing the intersection of race and sex: A Black feminist critique of antidiscrimination doctrine, feminist theory and antiracist politics. *University of Chicago Legal Forum, 1989*(1), 139–167.

Delgado, R., Stefancic, J., & HARRIS, A. (2012). *Critical Race Theory: An Introduction, Second Edition.* NYU Press. http://www.jstor.org/stable/j.ctt9qg9h2

Division of Counselling Psychology. (2005). *Professional practice guidelines.* https://doi.org/10.53841/bpsrep.2005.rep75

Duckworth, S. (2020). *Wheel of Power/Privilege.* Instagram.

Gunasinghe, C., Gazard, B., Aschan, L., MacCrimmon, S., Hotopf, M., & Hatch, S. L. (2018). Debt, common mental disorders and mental health service use. *Journal of Mental Health, 27*(6), 520–528. https://doi.org/10.1080/09638237.2018.1487541

Gunasinghe, C., Hatch, S. L., & Lawrence, J. (2019). Young Muslim Pakistani Women's lived experiences of izzat, mental health, and well-being. *Qualitative Health Research, 29*(5), 747–757. https://doi.org/10.1177/1049732318803094

Haverkamp, B. E., & Young, R. A. (2007). Paradigms, purposes, and the role of the literature: Formulating a rationale for qualitative investigations. *The Counseling Psychologist, 35*, 265–290.

Hawkins, J. M., Bean, R. A., Smith, T. B., & Sandberg, J. G. (2022). Representation of race and ethnicity in counseling and counseling psychology journals. *The Counseling Psychologist, 50*(1), 123–144. https://doi.org/10.1177/00110000211041766.

Howard, G. S. (1986). The scientist-practitioner in counseling psychology: Toward a deeper integration of theory, research, and practice. *The Counseling Psychologist, 14*(1), 61–105.

James, S., & Prilleltensky, I. (2002). Cultural diversity and mental health: Towards integrative practice. *Clinical Psychology Review, 22*(8), 1133–1154.

Johnson, A. W., & Nadirshaw, Z. (1993). Good practice in transcultural counselling: An Asian perspective. *British Journal of Guidance & Counselling, 21*(1), 20–29.

Linstone, H.A. & Turoff, M. (1975). *The delphi method: techniques and applications.* Addison Wesley Publishing Company.

Morrow, S. L., & Smith, M. L. (2000). Qualitative research for counselling psychology. In S. D. Brown & R. W. Lent (Eds.), *Handbook of counselling psychology* (3rd ed., pp. 199–230). Wiley.

Onwumere, J., Gentle, A., Obanubi, R., Davis, A., Karuga, M., Ali, R., BeFine Study Team, & Cardi, V. (2023). Amplifying the voices of Black racial minorities in mental health research through public involvement and engagement: The importance of advisory roles. *Health Expect, 27*, e13892. https://doi.org/10.1111/hex.13892

Ponterotto, J. G. (2005). Qualitative research in counselling psychology: A primer on research paradigms and philosophy of science. *Journal of Counseling Psychology, 52*(2), 126–136.

Rhead, R., Chui, Z., Gazard, B., MacCrimmon, S., Woodhead, C., & Hatch, S. L. (2020). The impact of workplace discrimination and harassment among NHS staff working in London Trusts: Results from TIDES study. *British Journal of Psychiatry Open, 7*(1), 1–8. https://doi.org/10.1192/bjo.2020.137

Roberts, S. O., Bareket-Shavit, C., Dollins, F. A., Goldie, P. D., & Mortenson, E. (2020). Racial inequality in psychological research: Trends of the past and recommendations for the future. *Perspectives on Psychological Science, 15*(6), 1295–1309. https://doi.org/10.1177/1745691620927709

Salter, P., & Adams, G. (2013). Toward a critical race psychology. *Social and Personality Psychology Compass, 7* (11), 781–793. https://doi.org/10.1111/spc3.12068

Salter, P. S., & Haugen, A. D. (2017). Critical race studies in psychology. In: Gough, B. (eds). *The Palgrave handbook of critical social psychology.* Palgrave Macmillan. https://doi.org/10.1057/978-1-137-51018-1_7

Walker, C. R., Gunasinghe, C., Harwood, H., Ehsan, A., Ahmed, F., Dorrington, S., Onwumere, J., Meriez, P., Stanley, N., Stoll, N., Woodhead, C., Hatch, S. L., & Rhead, R. D. (2024). Ethnic inequalities during clinical placement: A qualitative study of student nurses' experiences within the London National Health Service. *Journal of Advanced Nursing, 80*(4), 1497–1510, https://doi.org/10.1111/jan.15891

Willig, C. (2001). Introducing qualitative research in psychology. Adventures in theory and method. Open University Press.

Wilson, L. A. (2019). Qualitative research. In P. Liamputtong (Ed.), *Handbook of research methods in health social sciences.* Springer.

Woodhead, C., Onwumere, J., Rhead, R., Bora-White, M., Chui, Z., Clifford, N., Connor, L., Gunasinghe, C., Harwood, H., Meriez, P., Mir, G., Jones Nielsen, J., Rafferty, A. M., Stanley, N., Peprah, D., & Hatch, S. L. (2022a). Race, ethnicity and COVID-19 vaccination: A qualitative study of UK healthcare staff. *Ethnicity & Health, 27*(7), 1555–1574. https://doi.org/10.1080/13557858.2021.1936464

Woodhead, C., Stoll, N., Harwood, H., Alexis, O., Hatch, S. L., & TIDES Study Team. (2022b). 'They created a team of almost entirely the people who work and are like them': A qualitative study of organisational culture and racialised inequalities among healthcare staff. *Sociology of Health & Illness, 44*, 267–289. https://doi.org/10.1111/1467-9566.13414

Woolfe, R., Dryden, W., & Strawbridge, S. (2003). *Handbook of counselling psychology* (2nd ed). Sage.

Training

2

Andre Etchebarne

Overview

This chapter explores race and racism in Counselling Psychology (CoP) training. Though it focuses specifically on the context of training in the United Kingdom (UK), there are takeaways applicable to training pathways for applied psychology and in other contexts.

The key points of discussion will be:

1. The training context for CoP in the UK.
2. The significance of discussing racism in CoP training.
3. The concept of safe spaces and decolonising the curriculum.
4. Counternarratives of race and racism within CoP training.

Counselling psychology training

Awareness of racism and its impact on well-being is fundamental in developing Counselling Psychologists to become ethical practitioners (Nkansa-Dwamena & Ade-Serrano, 2023). Recent updates to the standards of proficiency from the Health and Care Professions Council (HCPC), the regulatory body for Counselling Psychologists and other applied psychologists, call for "an expansion of the role of equality, diversity and

DOI: 10.4324/9781003415244-3

inclusion … ensuring that our registrants can provide high-quality healthcare to all their service users" (HCPC, 2022).

There are two training pathways for aspiring Counselling Psychologists in the UK – the British Psychological Society's Qualification in CoP[1] or an approved professional doctorate offered by higher education (HE) providers. The professional doctorate pathway is the most common training route in the UK (Wynn & Winter, 2023). Therefore, the discussion below focuses primarily on training within HE settings.

Far from being post-racial, the literature indicates that racism remains a source of distress for academics and students in HE. Students who experience racism provide accounts of bullying from staff and a sense of isolation from their peers (Stoll et al., 2022). Unfortunately, similar issues of racism are also well documented for staff working in HE, impacting their wellbeing and leading some to look abroad for academic positions (Bhopal et al., 2016). Although less research looks specifically at CoP training, evidence suggests that trainee CoPs who experience racism feel unsupported and alienated from their peers in training (Daloye, 2022).

The professional doctorate training pathway for CoP combines academic teaching and skills training with practice-based placements. Trainees take up placement in various settings, including the NHS, third sector, and private organisations. Currently, trainees on placement are typically unpaid volunteers who rely on their supervisor's approval to satisfy course requirements. The nature of the power dynamics between trainees and supervisors can present challenges when concerns arise around race and racism, particularly if they stem from a supervisor's behaviour. Similar issues arise in academic supervision, particularly around the support trainees need with their research thesis.

If a trainee raises these issues, they may damage the supervisory relationship, which could influence the trainee's placement report or research goals. While there are likely mechanisms where the trainee can raise issues with the university, barriers can still exist. For instance, a trainee may be fearful that raising complaints will be viewed as an issue of personal compatibility with the supervisor and risk being labelled as a difficult trainee. Despite the documented need for more psychologists, the field is still relatively small, and there are concerns about being ostracised by others in the field.

Outside the supervisory relationship, trainees can also encounter racism from colleagues or their clients/patients. In practice, receiving support or even feeling able to ask for support is not always straightforward.

When a trainee raises concerns to a supervisor, the supervisor may feel unable to provide adequate support due to team dynamics, particularly if the trainee's difficulties stem from interactions with more senior colleagues. This is especially relevant as there are often fewer resources for pastoral support of trainees on placement compared to what is available at universities. Perhaps less discussed are the instances where a supervisor experiences racism from a trainee at university or on placement. While different power dynamics are at play, this does not necessarily make it easier for a supervisor to raise concerns or access support. A supervisor may fear experiencing subsequent issues after raising concerns, specifically if they already feel unsupported by senior colleagues. Supervisors are also likely to find it difficult to explain that rather than overt racial slurs, their experiences are influenced by more persistent microaggressions from their supervisees.

Anecdotally, it is not uncommon for placement providers to look to trainees for ideas on being more inclusive and anti-racist. However, the expectation to contribute to these service development initiatives tends to fall disproportionately on trainees who experience racism. If there is an emphasis on understanding racism within training, trainees who experience racism are well-positioned to design and support anti-racist service development projects. For example, patients who experience racism are likely to feel more able to discuss experiences of racism when interviewed by a trainee who also has experiences of racism. However, this type of work can have a detrimental impact on the well-being of trainees who experience racism. It can be traumatic to reflect on racism (Carter, 2007), which is especially relevant if a trainee is already feeling isolated from peers in their cohort. Finally, care needs to be taken to ensure that trainees who experience racism are not then faced with a larger workload of race-related tasks due to their experiences.

Discussing racism in counselling psychology training

Having discussed the specific context for CoP training in the UK, how can training better support trainees when it comes to race and racism? First, it is essential to acknowledge that from an academic perspective, race and racism remain subjective and unclearly defined (Burns & Vaughn, 2021). There is no consensus on the meaning of the terms or how best to achieve research and clinical goals in these areas. Even the definitions of relevant terms such as structural racism (Gopal & Rao, 2021), antisemitism (Ruth Gould, 2020), and Islamophobia (Allen, 2020) have generated fierce debate on both sides of the political spectrum. Fortunately, the pluralistic stance exemplified within CoP is well suited to sit with this ambiguity of definitions.

Talking about racism can be emotionally charged and elicits unpleasant physiological reactions (Nkansa-Dwamena, 2017). For trainees who experience racism, various responses and strategies may occur. They may choose to disengage from the discussion due to the traumatic nature of previous experiences of racism. They may also feel a sense of intellectualising the discussion to protect themselves from becoming upset or appearing angry. For those who experience racism, their responses can also be influenced by the degree to which they are a minority in the academic space. Individuals may find it less distressing when others who experience racism are present. The other side of this point is that a group discussion on racism where only one trainee who experiences racism is present could be particularly challenging for that individual.

Trainees who do not experience racism can also experience a host of reactions to discussions of racism during training. Seminar rooms may go silent when a lecturer invites comments on their understanding of racism in psychology, perhaps as a sign of fear of saying the wrong thing. Anecdotally, in these situations, it can be helpful for educators to share reflections as a sign that it is okay not to have all the answers or solutions to racism. However, radical honesty in discussions of racism can still be distressing to trainees who experience it, particularly when offensive or derogatory language is used (Denyer et al., 2022). Therefore, creating an environment that achieves open discussions about race and racism is a considerable challenge.

Safe spaces

Given the challenges associated with simply talking about racism, there have been efforts to create so-called "safe spaces" for reflective discussions. At face value, this makes sense and fits with the CoP ethos of being empathic and creating an environment where clients can express their complex thoughts and emotions. However, this raises two points: (1) it is unclear how successful this focus on safe spaces to discuss emotionally charged topics such as racism is and (2) a focus on safety can inadvertently reinforce unhelpful perspectives on racism (Arday et al., 2021). The discussion of safety highlights some broader questions to consider when exploring racism within training. What do we mean by safety in these contexts, and who needs to feel safe?

It is often individuals who do not experience racism who are most likely to feel threatened by these discussions. Therefore, an excessive focus on creating safe discussion spaces can inadvertently lead to surface-level and intellectual debates on the impact of racism. However, there is also the need to consider professional safety in such spaces. Academics and students alike must be conscious of their discussions of systemic racism that touch on politically controversial topics. An illustrative example is the Prevent strategy, created in the Counterterrorism and Security Act (2015). The Prevent policy has been criticised for disproportionally targeting Muslim academics and students as radical while limiting critical thinking and teaching (e.g., Danvers, 2021). Therefore, critical discussions of safe spaces require considering both emotional safety and the ability to safely discuss policies and systems that impact well-being in the UK and abroad.

Training courses should consider how all aspects of training reinforce racism or support anti-racism. For example, the course handbook is the most frequently checked document for trainees during training. The course handbook often refers to the need to act and dress appropriately in lectures and on placement. It is worth stating that what is deemed "appropriate" will differ between cultures. An unfortunate example is how traditional Afro-Caribbean hairstyles such as braids and dreadlocks have historically been labelled unprofessional. Since many courses provide the course handbook before trainees officially start training, course documents can play an essential role in framing the discussion of race and racism within training.

Decolonising the curriculum

HE has traditionally favoured a Eurocentric curriculum, with other canons of knowledge from the global south absent from the student experience (Arday, 2020). Due to this, there have been increasing attempts to decolonise the curriculum within HE. At a basic level, decolonial efforts can begin with changes to reading lists (Hall, 2021). For example, by discussing the perspectives of anti-colonial authors such as Frantz Fanon in the same way, students debate the therapeutic principles of Carl Rogers in classroom discussions. However, challenging racism without simultaneously reifying race by merely including authors who have experienced racism is a considerable task and requires critical reflection. To this point, a recent study found that even when psychology courses explicitly aim to increase the representation of authors from the Global South in the curriculum, minimal changes to reading lists are observed (Jankowski et al., 2022). More specifically, Jankowski and colleagues found that guest lectures on racism were quickly dropped from the curriculum, and departmental resources on decolonisation were rarely utilised by staff over a three-year period.

Attempts to change the curriculum in CoP training require a willingness to acknowledge that personal experiences of racism do not inherently make one a specialist in anti-racism, a challenge I have encountered while writing this chapter. To this point, even academics who experience racism will have been socialised into academia and may not be aware of how this influences their style of teaching. Therefore, decolonising the curriculum requires CoP training to challenge epistemic violence and broaden the ways in which teaching and learning occur. Historically, CoP has embraced qualitative research designs that emphasise the understanding of individual experiences. A research approach of relevance is the use of counter-narratives, which have been used to critique racism within educational settings.

Counter-narratives often use composite stories to highlight racism within HE and the experiences of staff and students (e.g., Doharty et al., 2020). Counter-narrative research articles could be used as suggested readings and brought into classroom discussions. The potential benefit is that it does not rely on trainees who experience racism to act as real-life case studies for their peers, which could be traumatic. Furthermore, discussing alternatives to traditional research methodology, such as counter-narratives during training, would align with the agenda for a pluralistic approach to research (e.g., Smith et al., 2021). Consequently, consider the counter-narratives presented below.

Counter-narratives

"Farhana"

Farhana is a third-year trainee who has achieved roughly 300 hours of clinical practice towards her required minimum of 450 hours. Farhana hopes to submit her thesis at the end of her fourth year. Following a recent tragedy that generated significant public discourse on racism, trainees who do not experience racism have created a White allyship group. The objectives are to "create a safe place" to reflect on bias and to become more informed practitioners when working with clients who experience racism. Regular meetings take place with good attendance for the remaining academic year.

During this same period, discussions around race and racism have also become more frequent at Farhana's placement. Before the latest news story on racism, the impact of racism and other forms of discrimination had not been featured in Farhana's supervision, despite working in a diverse London borough. The supervisor has a long-standing relationship with the course, and they are regularly asked to deliver guest lectures on the CoP course. Previous trainees had also recommended the placement to Farhana and emphasised how thoughtful the supervisor was on social exclusion when formulating supervision.

Farhana's supervisor has asked her to develop a service evaluation project, looking at dropout rates for patients from ethnic minority backgrounds. The supervisor suggested that Farhana reduce her caseload to allow her additional time to work on the project. At this stage of training, Farhana has several competing demands, but she feels unable to decline her supervisor's request. Furthermore, Farhana has overheard some fellow staff members making what she perceived to be racially insensitive remarks. After discussing this with her supervisor, Farhana was encouraged to join a support group within the organisation for Black, Asian, and minority ethnic professionals.

"Kobe"

Kobe is a lecturer on a CoP professional doctorate. As a student, he had written essays about the need to decolonise the curriculum. Therefore, he is keen to incorporate an anti-racist ethos throughout the modules he leads this academic year. While developing the module content for the upcoming year, he is reluctant to depart too far from the PowerPoint slides and group discussion format typically seen in teaching sessions. He wants to introduce less didactic teaching and a greater emphasis on reflective discussions; however, he worries that this will not be considered legitimate teaching and inappropriate for CoP trainees. Kobe also worries that students will judge him as a poor teacher for straying too far from the status quo.

Although he is passionate about social justice and anti-racism, Kobe is hesitant to talk about racism without it feeling like an attack on trainees without experiences of racism. He is also conscious of how careless discussions of racism could be unsettling for trainees who experience racism. Despite these reservations, Kobe decided to schedule a reflective session early on in the module for trainees to reflect on racism within psychology. During the reflective activity, Kobe and the trainees discussed experiences where they have witnessed or experienced racism in their professional roles.

The reflective session was well received by most of the students; however, two students left critical comments via an anonymised session feedback form. One student felt that the session was too emotional and questioned the scientific validity of terms like microaggressions and intersectionality. Another student suggested that Kobe had minimised the role of gender and social class in society during the reflective session. After becoming aware of this feedback, Kobe adapted the content for the remaining lectures with a return to more slide-based teaching. He also decided to emphasise gender and social class instead of race when discussing discrimination in psychology and health care more broadly.

Discussion

Kobe and Farhana's counter-narratives explored some of the challenges facing staff and trainees in CoP training. One of the commonalities was the expectation of what an anti-racist stance in CoP should look like, particularly for those who experience racism. For Farhana, there was an expectation that she should take an active role in the service evaluation project, looking at patients who experience racism. While acknowledging the potential benefits of such projects, several points are worth considering. First, there is the assumption that due to Farhana's skin colour, she will have specialist knowledge relevant to designing a service evaluation. Furthermore, the term community is sometimes used due to lazy generalisations based on nationality or religious faith, among other characteristics. Due to the power dynamics at play, it could be difficult for Farhana to decline her supervisor's request as they determine whether Farhana will pass or fail this placement.

Finally, the request to contribute to the project parallels the literature on academics who experience racism being designated the unofficial "diversity person". Consequently, leading such projects can be to the detriment of academics advancing in other areas, such as acquiring research funding. Similarly, suppose Farhana takes on this service evaluation project. In that case, it could result in Farhana taking longer to reach the minimum 450 clinical hours needed to qualify. Given the financial implications of being an unpaid trainee, Farhana may need to prioritise her well-being and decline to take on the service evaluation. Finally, the supervisor's encouragement to attend a staff support group may reinforce the notion that racism should not be discussed in supervision. Rather than difficult conversations with her supervisor, Farhana is encouraged to attend a support group where "safer" discussions can occur.

Farhana also encountered racialised experiences on the university side of training. Even if it was well-intended, the creation of the white ally group places those who experience racism as the other. In this fictional example, there were no discussions with Farhana or other trainees who experienced racism in the development of this group. While the ally group may be aimed at increasing inclusivity at a societal level, it could also be seen as exclusionary to Farhana and other trainees who experience racism. Although this short counter-narrative is intentionally ambiguous, it is worth considering whether the creations of such groups reflect motivations to being a racial justice ally or rather a racial justice saviour (Williams et al., 2022).

The creation of the allyship group also runs into the challenges discussed previously around safe spaces. In CoP, it is unfortunately common to have challenging conversations about violence and abuse with clients and colleagues. Despite the discomfort these conversations can generate, CoPs learn how to sit with the discomfort to benefit service users. To this point, it could be argued that the desire for the white ally group is inadvertently a form of safety behaviour in response to anticipated discomfort. Therefore, although discussing racism within the white ally group could be helpful in the short term, in the long term, avoiding similar discussions with trainees who experience racism due to a fear of saying the wrong thing could increase anxiety around race-related conversations for trainees in the white ally group.

While Farhana was placed into the role of anti-racist trainee by her supervisor, Kobe experienced a more unspoken tension regarding how to decolonise the curriculum. He experiences a hesitancy to be too persistent with discussions of racism for fear of being seen as overly focused on racism by trainees and colleagues. The initial enthusiasm for challenging the status quo was stopped by perceived negative criticism from trainee feedback forms. The trainee's critique of the scientific merits of intersectionality resulted in Kobe adjusting his teaching focus in subsequent lectures. As intersectionality has garnered more attention within applied psychology, there has been increasing criticism that it is not scientific and is politically motivated (Warner et al., 2020). Unfortunately, these types of critiques again place the burden on those who experience racism to justify their narratives as accurate and valid.

Conclusion

Previous authors have proposed models for embedding anti-racist practices into counselling training (Lee, 2021). Therefore, CoP training would benefit from incorporating and evaluating such models. Developing frameworks and evidence bases of best practices are necessary in response to criticisms of anti-racist initiatives being solely ideologically based. However, in keeping with decolonial thinking, there is also a need to challenge epistemic violence and broaden our understanding of what evidence is. As illustrated in this chapter, counter-narratives are one pathway for investigating the dynamics of racism in CoP training. However, conventional research approaches could also be adopted, such as qualitative explorations of anti-racism in CoP training or statistical analyses on the proportion of authors from racialised backgrounds found in CoP module reading lists. It would also be beneficial to reach out to anti-racist specialists from other academic disciplines and understand their views on what could benefit CoP training.

Our understanding of racism is as much influenced by our experiences and the political climate that exists. It was well documented that racialised individuals experienced discrimination throughout society before the murder of George Floyd. However, it was the political actions of world-wide protests, rather than carefully designed systematic reviews, that led to the acknowledgement of racism from psychological professions. Therefore, discussions on race and racism in training that do not acknowledge the activist component in enacting positive change are missing a fundamental piece of the puzzle. However, in speaking with colleagues within the field, a typical response is that CoP training did not develop the necessary skills to feel confident in challenging racism outside the confines of clinical practice. For instance, CoP could include assignments that require trainees to critically discuss existing government or organisational policies, such as changes to UK immigration laws and the impact on the well-being of individuals seeking asylum. Ultimately, research conducted during CoP training should aim to be socially helpful, and anti-racism research is a clear example of socially helpful research.

Chapter questions to provoke thoughts:

1. How can psychologists be more proactive in anti-racism between the major news events that generate the space for discourse?
2. How can discussions on race and racism take place without reifying race and othering those with different experiences of racism?
3. How can trainees engage in discussions of racism when it may be detrimental to their supervisory relationships?
4. How can the scholarly merits of anti-racist practice be emphasised in response to criticism of such work being unscientific?

Note

1. As of November 2023, this pathway is under review by the British Psychological Society and candidates are no longer accepted on to the programme. Those currently registered will be taught out. It has been confirmed as of March 2024, this pathway will no longer be a training pathway. As of 10 April 2024, it was confirmed that a consultation is currently underway pertaining to the future of affected qualifications.

References

Allen, C. (2020). Towards a working definition: Islamophobia and its contestation. In: *Reconfiguring Islamophobia. A Radical Rethinking of a Contested Concept. Palgrave Hate Studies*. Palgrave Pivot. https://doi.org/10.1007/978-3-030-33047-7_1

Arday, J. (2020). Fighting the tide: Understanding the difficulties facing Black, Asian and minority ethnic (BAME) doctoral students' pursuing a career in academia. *Educational Philosophy and Theory*, 53(10), 972–979. https://doi.org/10.1080/00131857.2020.1777640

Arday, J., Branchu, C., & Boliver, V. (2021). What do we know about black and minority ethnic (BAME) participation in UK higher education? *Social Policy and Society, 21*(1), 12–25. https://doi.org/10.1017/s1474746421000579

Bhopal, K., Brown, H., & Jackson, J. (2016). BME academic flight from UK to overseas higher education: Aspects of marginalisation and exclusion. *British Educational Research Journal, 42*(2), 240–257. https://doi.org/10.1002/berj.3204

Burns, M. A., & Vaughn, K. R. (2021). Race metatheory: Toward a dissolution of a calamitous concept. *Professional Psychology: Research and Practice, 52*(5), 487–493. https://doi.org/10.1037/pro0000416

Carter, R. T. (2007). Racism and psychological and emotional injury. *The Counseling Psychologist, 35*(1), 13–105. https://doi.org/10.1177/0011000006292033

Counter-Terrorism and Security Act 2015 (c.6). Available at https://www.legislation.gov.uk/ukpga/2015/6/contents/enacted

Daloye, D. (2022). The experiences of black and minority ethnic trainee counselling psychologists: An interpretative phenomenological analysis. *Counselling Psychology Review, 37*(1), 31–40. https://doi.org/10.53841/bpscpr.2022.37.1.31

Danvers, E. (2021). prevent/Ing critical thinking? The pedagogical impacts of prevent in UK higher education. *Teaching in Higher Education, 28*(6), 1264–1279. https://doi.org/10.1080/13562517.2021.1872533

Denyer, T., Wade, K., Whitney, M., Charura, D., & Proctor, G. (2022). Listen with love. *Psychotherapy & Politics International, 20*(1 & 2), 1–22. https://doi.org/10.24135/ppi.v20i1and2.06

Doharty, N., Madriaga, M., & Joseph-Salisbury, R. (2020). The university went to 'decolonise' and all they brought back was lousy diversity double-speak! Critical race counterstories from faculty of colour in 'decolonial' times. *Educational Philosophy and Theory, 53*(3), 233–244. https://doi.org/10.1080/00131857.2020.1769601

Gopal, D. P., & Rao, M. (2021). Playing hide and seek with structural racism. *BMJ, 373*(8289) n988. https://doi.org/10.1136/bmj.n988

Hall, D. (2021). Can you talk about race without going pink or feeling uncomfortable? In D. Charura & C. Lago (Eds), *Black identities + white therapies: Race, respect + diversity* (pp. 27–37). PCCS Books.

HCPC. (2022, August 1). *HCPC Updates Standards of Proficiency |.* www.hcpc-Uk.org. https://www.hcpc-uk.org/news-and-events/news/2022/sop-revisions-aug-2022/

Jankowski, G., Sandle, R., & Brown, M. (2022). Challenging the lack of BAME authors in a psychology curriculum. *Psychology of Women and Equalities Section Review, 5*(1), 18–36. https://doi.org/10.53841/bpspowe.2022.5.1.18

Lee, C. (2021). An anti-racist counselling training model. In D. Charura & C. Lago (Eds), *Black identities + white therapies: Race, respect + diversity* (pp. 52–64). PCCS Books.

Nkansa-Dwamena, O. (2017). Issues of race and ethnicity in counselling. In D. Murphy (Ed.), *Counselling psychology: A textbook for study and practice* (pp. 265–278). Wiley.

Nkansa-Dwamena, O., & Ade-Serrano, Y. (2023). Race, culture and ethnicity – What is your story? In T. Hanley & L. A. Winter (Eds.), *The SAGE handbook of counselling and psychotherapy* (pp. 67–74). SAGE.

Ruth Gould, R. (2020). The IHRA definition of antisemitism: Defining antisemitism by erasing Palestinians. *The Political Quarterly, 91*(4), 825–831. Portico. https://doi.org/10.1111/1467-923x.12883

Smith, K., McLeod, J., Blunden, N., Cooper, M., Gabriel, L., Kupfer, C., McLeod, J., Murphie, M.-C., Oddli, H. W., Thurston, M., & Winter, L. A. (2021). A pluralistic perspective on research in psychotherapy: Harnessing passion, difference and dialogue to promote justice and relevance. *Frontiers in Psychology, 12*, 1–15. https://doi.org/10.3389/fpsyg.2021.742676

Stoll, N., Yalipende, Y., Byrom, N. C., Hatch, S. L., & Lempp, H. (2022). Mental health and mental well-being of black students at UK universities: A review and thematic synthesis. *BMJ Open, 12*(2), e050720. https://doi.org/10.1136/bmjopen-2021-050720

Warner, L., Kurtiş, T., & Adya, A. (2020). Navigating criticisms of intersectional approaches: Reclaiming intersectionality for global social justice and well-being. *Women & Therapy, 43*(3–4), 262–277. https://doi.org/10.1080/02703149.2020.1729477

Williams, M., Faber, S., & Duniya, C. (2022). Being an anti-racist clinician. *The Cognitive Behaviour Therapist, 15*, E19. https://doi.org/10.1017/S1754470X22000162

Wynn, G., & Winter, L. A. (2023). Training in counselling psychology. In G. C. Davey (Ed.), *Applied psychology* (2nd ed., pp. 803–815). John Wiley & Sons Ltd. https://higheredbcs.wiley.com/legacy/college/davey/1119856744/4ProITCh/c43.pdf

Developing super-vision in a colour-blind world

3

Amelia Baldwin

Overview

The clinical and research supervisory relationship has the potential to address systemic issues of colour blindness in counselling and psychotherapy and further impact the wider context of our communities. Prioritising a critical intersectional and social justice lens subverts the tendency to blink off the central importance of race and racism to our societies. Our initial training, professionalisations, research practices, and supervisory relationships are often complicit in maintaining a system that continues to provide differential treatment to the marginalised in society. Supervision is a learning process that we are socialised into and internalised through our training, research, clinical practice, and clinical supervision. Movements to decolonise our practice often fall short because they take a piecemeal approach, which avoids the uncomfortable work that addressing racism entails. Supervision is critical to ensuring that the impact of the work continues beyond the triad of therapist-supervisor-client in ways that result in social justice. This requires maintaining focus on the uncomfortable work of addressing issues of race and racism within applied psychology. If this does not occur, supervision will collude with institutional and systemic racism.

DOI: 10.4324/9781003415244-4

Supervisory experiences

Garrett et al. (2001) share an anecdote of a supervisee joking that their supervisor would possess "[superpowers of] super-vision" (p. 147), initiating an important exploration of issues of difference as these pertain to the process of supervision and therapy at the beginning of the relationship. Conversely, supervision has the potential to perpetuate the dominance of particular perspectives by dismissing marginalised experiences, knowledge, and practices and by preventing entry altogether (Delgado & Stefancic, 2013; Dollarhide et al., 2021; Watkins & Shulman, 2008). In this chapter, I argue that the impact of supervision, as a learning and developmental process, can never be achieved without taking a critical, inclusive approach to address issues of race and racism. My reasons for taking this stance lie in part in my experiences as a Counselling Psychologist and supervisor who identifies as a Mixed-Race Neurodiverse Woman. Although I can "pass" as White in some contexts, my personal and professional experiences as a therapist, trainer, and supervisor have often resulted in the realisation that my social and professional worlds, and that of my supervisees and clients, are shaped by the ways in which power is constructed as processes at the intersection of raced, gendered, and ableist lines (Crenshaw, 1997).

Ryde (2000, 2009) highlights the potential for the position of Whiteness to become invisible and suggests the use of the seven-eyed model in supervision. The seven eyes are the culture of the client, supervisee, and supervisor, the unconscious supervisory process, the countertransference of the supervisee, the differences between the supervisee and the supervisor, and the broader socio-political and organisational context (Hawkins & Shohet, 2006). Sadly, inspection within supervision of the systemic and socioeconomic is not necessarily the norm (Constantine, 1997). Supervision is part of a cultural approach that can meaningfully apply anti-racist, social justice, and decolonial practices that reverberate through the communities we serve. For this to occur, issues of identifying and redressing racism need to be central to training, therapy, and supervision and not only considered when working with a racialised "other" as an expert, or in addition to what will then be viewed as the "real stuff" of therapy. Many have addressed how uninspected implicit power dynamics within supervision will reflect societal power differences, ensuring these differentials continue unchallenged and, therefore, unchanged (e.g. Constantine & Sue, 2007; Cook & Helms, 1988; Wind et al., 2021). Whether supervisees hold invisible normed positions has been shown to impact the supervisees' experiences and use of supervision in significant ways (e.g. Constantine & Sue, 2007; Granello et al., 1997; Ladany et al., 1997; Nelson & Holloway, 1990). These relational aspects highlight how supervisory processes can make visible or collude with structural privilege. Collusion may occur through what is coined microaggressions, which are an insidious and regular source of harm in the supervisory experience (and beyond) and refer to numerous indignities, invalidations, and inequalities (Constantine & Sue, 2007; Knox et al., 2003; Pieterse, 2018; Sue et al., 2007; Williams et al., 2017; Wind et al., 2021).

Constantine and Sue (2007) detail distinct types of racial microaggressions that manifest within supervisory relationships. Instances of microaggressions may involve the dismissal or avoidance of race-related material, labelling supervisees as too focused on issues relating to race and racism, perpetuating stereotypes, attributing blame for the racist context that has brought clients to therapy to explore their racial identity, and suggesting culturally inappropriate interventions based on personal biases and uninspected privileges. Supervisees may thereby internalise a deficit view of themselves, which can perversely decrease efficacy as it, in turn, increases anxiety (Garrison et al., 2022; Haley et al., 2015).

Negative experiences in supervision can result in a frightened supervisee who becomes unable to trust the supervisory process and may stop engaging with it altogether (Burkard et al., 2006; Crockett & Hays, 2015; Dollarhide et al., 2021; Jendrusina & Martinez, 2019). When supervisors ignore racialised elements approaching their work from a Eurocentric perspective, supervisees are landed with the burden of training their supervisors to understand the realities of racism, or working without the guidance and mentoring of supervision in order to try and address the crucial issues their clients bring (Hird et al., 2001; Jernigan et al., 2010; Washington et al., 2023). Research has found that although all supervisees are negatively affected by a supervisor's aversion to exploring issues of race, supervisees of colour experience more detrimental reactions, such as feelings of discomfort, fear, insult, and concern about the potential impact on their clients (Burkard et al., 2016). It is easy to see how ruptures in the supervisory relationship can occur in these scenarios (Lubbers, 2013), where supervisees may be presented with a difficult choice between their learning or negative responses from their supervisor (Eklund et al., 2014; Norton & Coleman, 2003). All of this results in barriers to the much-needed structural change of the very systems that therapy has the power to address in society.

Conversely, Burkard et al. (2006) found a direct relationship between supervisees' validation of their client's racial reality and their supervisors' ability to respond to and explore these experiences in supervision. Garrett et al. (2001) draw attention to the connection between racially marginalised clients' reluctance to participate in therapy or discontinuing it altogether (Sue & Sue, 1999) and the opportunity for supervisees to address this through the development of cultural awareness in supervision. The systemic impact of supervision is clear. Supervisors determine whether their supervisees will advocate and champion the practice needed to dismantle a racist system (Dollarhide et al., 2021; Eklund et al., 2014; Ellis et al., 2014). Helms and Cook (1999) point out that the failure to address power imbalances in supervision will disproportionately affect individuals with less power, particularly those who are marginalised. Consequently, clients and supervisees are more likely to bear the brunt of the negative consequences of inequality.

The supervisor of colour can also be subject to harm. Although microaggressions against supervisors of colour have been given less attention within literature, some highlight how supervisees and peers push back and challenge the presence of a supervisor or leader of colour (e.g. Pieterse, 2018). Experiences such as being monitored, facing complaints, and challenging relationships can lead to the supervisor ultimately leaving an organisation or profession altogether. These experiences are analogous to the concrete ceiling (Baxter-Nuamah, 2015; Chance, 2022; Davis, 2012). In comparison to the glass ceiling, a metaphor by which women are positioned to see what they are unable to attain or the reasons for lack of advancement, Chance (2022) extends this metaphor to the "concreteness" facing Black women, illustrating the impossibility of ever moving beyond these barriers (p. 44). Unsurprisingly, as Black women progress within leadership positions, they experience more questioning of their presence (Baxter-Nuamah, 2015; Chance, 2022).

Various levels of structural inequality mean that if supervision does not directly address the issues of power that bring clients into therapy (for example, regular experiences of racism or experiences of hate crime), supervision can become a process of whitewashing the very systemic issues that originate distress. As supervision redirects and distracts supervisees away from any meaningful response, this activity is likely to be reflected in the therapeutic relationship with clients, where they will be similarly distracted from addressing issues of racism within therapy (Mckenzie-Mavinga, 2020). We internalise our supervisors similarly to the process of internalisation of our therapists. Without supervisors modelling and mentoring the direction into the uncomfortable spaces needed to address issues of race and racism, this will not occur (Burkard et al., 2016; Chan, 2019; Dollarhide et al., 2021; Garrett et al., 2001; Ryde, 2000, 2009; Tarshis & Baird, 2021). In this way, racism will be perpetuated within us and our therapeutic relationships. Eventually, it becomes not racism but the response to racism that is problematised (Mckenzie-Mavinga, 2016). Supervisees are silenced, and power differences are reinforced without question. The client is positioned as disordered, defensive, and traumatised, and the intervention acts purely on addressing the client's response to inequality. The potential liberatory impact of supervision is thwarted, and supervision becomes a process of preventing challenges to and maintaining the status quo (Constantine et al., 2005; Washington et al., 2023). Every time an under-privilege is not addressed, so is an over-privilege reinforced and vice versa.

Supervision contextualised

A personal example of this experience occurred early in my career during a group supervision session. I was the only racially marginalised supervisee among approximately six older peers with a well-regarded White middle-class female psychodynamic supervisor. Within the supervision, a peer presented a case; her supervisory issue centred around her disapproval of social services' involvement with a Black African client due to the client's "caning" of their children. This peer stated that they had lived in an African country (albeit several hundred miles away from the country of their client) and stated that the client's distress was due to the cultural insensitivity of the social worker who could not see that "corporal punishment was a part of African culture". I was struck by a wave of emotion when considering how systematic violence had been implemented towards my family of origin in Southern Africa, particularly as a result of being racialised as "coloured" (a Southern African category for Mixed-Race people) within a British colonial apartheid system. By the time I had formulated a response, the group supervision had moved on to the next case. Apart from this one instance, racism was never brought up in any supervision or training sessions.

In addition to the emotional response, I had in relation to the material, I experienced a sense of responsibility to raise this as the only person of colour in the room. Due to the powerful position of Whiteness, it is easy to continue to have a blind spot to this power (Hays & Chang, 2003; Washington et al., 2023). This avoidance leads to a colour/privilege-blind approach to supervision. It is challenging to address an issue when the majority possess the dominant position and will not have experienced its absence. I felt shame that I did not raise this in the moment, particularly as it became clear that I was "passing as White". It seemed as though the only person considered racialised was the client, and this racialised difference was being generalised to all African people. At that moment, there appeared to be an unsaid agreement that the social worker, in this case, was incorrect and somehow acting from a racist position, which in turn resulted in all of us colluding with the racist assumption that Black people's culture includes violence to their children. However, there was another person of colour in the room – me. I still feel a strong wish to have paused and reflected on, as Ablack (2021) suggests, what was happening relationally in the room, as painful as this was.

Perhaps if the supervisor had simply paused to consider how this had landed with supervisees, how this was landing with themselves, and given space to explore issues of isms within supervision, I imagine this could have been a different supervisory experience. It is difficult to make such a judgement now; even so, this learning emphasised the importance of stopping and giving space to reflect on issues of race and culture, which are relational, after all (Ablack, 2021; Mckenzie-Mavinga, 2016; Patel et al., 1991). It is vital to continually develop supervisory skills to deliberately and conscientiously direct the work to recognise privilege-blind practice and conduct decolonisation at various levels. These skills have similar implications in another significant supervisory relationship, which is that of the research supervisor.

Super-vision in research

Research supervision is a neglected aspect of literature and research. Some point out the propensity for research supervision to determine doctoral trainee completion (Trudgett, 2014; Walker, 2020). It is not only the academy's ivory tower (Gullo et al., 2013; Walker, 2020) that results from structural inequality but also what knowledges are allowed to develop within this context (hooks, 2003a). Limits are placed on who is allowed in, colonising broader systems and knowledge bases (Broadfoot & Munshi, 2007).

A significant factor to consider here is the research supervisory relationship. The Indigenous Australian doctoral students in Trudgett's (2014) study wished to have relationships that did not reflect an expert-student power dynamic but rather a relationship that encouraged a student's exploration of their own research interests and methodology. Trudgett (2014) highlights that the reason for embarking on doctoral-level research was often to address issues facing student communities. Therefore, the potential for relational rupture is present when the supervisor directs research towards their unexamined positions of power. Limitations placed on what constitutes knowledge within academia can be evidenced through university practices, procedures, policies, and assessments (Broadfoot et al., 2010; Walker, 2020). Walker (2020) summarises this as "[controlling] the access Black people have to academia … [and maintenance of] white privilege" (p. 136). Supervisors must be mindful to attend to and validate critical aspects of experience.

A broader example from our society is the Macpherson report (1999) resulting from the inquiry into Stephen Lawrence's murder in 1993. The report brought to public attention the impact of secondary victimisation and made recommendations concerning the importance of not questioning the validity of the perception of racism. This recognition requires reflection on what the difference means to the client-supervisee relationship and, as this is brought into all supervisory relationships; what this means to the supervisee, supervisor, and their relationship.

Super-vision in practice

As hooks (2003b) points out, "One of the bitter ironies anti-racists face when working to end white-supremacist thinking and action is that the folks who most perpetuate it are the individuals who are usually the least willing to acknowledge that race matters" (p. 28). This does not exclude supervisors of colour, unsurprisingly, given therapy's Eurocentric knowledge base of mainly White European men (Katz, 1985; Mckenzie-Mavinga, 2020; Washington et al., 2023). Racialisation is a process that shapes all of us. As Dalal (2002) points out, we are not "[chromatically] ... black or white" (p. 3). We are all racialised and responsible for decolonisation, starting with the self, regardless of whether we are a person of colour or not. Power dynamics are continually reproduced, emphasising the importance of practices that develop awareness of our biases (Berzoff, 2023; Layton, 2006). Critical consciousness can only occur through the continual assessment of socio-political matters (Freire, 2005; Hernández & McDowell, 2010). Similarly, McIntosh's (1998) "Unpacking the Invisible Knapsack" builds on her feminist research and explores the function of, and what it means to face, one's privileges. It is only through the difficult work of analysing power and privilege that systemic racism can be understood and, therefore, changed (Hernández & McDowell, 2010).

Many point out that even though race impacts many parts of our lives, it is also one of the most challenging subjects to address. Awareness of bias naturally coincides with anger, anxiety, guilt, or shame (Berzoff, 2023; Ryde, 2009). Direction towards resistance and intense feeling can be used to guide and develop our continual learning (Ryde, 2009). Here lies the real-life work of how race operates in all its complexity (Burkard et al., 2016). Supervisors can normalise intense and defensive responses and use these as prompts to dive into contextual underlying issues (Eklund et al., 2014). Supervisors being prepared "to open the cultural door and walk through it with the supervisee" could be the most impactful aspect of their supervisory relationship (Bernard & Goodyear, 1998, p. 45).

Multicultural therapy, the fourth force of Counselling Psychology (Essandoh, 1996), emphasises the importance of using this lens. However, what this means in practice is contended: "Inclusives" take a view of multicultural practice that encompasses many forms of difference, including race, gender, or class (Stone, 1997, p. 264); "Exclusives" focus on racially marginalised groups, arguing that without this focus, the practice ends up allowing counselling/clinical professionals to fall back on a comfortable route of avoiding racial issues (Burkard et al., 2006; Stone, 1997, p. 265).

A common critique of multicultural supervision is its potential to develop into a practice of applying "a cookbook … [of] cultural stereotypes" (Stone, 1997, p. 270). Here, practices such as matching supervisees to clients based on race or ethnicity are implemented without considering what this means and the potential effects (Stone, 1997). Decentring Whiteness and an inspection of how power is exercised are necessary focuses of supervision.

Many point out the ethical responsibility to use an intersectional lens within supervision (Hernández & McDowell, 2010; Pieterse, 2018; Tarshis & Baird, 2021). The increase in neoliberal policies and a cost-of-living crisis urgently require supervisors to support action that addresses the impact (Berzoff, 2023; Layton, 2020). Black feminists (e.g. hooks, 2015) have brought to attention the potential failure of White feminism to consider the importance of the racialised experiences of Black women. The Combahee River Collective (2015) highlight how inseparable racism, classism, and sexism are when experienced together. An intersectional lens in supervision will deconstruct class, culture, and race as they systemically intersect in real-time, offering an ongoing praxis. Examples include identification and action to address binary categorisations, pathologisation, Eurocentricity, and empiricism (Berzoff, 2023; Collins, 1986; Renik, 1993).

Such intersectional practice acts as a form of critical race theory (CRT), illustrating how anti-Blackness is perpetuated through the application of "colorblind models of … supervision" (Washington et al., 2023, p. 150). Decentring Whiteness results in the recognition of unearned privileges (McIntosh, 1998) and CRT's full potential is limited by focusing on the individual rather than strategies to dismantle privilege (Collins, 2019; Grzanka, 2020; Washington et al., 2023). CRT supervision is an ideal space to identify and support anti-racist practices.

Supervision becomes part of a liberating act where critical awareness of the clients', supervisors', and supervisees' systemic reality is the focus (Dollarhide et al., 2021; Freire, 2005). Power is always relational and, therefore, can be redressed (Foucault, 1980); thus, a crucial aspect of supervision is the inclusion of a comprehensive assessment of the system. Bronfenbrenner (1979) provides a method to investigate systems, proposing levels of complex systems that interact with each other. The focus begins with the supervisee's self, moving to their relationships, then towards organisations and the political, ultimately leading to the examination of the dominant culture's ideologies. As power is redressed in the supervisory relationship, so can the same cascade throughout therapeutic encounters (Dollarhide et al., 2021).

Conclusion

It is essential to emphasise that anti-racist practice is not "for the too busy or the faint-hearted" (d'Ardenne, 2012, p. 119). As addressed here, discomfort in supervision is inevitable. The power of taking an anti-racist position is not pretending to be bias-free (Oluo, 2018). Instead, it is being open to recognise and take action to address racism, starting with the self. Supervision can be the space we provide each other to contain, recharge, nourish, and celebrate our work in solidarity.

Chapter questions to provoke thoughts:

1. What do I view as the purpose and remit of therapy, supervision, and research?
2. What would sharing privilege look like in supervision?
3. How do I heal from the effects of marginalisation?
4. What happens when it gets uncomfortable in supervision, and what causes the discomfort?
5. Whose voices, perspectives, knowledges, and practices are silent?
6. Who raises these questions in supervision, and what happens when they do?
7. How do my supervisory practices affect change to structural power?

References

Ablack, C. J. (2021). Who is transforming what? Ideas and reflections on training, practice and supervision in radical mode. In D. Charura & C. Lago (Eds.), *Black identities + white therapies: Race, respect + diversity* (pp. 141–151). PCCS Books.

Baxter-Nuamah, M. (2015). Through the looking glass: Barriers and coping mechanisms encountered by African American women presidents at predominately white institutions. *All Graduate Theses, Dissertations, and Other Capstone Projects.* https://cornerstone.lib.mnsu.edu/etds/414

Bernard, J. M., & Goodyear, R. K. (1998). *Fundamentals of clinical supervision* (2nd ed., pp. xiv, 354). Allyn & Bacon.

Berzoff, J. (2023). Intersectionality: Power differentials, impasses and enactments in clinical practice and in supervision. *Psychoanalytic Social Work, 30*(1), 64–76. https://doi.org/10.1080/15228878.2022.2073457

Broadfoot, K. J., & Munshi, D. (2007). Diverse voices and alternative rationalities: Imagining forms of postcolonial organizational communication. *Management Communication Quarterly, 21*(2), 249–267. https://doi.org/10.1177/0893318907306037

Broadfoot, K. J., Munshi, D., & Nelson-Marsh, N. (2010). COMMUNEcation: A rhizomatic tale of participatory technology, postcoloniality and professional community. *New Media & Society, 12*(5), 797–812. https://doi.org/10.1177/1461444809348880

Bronfenbrenner, U. (1979). *Ecology of human development: Experiments by nature and design* (1st ed.). Harvard University Press. https://doi.org/10.2307/j.ctv26071r6

Burkard, A. W., Edwards, L. M., & Adams, H. A. (2016). Racial color blindness in counseling, therapy, and supervision. In *The myth of racial color blindness: Manifestations, dynamics, and impact* (pp. 295–311). American Psychological Association. https://doi.org/10.1037/14754-018

Burkard, A. W., Johnson, A. J., Madson, M. B., Pruitt, N. T., Contreras-Tadych, D. A., Kozlowski, J. M., Hess, S. A., & Knox, S. (2006). Supervisor cultural responsiveness and unresponsiveness in cross-cultural supervision. *Journal of Counseling Psychology, 53*(3), 288–301. https://doi.org/10.1037/0022-0167.53.3.288

Chan, Y. (2019). Best practices in addressing diversity in clinical supervision: A survey of experienced supervisors [Psy.D., Pepperdine University]. In *ProQuest Dissertations and Theses*. https://www.proquest.com/docview/2306303037/abstract/B29C091C874E4E23PQ/1

Chance, N. L. (2022). Resilient leadership: A phenomenological exploration into how Black women in higher education leadership navigate cultural adversity. *Journal of Humanistic Psychology, 62*(1), 44–78. https://doi.org/10.1177/00221678211003000

Collins, P. H. (1986). Learning from the outsider within: The sociological significance of Black feminist Thought. *Social Problems, 33*(6), s14–s32. https://doi.org/10.2307/800672

Collins, P. H. (2019). *Intersectionality as critical social theory*. Duke University Press.

Combahee River Collective. (2015). A Black feminist statement. In G. T. Hull, P. Bell-Scott, & B. Smith (Eds.), *All the women are white, all the Blacks are men, but some of us are brave: Black women's studies* (2nd ed., pp. 33–37). The Feminist Press at the City University of New York.

Constantine, M. G. (1997). Facilitating multicultural competency in counseling supervision: Operationalizing a practical framework. In D. B Pope-Davies & H. L. K. Coleman (Eds.), *Multicultural counseling competencies: Assessment, education and training, and supervision* (pp. 310–324). Sage Publications, Inc.

Constantine, M. G., & Sue, D. W. (2007). Perceptions of racial microaggressions among Black supervisees in cross-racial dyads. *Journal of Counseling Psychology, 54*(2), 142–153. https://doi.org/10.1037/0022-0167.54.2.142

Constantine, M. G., Warren, A. K., & Miville, M. L. (2005). White racial identity dyadic interactions in supervision: Implications for Supervisees' multicultural counseling competence. *Journal of Counseling Psychology, 52*(4), 490–496. https://doi.org/10.1037/0022-0167.52.4.490

Cook, D. A., & Helms, J. E. (1988). Visible racial/ethnic group supervisees' satisfaction with cross-cultural supervision as predicted by relationship characteristics. *Journal of Counseling Psychology, 35*(3), 268–274. https://doi.org/10.1037/0022-0167.35.3.268

Crenshaw, K. (1997). Demarginalizing the intersection of race and sex: A Black feminist critique of antidiscrimination doctrine, feminist theory and antiracist politics. In K. Maschke (Ed.), *Feminist legal theories* (pp. 23–52). Routledge.

Crockett, S., & Hays, D. G. (2015). The influence of supervisor multicultural competence on the supervisory working Alliance, supervisee counseling self-efficacy, and supervisee satisfaction with supervision: A mediation model. *Counselor Education and Supervision*, *54*(4), 258–273. https://doi.org/10.1002/ceas.12025

d'Ardenne, P. (2012). Supervision, personal development and self-care in transcultural counselling. In *Counselling in transcultural settings: Priorities for a restless world. Counselling in transcultural settings: Priorities for a restless world* (pp. 115–128). SAGE Publications Ltd. https://doi.org/10.4135/9781473914926

Dalal, F. (2002). *Race, colour and the processes of racialization: New perspectives from group analysis, psychoanalysis and sociology*. Routledge.

Davis, D. R. (2012). *A phenomenological study on the leadership development of African American women executives in academia and business*. University of Nevada. https://doi.org/10.34917/4332702

Delgado, R., & Stefancic, J. (2013). *Critical race theory: The cutting edge* (3rd ed.). Temple University Press.

Dollarhide, C. T., Hale, S. C., & Stone-Sabali, S. (2021). A new model for social justice supervision. *Journal of Counseling & Development*, *99*(1), 104–113. https://doi.org/10.1002/jcad.12358

Eklund, K., Aros-O'Malley, M., & Murrieta, I. (2014). Multicultural supervision: What difference does difference make? *Contemporary School Psychology*, *18*(3), 195–204. https://doi.org/10.1007/s40688-014-0024-8

Ellis, M. V., Berger, L., Hanus, A. E., Ayala, E. E., Swords, B. A., & Siembor, M. (2014). Inadequate and harmful clinical supervision: Testing a revised framework and assessing occurrence. *The Counseling Psychologist*, *42*(4), 434–472. https://doi.org/10.1177/0011000013508656

Essandoh, P. K. (1996). Multicultural counseling as the 'Fourth Force': A call to arms. *The Counseling Psychologist*, *24*(1), 126–137. https://doi.org/10.1177/0011000096241008

Foucault, M. (1980). *Power/Knowledge: Selected interviews and other writings, 1972–1977*. Knopf Doubleday Publishing Group.

Freire, P. (2005). *Pedagogy of the Oppressed. 30th anniversary edition*. Continuum NY, London.

Garrett, M. T., Borders, L. D., Crutchfield, L. B., Torres-Rivera, E., Brotherton, D., & Curtis, R. (2001). Multicultural SuperVISION: A paradigm of cultural responsiveness for supervisors. *Journal of Multicultural Counseling and Development*, *29*(2), 147–158. https://doi.org/10.1002/j.2161-1912.2001.tb00511.x

Garrison, Y., Yeung, C. W., Ho, Y. C. S., Hong, J. E., Son, Y., Lin, C.-L. R., & Bermingham, C. (2022). Linguistic minority international counseling psychology Trainees' experiences in clinical supervision. *The Counseling Psychologist*, *50*(6), 813–844. https://doi.org/10.1177/00110000221094324

Granello, D. H., Beamish, P. M., & Davis, T. E. (1997). Supervisee empowerment: Does gender make a difference? *Counselor Education and Supervision*, *36*(4), 305–317. https://doi.org/10.1002/j.1556-6978.1997.tb00397.x

Grzanka, P. R. (2020). From buzzword to critical psychology: An invitation to take intersectionality seriously. *Women & Therapy*, *43*(3–4), 244–261. https://doi.org/10.1080/02703149.2020.1729473

Gullo, A., Li Volti, G., & Ristagno, G. (2013). New burns and trauma journal celebrating translational research. *Burns & Trauma, 1*(2), 2321–3868.118922. https://doi.org/10.4103/2321-3868.118922

Haley, M., Romero Marin, M., & Gelgand, J. C. (2015). Language anxiety and counseling self-efficacy. *Journal of Multicultural Counseling and Development, 43*(3), 162–172. https://doi.org/10.1002/jmcd.12012

Hawkins, P., & Shohet, R. (2006). *Supervision in the helping professions* (3rd ed.). Open University Press.

Hays, D. G., & Chang, C. Y. (2003). White privilege, oppression, and racial identity development: Implications for supervision. *Counselor Education and Supervision, 43*(2), 134–145. https://doi.org/10.1002/j.1556-6978.2003.tb01837.x

Helms, J. E., & Cook, D. A. (1999). Using race and culture in counseling and psychotherapy: Theory and process. *Adolescence, 34*(135), 642–642.

Hernández, P., & McDowell, T. (2010). Intersectionality, power, and relational safety in context: Key concepts in clinical supervision. *Training and Education in Professional Psychology, 4*(1), 29–35. https://doi.org/10.1037/a0017064

Hird, J. S., Cavalieri, C. E., Dulko, J. P., Felice, A. A. D., & Ho, T. A. (2001). Visions and realities: Supervisee perspectives of multicultural supervision. *Journal of Multicultural Counseling and Development, 29*(2), 114–130. https://doi.org/10.1002/j.2161-1912.2001.tb00509.x

hooks, b (2015). *Ain't I a woman Black women and feminism* (2nd ed.). Routledge, Taylor & Francis Group.

hooks, b (2003a). *Rock my soul: Black people and self-esteem*. Washington Square Press.

hooks, b (2003b). *Teaching community: A pedagogy of Hope*. Psychology Press.

Jendrusina, A. A., & Martinez, J. H. (2019). Hello from the other side: Student of color perspectives in supervision. *Training and Education in Professional Psychology, 13*(3), 160–166. https://doi.org/10.1037/tep0000255

Jernigan, M. M., Green, C. E., Helms, J. E., Perez-Gualdron, L., & Henze, K. (2010). An examination of people of color supervision dyads: Racial identity matters as much as race. *Training and Education in Professional Psychology, 4*(1), 62–73. https://doi.org/10.1037/a0018110

Katz, J. H. (1985). The sociopolitical nature of counseling. *The Counseling Psychologist, 13*(4), 615–624. https://doi.org/10.1177/0011000085134005

Knox, S., Burkard, A. W., Johnson, A. J., Suzuki, L. A., & Ponterotto, J. G. (2003). African American and European American therapists' experiences of addressing race in cross-racial psychotherapy dyads. *Journal of Counseling Psychology, 50*(4), 466–481. https://doi.org/10.1037/0022-0167.50.4.466

Ladany, N., Brittan-Powell, C. S., & Pannu, R. K. (1997). The influence of supervisory racial identity interaction and racial matching on the supervisory working Alliance and supervisee multicultural competence. *Counselor Education and Supervision, 36*(4), 284–304. https://doi.org/10.1002/j.1556-6978.1997.tb00396.x

Layton, L. (2006). racial identities, racial enactments, and normative unconscious processes. *The Psychoanalytic Quarterly, LXXV*(1), 237–269. https://doi.org/10.1002/j.2167-4086.2006.tb00039.x

Layton, L. (2020). *Toward a social psychoanalysis: Culture, character, and normative unconscious processes*. Routledge. https://doi.org/10.4324/9781003023098

Lubbers, L. (2013). Supervisees' Experiences Of Ruptures In Multicultural Supervision: A Qualitative Study. *Dissertations (1934-)*. https://epublications.marquette.edu/dissertations_mu/295

Macpherson, W. (1999). *The Stephen Lawrence inquiry.* London: Stationery Office.

McIntosh, P. (1998). White privilege: Unpacking the invisible knapsack. In M. McGoldrick (Ed.), *Re-visioning family therapy: Race, culture, and gender in clinical practice* (pp. 147–152). The Guilford Press. (Reprinted from 'Peace and Freedom,' July/August 1989, pp. 10–12. Also reprinted in modified form from 'White privilege and male privilege: A personal account of coming to see correspondences through work in women's studies,' Center Working Paper 189, 1989).

Mckenzie-Mavinga, I. (2016). *The challenge of racism in therapeutic practice: Engaging with oppression in practice and supervision* (2nd ed.). Bloomsbury Publishing.

Mckenzie-Mavinga, I. (2020). Engaging with racialized process in clinical supervision: Political or personal. In R. Majors, K. Carberry, & T. S. Ransaw (Eds.), *The international handbook of Black community mental health* (pp. 557–568). Emerald Publishing Limited. https://doi.org/10.1108/978-1-83909-964-920201034

Nelson, M. L., & Holloway, E. L. (1990). Relation of gender to power and involvement in supervision. *Journal of Counseling Psychology, 37*(4), 473–481. https://doi.org/10.1037/0022-0167.37.4.473

Norton, R. A., & Coleman, H. L. K. (2003). Multicultural supervision: The influence of race-related issues in supervision and outcome. In *Handbook of multicultural competencies: In counseling & psychology* (pp. 114–134). Sage Publications, Inc. https://doi.org/10.4135/9781452231693.n8

Oluo, I. (2019). *So You Want to Talk about Race.* Seal Press, Hachette Book Group

Patel, N., Bennett, E., Dennis, M., Dosanjh, N., Mahtani, A., Miller, A., & Nadirshaw, Z. (1991). *Clinical psychology, 'Race' and culture: A training manual* (1st ed.). Wiley.

Pieterse, A. L. (2018). Attending to racial trauma in clinical supervision: Enhancing client and supervisee outcomes. *The Clinical Supervisor, 37*(1), 204–220. https://doi.org/10.1080/07325223.2018.1443304

Renik, O. (1993). Analytic interaction: Conceptualizing technique in light of the analyst's irreducible subjectivity. *The Psychoanalytic Quarterly, 62*(4), 553–571.

Ryde, J. (2000). Supervising across difference. *International Journal of Psychotherapy, 5*(1), 37–48. https://doi.org/10.1080/13569080050020254

Ryde, J. (2009). *Being white in the helping professions: Developing effective intercultural awareness.* Jessica Kingsley Publishers.

Stone, G. L. (1997). Multiculturalism as a context for supervision: Perspectives, limitations, and implications. In D. B. Pope-Davis, & H. L. K. Coleman (Eds.), *Multicultural counseling competencies: Assessment, education and training, and supervision* (pp. 263–289). Sage Publications, Inc.

Sue, D. W., Capodilupo, C. M., Torino, G. C., Bucceri, J. M., Holder, A. M. B., Nadal, K. L., & Esquilin, M. (2007). Racial microaggressions in everyday life: Implications for clinical practice. *The American Psychologist, 62*(4), 271–286. https://doi.org/10.1037/0003-066X.62.4.271

Sue, D. W., & Sue, D. (1999). *Counseling the culturally different: Theory and practice* (3rd ed., pp. xiii, 368). John Wiley & Sons Inc.

Tarshis, S., & Baird, S. L. (2021). Applying intersectionality in clinical supervision: A scoping review. *The Clinical Supervisor, 40*(2), 218–240. https://doi.org/10.1080/07325223.2021.1919949

Trudgett, M. (2014). Supervision provided to indigenous Australian doctoral students: A black and white issue. *Higher Education Research & Development, 33*(5), 1035–1048. https://doi.org/10.1080/07294360.2014.890576

Walker, S. (2020). Racism in academia: (How to) stay Black, sane and proud as the doctoral supervisory relationship implodes. In R. Majors, K. Carberry, & T. S. Ransaw (Eds.), *The international handbook of Black community mental health* (pp. 93–111). Emerald Publishing Limited. https://doi.org/10.1108/978-1-83909-964-920201007

Washington, A. R., Williams, J. M., & Byrd, J. A. (2023). Exposing blindspots and the hidden curriculum within counselor supervision models. *Counselor Education and Supervision, 62*(2), 149–156. https://doi.org/10.1002/ceas.12260

Watkins, M., & Shulman, H. (2008). *Toward psychologies of liberation.* Palgrave Macmillan UK. https://doi.org/10.1057/9780230227736

Williams, T. D., Shamp, L. M., & Harris, K. J. (2017). Microaggressions in psychotherapy. *Psychotherapy Bulletin, 52*(4), 12–18.

Wind, S. A., Cook, R. M., & McKibben, W. B. (2021). Supervisees' of differing genders and races perceptions of power in supervision. *Counselling Psychology Quarterly, 34*(2), 275–297. https://doi.org/10.1080/09515070.2020.1731791

Ethics and ethical practice   **4**

Jaspreet Tehara, Ohemaa Nkansa-Dwamena, and Yetunde Ade-Serrano

Right conduct is relative always to the *human* situation and morality is oriented not from any absolute standards of honesty or truth but from the *social good* in each situation. Conduct that promotes smooth relationships, that upholds the social structure, is good; conduct that runs counter to smooth social relationships is bad.

(J. D. and E. J. Krige in Forde, 1954, p. 78)

Overview

Ethics and ethical practice are well-documented areas of interest in the UK for many professions including psychology. Due to the nature of guidelines psychologists have to adhere to, we postulate the critical intention and dissection of meaning, overlaying these with consideration of race on three levels, macro, meso, and micro. We highlight the interconnection within and between them reinforcing the notion that they are not mutually exclusive. At the conjunction of race, ethics, and ethical practice, the discussions provide the context necessary for reframing moral and professional codes of conduct.

DOI: 10.4324/9781003415244-5

Introduction

As UK Applied Psychologists, we are bound by a professional code of conduct (BPS, 2021) which is outlined within the British Psychological Society (BPS) and the Health and Care Professions Council (HCPC) literature, in addition to an ethics guidance that informs and underpins psychological practice. The absence of multicultural and anti-discriminatory lenses within the development of these guidelines has meant harmful gaps within professional standards and ethical practice, perpetuating biases, and assumptions in our work with minoritised communities. This is exacerbated by professionals who work within systems that lack ethical congruence in its approach to culturally attuned care.

The importance of this is underscored when there is a lack of or minimal interrogation of values and bias pertaining to race and ethical practice which has implications for professional development and an ongoing enactment of power differentials in practice.

Ethics in psychological professions in this chapter will be observed through the interaction between three levels (the macro – pertaining to society, the meso – pertaining to the groups within societies, and the micro – pertaining to the individual, see Figure 4.1), and how the impact of wider societal shifts can cause unexpected reverberations between and within these levels (or systems).

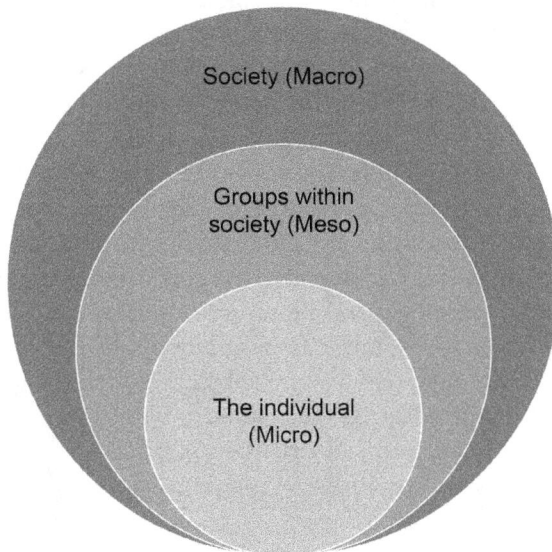

Figure 4.1 A visual representation of how the individual sits within meso and macro levels that modulate their experiences.

The ethnic practitioner at the macro-level

The high-profile Bawa-Garba case[1] (Emery et al., 2021) exemplifies the ways in which there can be a building sense of persecution towards professionals of ethnic backgrounds from the institutions in which they work showcasing the dynamics of race, ethics, and ethical practice. Ethical (mis) practice on a macro level often contradicts the professional's efforts and experiences impaired by the intrinsic unconscious bias (Agarwal, 2020) existing within it.

As that case unfolded, there was an interesting observation to be made about the institution as a site of power that imposes on the practitioner and exposes the undertakings of the institution to uphold their power. In this instance, the practitioner is framed as the perpetrator held accountable for abstention of protocol in the quest of preserving the institution's reputation. The General Medical Council (GMC) was publicly criticised for its actions and the ways in which Dr Bawa-Garba had been treated following the findings of the investigation into the events leading to the loss of life (ibid).

Qualitative research commissioned by HCPC and conducted by Maben et al. (2021) into registrants' experiences of fitness-to-practice (FTP)[2] procedures concluded that improvements were crucial to better support the psychological wellbeing of registrants during and after the process. To the point of power and the institution's propensity to offer up individual practitioners to the slaughter as opposed to highlighting the systemic failures contributing to (in extreme cases, loss of life) the dysfunction of the system. Maben et al.'s research denoted staff shortages, IT system failures and a lack of access to available data as the "systemic issues" for "corporate responsibility". We would argue that the inconsideration of race overlaying ethics and ethical practice conceals additional layers intertwined within the FTP process experience. There is insufficient data from HCPC (HCPC, 2023) to confidently consider the outcomes for ethnic practitioners when subjected to and held accountable for failures in the system.

Ethnic practitioners can find that they are censured in several ways due to dynamics of power, privilege, and prejudice within society. They can often be found to be blamed for systemic issues, they can be targeted as a method of deflecting responsibility, they can be subject to issues of political exploitation (in relation to the interpersonal politics within a local system, or as part of a wider national political discussion), and they can be subject to racialised stereotypes and prejudices (and as such can be targeted for cultural differences).

Ethically, it is imperative to then explore ways of developing a culture around psychological practice that can produce robustness in the investigation of complaints and with a nuance of understanding and implementing learning outcomes that are not necessarily punitive but are intent on understanding the entirety of the issue with cause for further development.

Ethics and ethical practice on a macro level is also about addressing the social realities and social context in which practitioners and clients exist. This also warrants acknowledgement, challenge, and engagement to impact meaningful shifts on a meso and micro level. The ethical challenge on the macro level requires a transformation of theory and practice – drawing in and authentically listening to the experiences of individuals. The body of existent research, policy, and documentation of lived experience continues to be an exercise in harm if recommendations arising from these are not tangibly implemented in a way that strongly shapes and upholds ethical practice across all mental health professions.

This can be further complicated as the profession itself is known to be institutionally biased. In 2020, the Chief Executive of the BPS, Sarb Bajwa, recently appointed at the time, acknowledged that the BPS could be considered institutionally racist. Sarb also went on to address various issues of intersectionality across the BPS, indicating that while the profession was "predominantly white and female" it was not "reflected in leadership positions across the profession, which are disproportionately white and male" (Bajwa, 2020).

The following year, Fernando et al. (2021) delivered a landmark presentation at the Division of Clinical Psychology annual conference where they asked the division itself if it was doing enough to change the face of the division (and it can be argued by proxy the BPS itself due to the overwhelming size and number of clinical psychologists the BPS represents) in light of its work with both ethnic community practitioners and patients. It could be suggested that the lack of action itself is unethical because of the effect this lack of intervention has had cascades through to the directions and decisions made about end-user care through appropriate exploratory or targeted research, strategy for intervention, and review of those interventions once designed and implemented. Given these acknowledgements, is it ethical no sustainable changes have been made thus far three to four years on?

The ethnic practitioner at the meso-level

Slay and Smith (2011) discuss the inherent conflict in the development of practitioners from minoritised backgrounds, positing that there could be incongruence between the "possible self", and the "provisional self" (see also Markus & Nurius, 1986), meaning that during the course of developing a professional identity, minoritised professionals wrestle (consciously or otherwise) with the concept of their cultural backgrounds and the cultural expectations of what is negotiable professionally as they begin to transcend those expectations.

On a meso level, the interconnection of race, ethics, and ethical practice have impact(s) in a myriad of ways. The ethics (personal and professional) and values of practitioners are shaped by the healthcare culture and professional bodies, in ways that are incongruent with the communities served or engaged with. Practitioners therefore may find themselves negotiating knowledge, beliefs, morals, and customs within systems which misalign with their own positioning and experiences. In this regard, the role we play as a group of practitioners within systems that may not uphold ethical and racial values is integral – the ethical standards that guide practitioners are rendered inadequate in these circumstances. This may require learning, training, challenging, and adopting anti-discriminatory stance and cultural humility to help propel systemic shift and support a more client, community-driven culture. It is also therefore imperative for practitioners as a group to live in their authenticity despite the challenges the systems lurch at us.

In living in our authenticity as ethnic practitioners, we may need to consider the quality of our practice, fears around exploitation, transparency about our expectations, and outcomes measured against that of the system we exist in, equity to achieve, the nature of support we subscribe to (including clinical/research supervision) and guidance to develop individually. Our positionality on value, norms, and behaviours are not absent of systemic power influences. Hence, we need to adduce together strategic aims of long-term stability for the profession, and in particular the impact that has on shaping our work with ethnic community patients, clients, and/or service users.[3]

As part of the exploration of the ethnic practitioner within the meso-level, it is relevant to address the offerings of superficial overtures surmised by the strategies of equality diversity and inclusion (EDI), particularly as these often fall to existing research or theoretical underpinning from Western or European perspectives. In this way, the ethical standards and hence the ethical practice required for ethnic practitioners to follow devalues the essence of their individual and collective origin. We acknowledge the assiduous work of individuals and groups who unequivocally devote time to incorporate African and Eastern values within EDI strategies. It is therefore imperative to interrogate which groups or individuals' ethical guidelines protect and speak for. If ethics and ethical practice do not explicitly and tangibly consider the experiences of ethnic communities, then it remains that they are interpreted and considered for the privileged few.

The ethnic practitioner at the micro-level

Daloye (2022) conducted an IPA (interpretative phenomenological analysis) study with trainee Counselling Psychologists from Black and Minority Ethnic (BME) backgrounds and investigated the experiences of what being a trainee Counselling Psychologist feels like. The broad themes of the participants within this research indicated that there was a difficulty in their experience of (1) "a need to belong", (2) a lack of diversity, (3) the impact of support on the self, (4) versatile BME trainee identity, and (5) managing a range of challenges.

Fifteen years prior, Tan and Campion (2007) discussed issues of the identity process and how there is an assimilative experience in doctoral Clinical Psychology training that indicates adopting the etiquette of a professional (including the shift to the perception of an empathic stance).

These exemplars of research while focused on trainee practitioners highlight the extensive implications of identity within ethics and ethical practice. If we examine this from an attachment lens, it is highly likely that ethnic practitioners can experience feelings of insecurity through their relationships with various institutions and would need to maintain appropriate attachment scaffolding to establish secure working relationships. In the shadow of this is the socialisation of not being good enough (Holden et al., 2021) or that these particular brands of practitioners have to work extra hard – not just extra hard but harder than their peers in order to be in with a chance. We argue then that the shadow of such socialisation hinders the attachment style when considered within the context of racial inequity and the basic need for survival.

Institutions are ethically bound by contract to guide practitioners through their professional journey. It is important to note we promote shared responsibility without locating the institution's duty within individual practitioners. Offering additional support and resources (not tokenistic) tailored to the needs of ethnic practitioners by just being aware and taking it into consideration begins to lay the foundation for ethical practice.

What does this all mean for the transmission to the communities' ethnic practitioners serve? Much has already been written about the ethical issues of offering interventions that are not designed suitably for ethnic service users, but less has been explored around the experience of developing therapeutic interventions geared towards ethnic patients from ethnic practitioners, in more of a view akin to the hermeneutic turn (Sloane & Bowe, 2014). What occurs when an ethnic practitioner misses the mark in the service of the community they serve? What ethical grounding can support in repairing the damage that can be done?

Arundell et al. (2021) explored adapted practices for working with ethnic community clients and reported through their metanalysis that a medium effect size (with significant difference between adapted and non-adapted intervention outcome) was found for those who had accessed group work, however, due to the conflation in the studies it was difficult to understand if the effect occurred due to the group setting or other adaptive factors that were implemented as part of the treatment adaption process not forgetting the self of the practitioner. Holistically, race, ethics, and ethical practice as alterations will not occur in isolation.

A personal reflection

I have previously written about an experience of racism faced in a therapeutic setting (Tehara, 2023) and wrestled with the idea of what that meant for me as an individual, and the myriad manners of reaction one could take – with time and consideration – to being subjected to acts of racism and prejudice in the therapeutic encounter.

At the close of the reflective element in writing the aforementioned chapter, I expressed that I was upset with myself for being unaware of how to contain and interpret those kinds of interactions with patients, to be a good enough container (Bion, 1985) for those anxieties. I wrote of becoming trapped between the notion of being authentically myself in the therapeutic space and being upset with myself in a professional capacity. Retrospectively, I found myself surprised with the reflection about how I had remained distanced from the training institute; instead, seeking solace from peers, through my placement supervision, and in the depths of existing literature, trying to work out an answer for what to do by myself, initially.

It struck as the chapter had concluded that there was an unconscious move to distance myself from the academic institute. The defence of distancing oneself from the institute brought up wider questions as to why working through it alone may have been a preferred method to explore an issue of race in therapeutic relationships. One reading would locate the issue within, as a replay and re-enactment of attachment dynamics with supervisors. However, subsequent thinking around the peripheral information I had been offered through the training route indicated to me that issues of racial disparity, lack of non-Western concepts around therapeutic intervention, economic hardship, and lack of acknowledgement around racism and othering through the institution itself were not considered within the intersect of ethics and ethical practice. I was concerned with the way I would be perceived for my non-therapeutic termination of clinical work with a patient – rather than being seen for someone, a trainee, who had been wounded by racial transgressions and was not aware of how to cope when such an incident arose.

I now reflect on what it meant to experience racism at an interpersonal level between myself and a patient and how I could not be contained by an institutional system that perpetuated and communicated the same problem to me about my otherness and what that meant for professional development. It is my perspective as a practicing clinician that there is great difficulty in separating the experience of the practitioner from the experience of the trainee, where precedent is set around an institutional lack of ethical consideration to the ethnic trainee, which follows on through their working lives as psychologists. When considered in relation to the experiences of ethnic trainees, these observations take on an additional layer of complexity in the realm of intersectionality (Bilge & Collins, 2016; Crenshaw, 1989, 1991) through further identities these people also hold concomitantly, including, but not restricted to their bodily abilities, sexuality, gender, care-provider roles, or additional national identities.

How do we integrate race and ethical practice?

Ethical decision making – what framing, and information informs the decisions and approaches practitioners take? The transcultural integrative ethical decision-making model (Garcia et al., 2003) is one example of a framework to advance practice in this regard. It is a model which intertwines a culturally attuned lens with ethical principles, based on the premise that both can inform one another. However, centring on other frameworks and points of reference, including intersectionality and cross-cultural beliefs and values can also expand an ethical practice lens.

Cultural humility and sensitivity – stepping away from the notion of cultural competence, and instead engaging with cultural curiosity, and humility in terms of how clients' experiences are formulated and understood. This is also integral on a systemic level. By adopting a multicultural approach, the practitioner embraces a duality of moral pluralism and ethical relativism (Beauchamp, 2014; Johnson & Melton, 2020).

A re-consideration of therapeutic intervention – other forms of therapeutic intervention could be explored and understood as an ethical consideration to developing competent practitioners; various ethnic population groups place emphasis on community for example, an exploration of group therapeutic models in application to these communities could be one avenue for further implementation. Part of the ethos in Counselling Psychology is the relational element and the strength and depth in therapeutic relationships built within communities – for example, in the group setting, or taking into consideration group experiences as bonding, especially following traumatic experiences such as the Grenfell fire (Ababio, 2022; Hammad et al., 2020; Patel, 1997; Sennik, 2023). This ethos is ideal for beneficial work for those who need longer-term interventions, such as people on long-term stays in low to medium-secure psychiatric wards, those with issues that may need longer-term structured clinical approaches in community settings, those with group analytic needs, or those imprisoned. Often approaching work with marginalised communities is a multi-year project and ethnic community Counselling Psychologists are very well placed to think about the longer-term imprinting of their work towards projects that take time to shape beneficial outcomes for ethnic community service users.

Training courses, the mediating (meso-level) factor between societal issues and the impact towards ethnic community practitioners – in consideration of practical elements that could be addressed to change the direction of travel and develop conscientious practitioners who then are able to affect change when in positions of influence, tentative exploration of strategies pertaining to diverse input, review and tangible change within curricula, mentorship for ethic community practitioners to minimise otherness and meaningful collaboration with ethnic community practitioners to incorporate a diversity of thought.

Conclusion

Simply put, the weave of race, ethics, and ethical practice is intentional. Applied psychology in the United Kingdom appears to remain within peripheral spheres of influence, focussed primarily to the delivery of thorough therapeutic intervention at the interpersonal level. In this regard, with consideration of ethnicity in mind, it mimics existing power dynamics – unable to address systemic inequalities or implement better promotion of experience for ethnic community students and practitioners so that they are able to further develop ideas, strategies, and interventions when they are able to rise into positions of direct influence and steering.

Applied psychology in the United Kingdom is already an area that is highly selective and skewed predominantly to cis-gendered, able-bodied, heterosexual, middle-to-upper class, White-British women (Ahsan, 2020; Ong, 2021) for various reasons. The landscape for psychology in the UK in its purity interdicts ethnic practitioners. Compounded by race, ethics, and ethical practice relays a road less travelled. That is conquered, it is now a path well-travelled. Therefore, the land has been toiled and it is ready for imbedding.

Chapter questions to provoke thinking:

1. How do personal values, beliefs, and experiences impact the way in which we engage with race and clients who are different to us, and may have different experiences or beliefs?
2. What are your professional and ethical obligations in ensuring that all ethnic community individuals can access quality, relevant, and appropriate therapy services?
3. How do the ethical guidelines you subscribe to account for ethnic diversity of experience and multiculturalism?
4. In considering race, ethics, and ethical practice, what are the pressure points within you and the systems you exist in?
5. How do you place history and context within race, ethics, and ethical practice in a meaningful way?

Notes

1. The case of Dr Hazida Bawa-Garba, who was prosecuted for being involved in the loss of life to a young child in 2015 following a series of systematic failures, including the absence of the on-call consultant on the evening of the child's death and issues with the information system. Dr Bawa-Garba was suspended by the GMC and then stricken off in January 2018, only to have this decision overturned later in August 2018.
2. The regulatory body for applied psychologists in the UK is the HCPC.
3. It should be acknowledged that preference for various terms as ways of relating to one another evolve in consideration of power dynamics.

References

Ababio, B. (2022). Nafsiyat therapy centre: Challenges, insights, and developments. *Psychoanalysis and History, 24*(3), 311–318.

Agarwal, P. (2020). *Sway: Unravelling unconscious bias*. Bloomsbury Publishing.

Ahsan, S. (2020). Holding up the mirror: Deconstructing whiteness in clinical psychology. *Journal of Critical Psychology, Counselling and Psychotherapy, 20*(3), 45–55.

Arundell, L. L., Barnett, P., Buckman, J. E., Saunders, R., & Pilling, S. (2021). The effectiveness of adapted psychological interventions for people from ethnic minority groups: A systematic review and conceptual typology. *Clinical Psychology Review, 88*, 102063.

Bajwa, S. (2020, June 30 – July 1). Chief Executive Address [Psychology of the future: changing landscapes]. BPS 2020 Conference, Online, UK. https://www.youtube.com/watch?v=vk8QGD6FhJQ&t=11s

Beauchamp, T. L. (2014). The compatibility of universal morality, particular moralities, and multiculturalism. In Wanda Teays, John-Stewart Gordon, & Alison Dundes Renteln (Eds.), *Global bioethics and human rights: Contemporary issues* (pp. 28–40). Rowman & Littlefield.

Bilge, S., & Collins, P. H. (2016). *Intersectionality*. Polity.

Bion, W. R. (1985). Container and contained. *Group Relations Reader*, 2(8), 127–133.

BPS. (2021). *Code of ethics and conduct*. The British Psychological Society. https://explore.bps.org.uk/content/report-guideline/bpsrep.2021.inf94

Crenshaw, K. (1989), Demarginalizing the intersection of race and sex. *The University of Chicago Legal Forum*, pp. 139–167.

Crenshaw, K. (1991). Mapping the margins: Intersectionality, identity, and violence against women of color. *Stanford Law Review*, 43(6), 1241–1300.

Daloye, D. (2022). The experiences of Black and minority ethnic trainee counselling psychologists: An interpretative phenomenological analysis. *Counselling Psychology Review*, 37(1), 31–40.

Emery, L., Jackson, B., & Herrick, T. (2021). Trainee engagement with reflection in online portfolios: A qualitative study highlighting the impact of the Bawa-Garba case on professional development. *Medical Teacher*, 43(6), 656–662.

Fernando, S., Klein, R., & Kessedjian, A., (2021) *Addressing systemic racism in clinical psychology: A call to action*. http://www.sumanfernando.com/DCP%20Annual%20Conference%202021%20.pdf (accessed May 23, 2023).

Forde, D. (Ed.). (1954). *African Worlds, studies in the cosmological ideas and social values of African peoples*. Oxford University Press.

Garcia, J. G., Cartwright, B., Winston, S. M., & Borzuchowsk, B. (2003). A transcultural integrative model for ethical decision making in counselling. *Journal of Counseling & Development*, 81(3), 268–277. https://doi.org/10.1002/j.1556-6678.2003.tb00253.x

Hammad, J., El-Guenuni, A., Bouzir, I., & El-Guenuni, F. (2020). The hand of hope: A coproduced culturally appropriate therapeutic intervention for Muslim communities affected by the Grenfell tower fire. *Journal of Muslim Mental Health*, 14(2), 15–62.

HCPC. (2023). *Fitness to practice annual report 2022–23*. https://www.hcpc-uk.org/about-us/insights-and-data/ftp/fitness-to-practise-annual-report-2022-23/ (accessed December 20, 2023).

Holden, C. L., Wright, L. E., Herring, A. M., & Sims, P. L. (2021). Imposter syndrome among first-and continuing-generation college students: The roles of perfectionism and stress. *Journal of College Student Retention: Research, Theory & Practice*. https://doi.org/10.1177/15210251211019379

Johnson, M., & Melton, M. L. (2020). *Addressing race-based stress in therapy with Black clients: Using multicultural and dialectical behaviour therapy techniques*. Routledge.

Maben, J., Hoinville, L., Querstret, D., Taylor, C., Zasada, M., & Abrams, R. (2021). Living life in limbo: Experiences of healthcare professionals during the HCPC fitness to practice investigation process in the UK. *BMC Health Services Research*, 21, 1–14.

Markus, H., & Nurius, P. (1986). Possible selves. *American Psychologist*, 41(9), 954.

Ong, L. (2021). *White clinical psychologists, race and racism* (Doctoral dissertation, University of East London).

Patel, G. (1997). Communities in struggle: Bengali And refugee groupwork in London. In T. Mistry & A. Brown (Eds.), *Race and groupwork* (pp. 160–187). Whiting and Birch Ltd, Human Science Publishers.

Sennik, B. (2023). *"It's that Internal Struggle": Grenfell residents lived experience of psychological distress, post-fire, 14-06-17. An interpretative phenomenological analysis* (Doctoral dissertation, University of East London).

Slay, H. S., & Smith, D. A. (2011). Professional identity construction: Using narrative to understand the negotiation of professional and stigmatized cultural identities. *Human Relations, 64*(1), 85–107.

Sloan, A., & Bowe, B. (2014). Phenomenology and hermeneutic phenomenology: The philosophy, the methodologies, and using hermeneutic phenomenology to investigate lecturers' experiences of curriculum design. *Quality & Quantity, 48,* 1291–1303.

Tan, R., & Campion, G. (2007). Losing yourself in the moment: The socialisation process of clinical psychology training. *Clinical Psychology Forum,* 180(1), 13–16.

Tehara, J. (2023). "(inter)Racial transference: A case of projective identification. In N. Zahid & R. Cooke (Eds.), *Therapists challenging racism and oppression: The unheard voices* (pp. 138–153). PCCS Books.

PART 2
LANDSCAPE

Mental health   **5**

Hayat Hussein

Overview

This chapter delves into the intersection of mental health with race, culture, social class, and spirituality. The aim is to stimulate reflection among mental health professionals on practical applications within the communities they engage with. Drawing from personal experiences as a practitioner and collaboration with the grassroots organisation 'Midaye Somali Development Network', the chapter emphasises the diverse conceptualisations of mental health within communities. Understanding culturally specific meanings of distress is crucial for overcoming barriers to mental health care in the UK. Insights from the work with Midaye underscore universal principles applicable across diverse communities.

Introduction

We live in a diverse and culturally rich society where there are cultural differences with regards to expressing distress and help-seeking behaviours for alleviating distress. Applying a Western or Eurocentric concept of distress/mental illness/disorder to individuals from different communities and ethnicities runs the risk of misdiagnosis, over-diagnosis, and misunderstanding that hinders an individual from receiving care for their distress.

DOI: 10.4324/9781003415244-7

It could be argued that even in textbooks and taught programmes centred around mental health, which promote a biopsychosocial model, psychiatric diagnoses are primarily used to shape our understanding by normalising the use of labels and explanations of diagnoses to present learning (Cromby et al., 2013). It can also be argued that there is a geopolitical element in the focus of a biological approach to explaining distress as this may relieve responsibility from politicians and governmental agencies as well as pharmaceutic companies in their contributions to people's distress (Cromby et al., 2013). For example, the conditions associated with social inequalities, such as poor housing and poverty, are often blamed on individual pathology when a biological approach is promoted (Gopalkrishnan, 2018).

Overall, there have been many attempts throughout history to conceptualise human distress, mental health, mental ill-health, etc. These descriptions have changed according to the social and cultural norms of society. Racial trauma has only recently been recognised within psychology as a distinct type of trauma, despite the overwhelming evidence over the years highlighting the adverse impact of racial discrimination on mental and physical health (Chin et al., 2020). These examples highlight the influence of social and cultural values on how we understand, classify, help-seek, and treat mental health. Furthermore, when individuals from marginalised communities do not align with the dominant cultural norms, it can be more challenging to conceptualise and recognise mental ill-health, as the prevailing cultural framework may not fully encompass or understand their unique experiences and perspectives. This underscores the importance of considering diverse cultural perspectives in mental health conceptualisations and practices. This chapter will explore what mental health is for different cultures using experiences from my work and raise questions on the differences in approaching those from individualist and collectivist cultures when thinking about support/interventions, and finally how we as practitioners can collaborate with different communities.

Cultural perspectives on mental health

Many marginalised groups often regard mental health as a taboo subject and the role of stigma has been heavily evidenced to be a contributing aspect to how mental health has been perceived (Shefer et al., 2013; Whittaker et al., 2005). From my experiences in working with marginalised groups in the UK and grassroots organisations, as well as my position as a Somali British Muslim woman, the level of shame and secrecy of mental health seems to be a powerful component linked to stigma. The implications of this shame and secrecy within the Somali community regarding mental health are that it leaves those with mental health difficulties with limited options for seeking support, as there would be some mistrust of external individuals and even individuals within their own family or community network.

In the Somali language, the only term to come close to the meaning of mental health is translated to the words 'goof walan' which means crazy/mad person. What came across from my doctoral research as well as my work with the Somali community over the years is that there is a fear of families being ostracised and isolated from the community as the shame and stigma is long-lasting, and the family may be perceived to have lost its honour. Therefore, the implication of being labelled as a crazy/mad person may hinder help-seeking behaviours. It is important as a practitioner to be mindful of what the term mental health may mean in different communities and languages.

Furthermore, mental health is conceptualised differently within various communities which highlights the importance of collaborating with communities to understand what distress means to them to find ways that support them better. There are different cultural meanings of distress which may create different barriers to accessing mental health care in the UK if this is not taken into consideration and put into practice. It can be easy to allow a Eurocentric view to dominate ways of practice and understanding, but it is essential to understand the communities we work with in order to co-create support that is meaningful to the client's recovery.

This approach is demonstrated in one grassroot organisation that I work for 'Midaye Somali Development Network', which aims to develop a community-based emotional well-being model called 'Journey of Hope' that would work better for Somali and Arabic-speaking communities and develop links with partners that can support the community.

The project 'Journey of Hope'

This project is a Somali and Arabic-speaking led women's project which allows women to shape culturally appropriate interventions for their community. One notable contribution was the need to ban the word mental health from the model replacing it with emotional well-being. They justified this by sharing that they did not find the term mental health relatable rather they found it fearful. Community members further expressed that in Somalia mental health is only recognised when someone presents as a risk to themselves or others and presents this overtly. They highlighted that in Somalia people are chained and locked up to reduce the risks, which they

understood this to be a cruel form of treatment. By having this open dialogue with the community members fostered the feeling of being heard,
included and engaged with the programme.

This experience with the community showcases that asking about distress, allowing the space to describe what it means to them and how they
make sense of their difficulties, can co-produce a space of recovery. Once
we changed the label of mental health to emotional well-being the women
experienced this more normalising, as everyone has emotions and daily
life stressors that fluctuate. Emergent topics included motherhood, socio-
economic issues, relationship/family issues, pre-migratory trauma, and
intergenerational disparity with their children such as the push and pull
between a Somali collectivist culture and a British individualistic culture.
Without the fear of being labelled with mental illnesses, these women felt
secure to openly express their thoughts and feelings, fostering a supportive
community for mutual learning. This underscores the contrast in mental
health conceptualisation between Somalia and the UK. Acknowledging
diverse interpretations enriches the discourse, and creating similar spaces
in other communities might reveal varying perspectives on distress, showcasing distinctions between the UK and other cultural contexts.

Seeking to learn from community members, they proposed workshops
on managing emotions and behaviours. This highlights the value of
acknowledging the intersectionality of race, gender, social class, and religion in discussions. Recognising the impact of systemic inequalities reduces
blaming communities for distress. Practitioners should reflect on systemic
factors, avoiding solely attributing issues to individuals, which depoliticises
distress. Understanding historical and current oppressive structures, racial
trauma, social class, faith, and other societal contexts is essential when
addressing psychological distress in the context of race in the UK. For
example, in therapy if we formulate some of these community members
distress with a cognitive lens, it may not emphasis the impact or even
acknowledgement of race and social inequalities and how it appears to play
a role in their emotional well-being. However, culturally adapted Cognitive
Behavioural Therapy (CBT) has allowed more inclusion of the client's cultural background, which is a step towards making therapy more flexible.
Notwithstanding, it prompts the question of whether culturally adapted
CBT adequately fully encapsulates the complexity of the therapeutic process, especially when working with specific client groups. There might
be a desire for a more nuanced exploration of how the therapy is not just
adapted to cultural backgrounds but also how it is conceptually understood,
the theoretical underpinnings and how they are applied in the context of
the communities.

This prompts reflection on how services develop inclusion and exclusion criteria for therapy or support for emotional distress. A common theme of inclusion for some National Health Service (NHS) services can be stable housing and being psychologically minded which may cause a barrier for some communities. The requirement for stable housing and psychological awareness as key inclusion factors might not resonate equally with all communities who are facing social inequalities and limits inclusivity. This prompts considerations about whether the interplay of race, gender, social class, and religion influences the way marginalised groups in the UK access adequate mental health care. This highlights the need to continue the work of demystifying the different prejudices that professionals, services, and institutions hold but also the need to promote agency within marginalised communities by sharing information about the possible services and treatments so that they can make a more informed choice about the required support. In addition, collaborating and developing partnerships with various communities to develop culturally sensitive interventions and training to practitioners can promote further agency within the community.

The implication of culturally insensitive or unattuned interventions, services, or practitioners are that certain communities will not have equitable access to mental health care and that this could further impact their distress. Within the work with 'Midaye Somali Development Network' many of the community members have asked to promote their learning about how mental health is viewed in the UK and information about available treatment. Community members shared this empowered them as well as increase their knowledge, skills, and resources. Furthermore, they also felt empowered by having a voice in shaping the interventions that were delivered, which led to many wanting to create their own groups that they felt would help. For example, some community members who were Arabic speaking created their own peer support group for mothers with children with special needs, others from the Somali community created a sewing group. They all shared that from their cultures this is how women connected to support each other and talk.

These examples hope to provoke reflection on the helpfulness of the term mental health in marginalised communities and if this aids or rather ostracise, isolate, and create fear in communities. If this helps to create the latter then it questions whether these labels are more helpful to practitioners, institutions, and governments rather than the communities we are trying to support and work with. Counselling Psychology can play a significant role in addressing and understanding the intersectionality of race, gender, social class, and religion whether it is through community collaboration, education and training, social justice work, and advocacy that can impact policies, therapy, addressing biases, cultural competence, and research. Furthermore, Speight and Vera (2004) embrace that Counselling Psychologists have unique opportunities to investigate the processes involved in maintaining systems of oppression and provide strategies of combating injustices as research practitioners. As such, Kelly's (1970) ideas to produce transformational change in the world carry significant weight within the field of psychology.

Barriers to accessing mental health services in the UK

Applying Western mental health concepts to diverse communities' risks misdiagnosis and misunderstanding, hindering access to care and contributing to barriers in mental health services. For example, many of the community members from 'Midaye Somali development network' shared the difficulties of communicating with the General Practitioner (GP) whether speaking on their own behalf or a family member. As they could not understand the threshold of severity for mental health difficulties. Guerin (2004) also emphasised that Somali clients hold the view that mental illness is reserved for severe and untreatable cases. This could perhaps account for why some Somalis feel discouraged to seek support and highlight certain structural issues in mental health services in this regard. Furthermore, it can be important for practitioners to understand the role and influence of family within certain communities as this can be important for treatment.

Shefer et al. (2013) found that opposing views within families can act as a barrier to an individual seeking support from mental health services. They further argued that this resistance can be due to the stigma surrounding mental health (Shefer et al., 2013). There can be several explanations for this such as stigma, shame and secrecy as mentioned earlier in this chapter. This highlights the potential for Counselling Psychologists and Applied Psychologists to link with GPs which are often the gatekeepers in accessing specialised mental health services. This may allow for training on how to discuss mental health with different communities and cultural awareness of distress. Therefore, it is important to reflect on a client's journey in accessing mental health care and whether there are barriers which are furthering inequalities. By identifying barriers practitioners and can work with communities in addressing better access and routes to care.

In addition, it is important to mention language, and if information is being communicated and understood or is it another barrier in accessing mental health services (Aggarwal et al., 2016). Bhattacharyya and Benbow (2013) suggest that language barriers are one reason why services are under-utilised.

When working with translators, inquire about the client's specific language, dialect, and gender preference influenced by faith or culture. Knowing cultural context and potential issues within communities is crucial for effective communication, as dialects may be challenging, leading to misunderstandings and potential discrimination, impacting the client's experience.

Furthermore, as mentioned earlier community members expressed that in Somalia mental health is only recognised when someone presents as a risk to themselves or others and presents this overtly. They highlighted that in Somalia people are chained and locked up to reduce the risks, which they understood this to be a cruel form of treatment. Research has highlighted that marginalised groups in the UK endure psychological distress longer getting to a crisis point before knowing how to act. Which may eventually lead to having to employ the help of law enforcers in order to restrain and at times section family members. This is concordant with Appleby's (2008) study which evidenced that there are disproportionate high rates of admissions and sectioning within marginalised communities from police intervention, which can be due to institutionally racist practice by the police. Moreover, Jeraj et al. (2015) describe how different marginalised groups have experienced seeking support at a crisis point. They conveyed that the police are often contacted as an act of desperation as all previous attempts for support have failed. Similarly, issues with accessing services at earlier points appeared to be the catalyst for further deterioration and police involvement (Jeraj et al., 2015).

This raises questions on when marginalised groups access services how they are being approached. When asking questions around risk, is this being done with sensitivity keeping in mind the client's faith and culture? From my experience, working with Midaye when some community members tried to get help from NHS services, they have reported being triggered by questions surrounding risk. For example, a mother shared that she felt her 18-year-old son had shown signs of neurodiversity most of his life and was not offered support from external services. She expressed worry around his neurodiversity and how not having support was impacting his mood. She spoke to an autism service who asked her if her son wanted to end his life and informed her that she had to go back and ask her son this. The mother expressed that this increased her anxiety and fear, and that she felt extremely uncomfortable to approach this with her son. She stated she had asked her son like the service suggested and he said no of course he did not want to harm himself as he had faith in God. The mother went back to the service, and they then explained they cannot help her son as there is no risk. This mother was left confused as she did what the service wanted but her son was not offered any support. This is an example highlighting the need to be transparent with clients from the beginning and discuss their options and to have conversations with clients about how they view risk in accordance with their beliefs and culture.

Inclusion and exclusion criteria of services may not at times match with the variations of distress that are presented with different communities. For example, the son discussed above had many strengths and skills such as getting through the education system with no special needs support and is attending university now. The service understood this as him not requiring support, as he had managed on his own and his risk is low. However, the son was struggling socially at university and was extremely isolated which increased his low mood and self-esteem. When he would come home from university, he would cry to his mother that he has no friends and self-neglected. He presented with low self-worth which is why he did not approach services for support.

Many recognise that support is out there for mental health but agree that this support can only be utilised when the individual suffering with poor mental health seeks it, as this is how Eurocentric services are setup. It may be helpful at these times to consider how the individual's family or social network can be supported when they are reporting concerns and considering the individual's culture and faith. This can be a difficult situation to tackle as at times individuals find it hard to access services independently, to report and recognise symptoms of mental health (McCabe & Leas, 2008). Tucker et al. (2011) reported that there are links between how clients perceive providers' cultural sensitivity and how well they adhere to interventions recommended by those providers. They emphasised the importance this has on health behaviours and outcomes, and therefore suggested the significance of having a model that is patient-centred and culturally sensitive (Tucker et al., 2011). Furthermore, it is important that practitioners and services place enough importance on faith and the role of family. Sue (2001) expressed that monocultural policies and practices create invisibility for other diverse cultural groups.

Collaboration with communities

This section of the chapter will focus heavily on the work of 'Midaye Somali Development Network' and their programme named 'Journey of Hope'. Their vision is to transform the effectiveness of mental health services for marginalised migrant women in London, so that these women will have a say in how services are developed and delivered. Midaye are also in the process of offering training and small funding to other community groups on their model to allow other communities to explore how they can further develop members of the community. Midaye also aims to develop a trusted community-led emotional well-being service, which will play a central role – in community views; providing culturally informed, high quality therapeutic interventions in community languages; and help transform the accessibility and relevance of mainstream mental health services. The process of this has led to co-producing with the community in developing emotional well-being groups, workshops, and social groups. The community shares their needs, and the aim is to develop a community-led service for this.

The activities provided aim to empower, advocate for and support these communities. This programme highlights the strengths, skills, and knowledge of this community members. The emotional well-being groups involve providing a therapeutic space for emotional well-being, psychoeducation as well as a processing space to share experiences. What has helped this group develop is acknowledging and allowing their faith, culture, race, and gender be a part of the work and using this as their strengths. For example, the women like the groups to end with a prayer as this allows them to openly share parts of themselves in the work. Furthermore, when we discuss low mood, the women find it helpful to explore how this is viewed within their Islamic faith, and find it comfortable that their faith advocates for everyone to take care of themselves emotionally, physically, and spiritually. This has led to some women opening up about domestic violence and how they sometimes feel their partners may spiritually abuse them. This led to creating a session on domestic abuse with an Islamic lens and consulting with religious leaders for advice. In each topic we presented what the women wanted to explore, we ask them questions of how they understand this in their culture and faith. This project initially worked with Somali and Arabic speaking women who came from African and middle Eastern countries. This has now slowly branched out to other African countries as these women are sharing how they feel empowered with other community members and friends which then calls for staff to learn more about other cultures and faiths and bringing this into the work. The community members have shared in consultations that their social networks have shared their curiosity in the positive changes they have noticed in them, which has led to them sharing what has helped them and inviting them to join Midaye.

The community members also asked for workshops which involves providing spaces for practical support and inviting different services/agencies. This helps the community to learn, engage, and feel empowered. For example, the women expressed being worried about their children being a part of gangs or joining them. This led to us partnering with a service that are an expert in gangs and they provided four workshops to the mothers. In addition, the women asked for social groups which involves an opportunity to connect with each other and the wider community – e.g., offering physical activity, coffee mornings, gatherings. Many of them described feeling isolated as they were used to been around others in their country where it is a collective community. Such as in Somalia, doors are left open, and the front porch is an extension of the home where people would sit outside in the sun and bond. However, they described that in the UK everyone is too busy to connect and that it is more of an individualistic culture where you focus on yourself. Many described this has been a culture shock as they feel isolated from others and sometimes this impacts low mood.

Furthermore, this led to developing the concept of reflective dinners where the group would go over what they have learnt from the emotional well-being groups, workshops, and social groups. They would describe what was going well with the groups and what Midaye could improve. The more we had these reflective dinners the more the women became more confident, assertive, and empowered. They would share that these dinners are not only reflective but also a celebration for continuing to look after themselves and learn. They would come dressed in traditional clothes like it was a wedding and dance after the reflections. Those that did not have any support to look after their children were offered babysitting services from Midaye so they could join the reflective dinners. Many of the women described that these dinners would be something they would look forward to, and that their children would comment on the positive changes they could see in their mothers.

The collaborations between practitioners and the communities can empower others and resolve misunderstandings. One study shared the same views and suggested the need to present a more positive view of mental health care to marginalised communities by linking with community groups and local leaders (Appleby, 2008). Furthermore, Codjoe et al. (2019) emphasised the need to collaborate and co-design acceptable programmes with cultural sensitivity that will reach marginalised communities. Vahdaninia et al.'s (2020) systematic review suggested that mental health services designed for marginalised communities are practicable and achievable. Vahdaninia et al. (2020) emphasised the importance of designing mental health services that are not based in settings such as clinics but rather in community centres and schools to reduce the stigma that hospitals carry for certain cultures. There does not seem to be enough of these spaces now. This was something that was practiced at Midaye, the emotional well-being group ran in the evening on Zoom as many of the women are single mothers. If someone did not have access to a smartphone, laptop, or internet this was something they were supported with from Midaye to access. The workshops would either be in the day during school hours or evenings.

The more we worked with the community the more we identified their strengths and the impact of the narratives they carry. This is when we introduced Tree of Life groups (Ncube, 2006) and Recipe of life groups (Wood, 2012). The women responded well to this, as it was based on knowing our communities, context and history, i.e., war, migration, racism, avoiding re-traumatising by sharing control and power, honouring how people respond to trauma and how we provide the service. Another important aspect of our work is facilitating and encouraging leadership roles within the community. We have noticed that community members share that they feel empowered from our groups, and they would like to share their knowledge and skills to others. Therefore, participation and empowerment have been a key element of the 'Journey of Hope' as it aids community members in their personal journeys. We have trained others in interests they have i.e., peer support Special Education Needs (SEN) group, teaching children, joining our steering panel, etc.

Midaye's principles of working that have worked with these communities are shown in Figure 5.1. The work of Midaye emphasises how we can

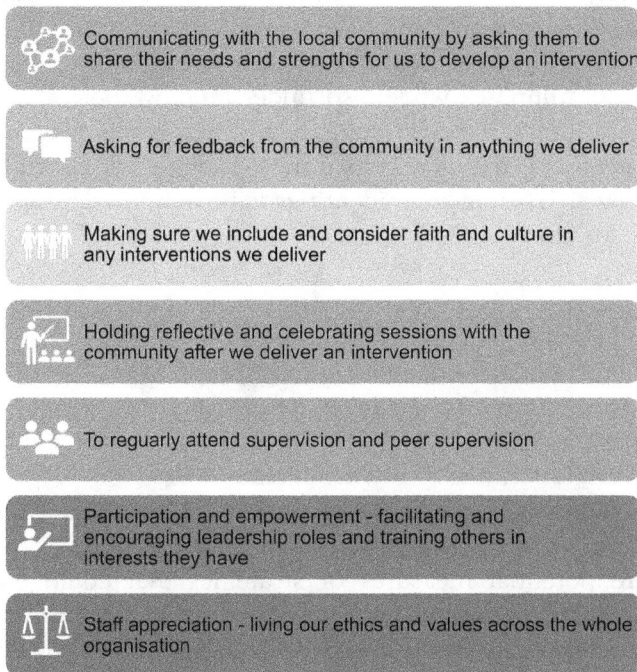

Communicating with the local community by asking them to share their needs and strengths for us to develop an intervention

Asking for feedback from the community in anything we deliver

Making sure we include and consider faith and culture in any interventions we deliver

Holding reflective and celebrating sessions with the community after we deliver an intervention

To regularly attend supervision and peer supervision

Participation and empowerment - facilitating and encouraging leadership roles and training others in interests they have

Staff appreciation - living our ethics and values across the whole organisation

Figure 5.1 Midaye's principles of working

empower certain marginalised communities, as well as how the community can empower themselves from within to meet the needs of the community through co-production.

Conclusion

Overall, the effects of oppressive practices and systemic and structural problems highlight the inequalities in mental health care, as well as how intersectionality of race, gender, social class, and religion appears to play on marginalised communities' ability to access good mental health care in the UK. This chapter highlights the influence of social and cultural values on how we understand, classify, help-seek, and treat mental health. Furthermore, conceptualisations of mental health can be more difficult when one may not hold the dominating cultural values of the society one lives in, as is true of marginalised groups in the UK. There are multiple variations in defining mental health and distress. Therefore, this questions the set definition of mental health that applies across cultures. It may be more helpful to focus on the distress of the individual and the community collectively. In addition, the work with Midaye can be applied to other communities and spaces. As the core principles of working highlighted in Figure 5.1 help facilitate these discussions, it hopes to bring out the needs of different communities while also understanding their social, cultural, and spiritual contexts. A key learning from Midaye was that communities hold many practices that have helped them survive distress and that facilitating spaces which fosters their identities to be honoured brings with it the opportunity for good work.

Chapter questions to provoke thoughts:

1. What is your understanding or perception of mental health and what factors or influences have shaped your conceptualisation? Reflect on the sources, experiences, or knowledge that have contributed to your personal understanding of mental health.
2. How do you bring in an individual's race, culture, social class, and spirituality into therapy and formulation?
3. What are potential measures or strategies that could enhance the service's ability to reach and engage with different communities, to improve accessibility, and inclusivity in the services provided by your organisation, particularly in reaching out to diverse communities?

4. Are you aware of any local, community-based organisations related to your work that your organisation could potentially collaborate with? Additionally, how might your employer react or respond to the idea of forming partnerships with such grassroots organisations?

References

Aggarwal, N. K., Pieh, M. C., Dixon, L., Guarnaccia, P., Alegria, M., & Lewis-Fernandez, R. (2016). Clinician descriptions of communication strategies to improve treatment engagement by racial/ethnic minorities in mental health services: A systematic review. *Patient Education and Counseling, 99*(2), 198–209.

Appleby, L. (2008). Services for ethnic minorities: A question of trust. *Psychiatric Bulletin, 32*(11), 401–402.

Bhattacharyya, S., & Benbow, S. M. (2013). Mental health services for Black and minority ethnic elders in the United Kingdom: A systematic review of innovative practice with service provision and policy implications. *International Psychogeriatrics, 25*(3), 359–373. https://doi.org/10.1017/S1041610212001858

Chin, D., Loeb, T. B., Zhang, M., Liu, H., Cooley-Strickland, M., & Wyatt, G. E. (2020). Racial/ethnic discrimination: Dimensions and relation to mental health symptoms in a marginalized urban American population. *American Journal of Orthopsychiatry, 90*(5), 614.

Codjoe, L., Barber, S., & Thornicroft, G. (2019). Tackling inequalities: A partnership between mental health services and black faith communities. *Journal of Mental Health, 28*(3), 225–228. https://doi.org/10.1080/09638237.2019.1608933

Cromby, J., Harper, D., & Reavey, P. (2013). *Psychology, mental health and distress.* Palgrave Macmillan.

Gopalkrishnan, N. (2018). Cultural diversity and mental health: Considerations for policy and practice. *Frontiers in Public Health, 6*, 179. https://doi.org/10.3389/fpubh.2018.00179

Guerin, B. (2004). Somali Conceptions and expectations concerning mental health: Some guidelines for mental health professionals. *New Zealand Journal of Psychology, 33*(2), 59–67.

Jeraj, S., Shoham, T., & Islam-Barrett, F. (2015). *Mental health crisis review: Experiences of black and minority ethnic communities.* Race Equality Foundation.

Kelly, J. G. (1970). Antidotes for arrogance: Training for community psychology. *The American Psychologist, 25*(6), 524–531. https://doi.org/10.1037/h0029484

McCabe, M. P., & Leas, L. (2008). A qualitative study of primary health care access, barriers and satisfaction among people with mental illness. *Psychology, Health and Medicine, 13*(3), 303–312.

Midaye Somali Development Network. (2022). https://www.midaye.org.

Ncube, N. (2006). The tree of life project. *International Journal of Narrative Therapy & Community Work, 2006*(1), 3–16.

Shefer, G., Rose, D., Nellums, L., Thornicroft, G., Henderson, C., & Evans-Lacko, S. (2013). 'Our community is the worst': The influence of cultural beliefs on stigma, relationships with family and help-seeking in three ethnic communities in London. *International Journal of Social Psychiatry, 59*(6), 535–544. https://doi.org/10.1177/0020764012443759

Speight, S. L., & Vera, E. M. (2004). A social justice agenda: Ready, or not? *The Counseling Psychologist, 32*(1), 109–118. https://doi.org/10.1177/0011000003260005

Sue, D. W. (2001). Multidimensional facets of cultural competence. *The Counseling Psychologist, 29*(6), 790–821.

Tucker, C. M., Marsiske, M., Rice, K. G., Nielson, J. J., & Herman, K. (2011). Patient-centered culturally sensitive health care: Model testing and refinement. *Health Psychology, 30*(3), 342.

Vahdaninia, M., Simkhada, B., Van Teijlingen, E., Blunt, H., & Mercel-Sanca, A. (2020). Mental health services designed for Black, Asian and minority ethnics (BAME) in the UK: A scoping review of case studies. *Mental Health and Social Inclusion, 24*(2), 81–95.

Whittaker, S., Hardy, G., Lewis, K., & Buchan, L. (2005). An exploration of psychological well-being with young Somali refugee and asylum-seeker women. *Clinical Child Psychology and Psychiatry, 10*(2), 177–196.

Wood, N. R. (2012). Recipes for life. *International Journal of Narrative Therapy & Community Work, 2*, 34–43.

Racial trauma

6

Divine Charura and Byron Al-Murri

Overview

This chapter critically discusses and broaches the highly sensitive and extremely important area of racial trauma. We start with a brief introduction on the importance of an awareness of racial trauma and its impact, and we then shift to a critical review of the history of racism and its continued manifestation in contemporary society. We offer reflections of our positionality, within our own contexts, thus illuminating how we align with Counselling Psychology's emphasis of phenomenological, humanistic, and reflective practice. Furthermore, we discuss the mental and physical health impacts and consequences of racial trauma from systemic perspectives, relating to ideas of power, capital, threats, and meanings. Additionally, the chapter examines how practitioners can employ the Power Threat Meaning Framework to explore racial trauma with clients. The chapter ends by posing five concluding questions that seek to challenge and inspire you. This is to reflect on how to realise the theory and practicum indicated here, into your pedagogy, supervision, and therapeutic practice.

DOI: 10.4324/9781003415244-8

Introduction

This chapter seeks to elucidate and critically discuss racial trauma from a uniquely British and European lens. We will critically review the concepts, terminology, socio-historical-political contexts of racial trauma, as well as explore the profound implications, effects and damages this trauma has, and is, having on people from minoritised racial and ethnic identities. We offer a critical overview, discussion and synthesis on the contemporary issues and debates relating to racial trauma. These for example include a critique to the history and origins of the concept of race, racism, colonialism, systemic oppression, and injustices. This chapter is for those interested in and affected by racial trauma. It was written by two Practitioner Psychologists, as such the discussions on racial trauma are framed and informed by the authors' lived experiences which include experiencing racism in addition to working in clinical practice with individuals, couples, and families impacted by racial trauma.

Firstly, we establish and broach our own positionality and philosophical underpinnings. Terms, language, and historical locations of salient constructs are examined to showcase the complexities and challenges in detangling often interchangeably used or misunderstood concepts. The underpinning foundations of this chapter also include Critical Race Theory (CRT) because of its focus on engaging voices of those with the lived experience of being marginalised by the dominant culture and the value of their counter-storytelling of how they experience racism. Their counternarratives include an openness to learning about the embodied nature of racial trauma as well as its transgenerational and personal impact. Additionally, we also draw from the literature indicating that the therapeutic relationship can only be understood in the context of social factors, including systemic racism and oppression of those from ethnically diverse communities (Charura & Clyburn, 2023; Maharaj et al., 2021).

Counselling Psychology as a Western and Eurocentric endeavour is compromised by racism. This relates to its theoretical historical foundations, to the mainstream theoretical orientations we teach, which are steeped in Eurocentric epistemologies that do not always appreciate the diversity of perspectives on mental health from other cultures (Charura & Clyburn, 2023). Additionally, there are also cultural limitations within psychology research designs and methods which often mean that findings are generalised to diverse groups, even when they do not necessarily apply. As ethical practitioners committed to the ethical principle of nonmaleficence (alongside other principles such as beneficence, autonomy, justice, and fidelity), 'doing no harm' then means, we cannot ignore, avoid, sidestep, or intellectualise the concept of racial trauma. Treating racial trauma through a purely psychiatric/medical (diagnostic trauma lens), or conceptualisation of embodied distress arising from the impacts of racism, without cultural, racial sensitivity, knowledge, and humility, denies the fundamental aspect of a client's/community's identity, lived experience and oppression. We therefore argue that such a 'power-over-other' approach aligns with maleficence, injustice, psychiatric or psychological imperialist, and colonialist agendas of continuing to oppress racialised groups. That is because it wrongly locates the problem within the client, thus reinforcing the dominant narrative of inaccessibility, and exclusion from mainstream therapeutic services.

Consequently, it incorrectly positions the individual/community as incompatible and separate from the dominant system. Thus, racism as trauma, epistemic violence, its acute and lasting psychological and embodied traumatic impact are reviewed in this chapter through an ethical and social justice lens. This will compliment historical and enduring epigenetic perspectives of race-based traumatic stress and transgenerational trauma. In contrast, there will also be a discussion around the use of working phenomenologically with racially-minoritised clients. Whilst there is a diversity of ways in which clients/patients presenting with racial trauma can be supported, we offer an adapted racially sensitive and racial trauma-informed version of the Power Threat Meaning Framework (PTMF) template (Johnstone et al., 2018). The chapter concludes with some reflective questions to support further discussion and development.

A brief note on race and racism: History, terminology, and language

Given the complexities, misunderstandings, and profound impact and implications of such concepts, it is vital to critically appraise and attend to the bio-psycho-social-political and historical provenance of such terminology used in the chapter and in wider research. Within this chapter, we acknowledge the evolving nature of language and use the term 'racial trauma' to be associated with those 'who experience and have been impacted by racism'. We are also aware that in different contexts language descriptors, that have been used includes: 'people of colour (POC)', 'Black, Asian, and Minority Ethnic', 'Minority groups', and 'ethnically diverse communities' (Denyer et al., 2022). It is vital to acknowledge that those who experience racism are not a homogenous group, and there are a wide range of ethnicities, cultures, and backgrounds, who happen to share experiences of being discriminated against due to racism.

As Counselling Psychologists our use of language is paramount as language can be and has been used to offend, oppress, and discriminate against individuals and groups. We thus assert the importance, holding in mind that the use of language to subjugate and separate others is prevalent and salient to clinical/therapeutic practice when working with racial trauma. Within our chosen terminology, the aim is to convey a reflective depth whilst also using language sensitively, and appropriately, to avoid repetition of othering.

Positionality, ontology, and epistemology

We agreed on writing this chapter that it is important to be transparent about our own positions because where you sit, will determine where you stand. As we are drawing in this chapter from a number of critical theories, i.e., CRT, which are far from politically neutral, our worldviews, social positions, perspective, and interests of the theorists we align with, are reflected. We argue that it is important for Counselling Psychologists, as reflective, scientist practitioners to make explicit the philosophical and epistemological paradigms and ontological assumptions that underly their practice and research. Therefore, this section transparently engages with our own contexts and positions, which are important to reflect on to highlight the lived-experiences and to ground this chapter both academically and phenomenologically akin to the scientist-reflective-practitioner values of Counselling Psychology (HCPC, 2023).

Both authors are Practitioner Counselling Psychologists who are positioned as being minority ethnically diverse groups in the UK. We both have background and practice in psychodynamic psychotherapy, cognitive behavioural therapy, coaching and relational approaches. The first author (DC) identifies as Black British of African heritage. The second author (Byron Al-Murri) identifies as British-Arab of English and Middle Eastern heritage. Our ontological and epistemological positions that inform our research, teaching, and practice are grounded in phenomenology, interpretivism, and relativism. Thus, in line with this, we conceptualise that from this positionality, no single reality or truth exists, but rather there are multiple realities, which are rooted in an individual's lived experience and sense-making of their own realities and of phenomena (Smith et al, 2022). We are also informed by perspectivism (Blackburn, 2017), which asserts that each unique personal experiences and realities of a phenomena rely on one's position and one's viewpoint of it, which is subject to change and difference, if positioned differently. This also links with our post-modernist philosophical tenet of dialectics in being able to hold and reconcile two positions, accepting the 'both/and' rather than 'either/or' positions. This allows us to gather additional positionality and perspective to better synthesise and analyse various viewpoints (Charura & Lago, 2021a). In our work, we view difference and diversity from an intersectional paradigm. We reflected upon our own diverse identities and difficulties in writing such an emotive and personally meaningful chapter.

We started this chapter by critiquing the concept of 'race' and we challenge its misuse. Our first provocation is that the term 'race' is redundant as a term because it refers to just an individual's outward appearance based on the colour of their skin. Thus, in some ways it is not meaningful because as people we are all in the same category of 'human'. Biological and scientific 'race' is rooted in racism, used as a colonial tool to divide, and conquer, rationalised by objectifying and demonising those to be dominated. However, we note that our argument here is not to ignore ethnicity, culture, as these are significantly linked to identity and lived experiences but rather, we are inviting critique and meaningful exploration of the underlying dynamics in the conceptualisation of discussions on race.

Critical review of the history of racism and its continued manifestation in contemporary society

In this section we engage in a critical review of the history of racism and its continued manifestation in contemporary society. Racism involves attitudes, dispositions, behaviours, and assumptions of Whiteness (Green et al., 2007; Gunew, 2007; Owen, 2007). There is a long history of racism, which are evident throughout history and pre-history, evidenced in the existence of and maintenance of slavery and enslavement. In the 21st century, these concepts and artefacts continue to exist more actively, via criminal, radical and extreme factions, for the purposes of modern-day slavery, and the trafficking of peoples across borders for sexual and economic exploitation.

Moreover, institutionalised, and systemic racism have come into sharp focus in recent years through the awareness and exposure of police brutalities, killings, and endemic discrimination in the judicial system and wider social inequalities and oppressions. Colonialism was underpinned by the mass commercialisation and industrialisation of slavery, which itself was fuelled by racist and extreme-religious ideologies such as the 'mission to civilise' and pseudo-scientific and biological distinctions of race. These attempted to rationalise exploration, conquest, exploitation, and domination of indigenous peoples. Moreover, the financial gain from slavery facilitated the imperial conquests and subjugations of indigenous people from Africa and the Americas. Both White and minority-ethnic peoples were involved in the capture, transportation, and ownership of slaves, including Black slavers and free African American owners of Black slaves.

Post-emancipation, with slaves becoming subjects, freed peoples were often separated, segregated, and partitioned from the White settler community (Banaji et al., 2021). Through the rise of empiricism and evolutionary theory, the religious emphasis became pseudo-biological, with the idea of polygenism, meaning people of colour (POC) were viewed as originating from different species, including animals, which further dehumanised and propagated the mythology of their 'savagery, unintelligence, sexual promiscuity, and violent tendencies' (Fanon, 1952). This, in turn, internalised and externalised stigma and fears, and was exacerbated through racial and racist segregation and sustaining 'othering'. In the 19th and 20th centuries, this ideology became more radical and brutal through eugenics (sterilisation), White supremacy and through actions and inactions that sought to excuse the decimation of the endemic global majority populations through famine, destitution, or genocide, via their dehumanisation and objectification.

Saini (2019) noted the history of race with European Enlightenment naturalists and scientists categorised humans into discrete groups in the same way as some other animal species. This then led to the arbitrary setting of the boundaries for the categories they had decided, based on skin colour, and established sweeping generalisations of cultural, stereotypes about temperament, intelligence, behaviour, and innate differences between populations (Charura & Clyburn, 2023). Ultimately, these 'pseudoscientific' ideas which in themselves were to oppress, discriminate and champion White supremacy became the bedrock influence of Western medicine for centuries and formed the basis for the Nazi eugenics programme of racial cleansing and the Holocaust (Saini, 2019).

Sadly, and disgracefully, in the 21st century we continue to see dehumanising rhetoric, policies, and actions in relation to migrants, refugees and asylum seekers from various governments. This is in addition to the rise of the influence of right-wing anti-immigration political parties globally. Thus, the history of race is a reminder that what may be called 'science' (including diagnostic systems) and politics should not just be about theories and data; but also about which facts and stories regarding human diversity are given pre-eminence and by whom (Charura & Clyburn, 2023). Considering these historical and current considerations, it is important to be clear in the use of language and terminology (Table 6.1). This next section will detail common theoretical concepts relevant to the research and experiences of racial trauma.

Table 6.1 Key terminology and definitions

Term	Attributed to	Viewed as	Assumed to be	Actualities
Race	External Physical appearance (skin pigmentation and shape)	Physically based and permanent	Genetically determined	Socially constructed, which serves to maintain socio-political-structural disseminations of power and access to various 'capitals' to population groups.
Culture	Behaviours and attitudes	Socially derived and non-static	Passed down by parents, caregivers, important relational others	Variable and changeable blueprint for living
Ethnicity	Sense of belonging	Psychosocial and expression of cultures, partially subject to change	How people see themselves in terms of background and parentage	Culture-race conflation
Identity	Subjective feelings and perceptions	Psycho-personal, multiple identities and consistent across time	Formed through upbringing and experience, self in relation to others, different to and from others	Feelings about heritage; personal choice, changeable and context specific, intersectional, synthesis of similarities and differences
Oppression	Discrimination, barriers, prejudicial treatment, and actions and preventions to limit civil engagement, opportunities, rights, and freedoms	Systemically located, external to the individual and communities	Pre-existing, but changeable	Internalised oppression and external oppression, socio-cultural-historically located through colonialism and 'othering', microaggressions, racial shaming

(Continued)

Table 6.1 Key terminology and definitions (*Continued*)

Term	Attributed to	Viewed as	Assumed to be	Actualities
Colonialism	Active subjugation, enslavement, diminishment of indigenous cultures, and control and exploitation of territory, resources, and populations	Historical, imperialism, marked by systematic violence, oppression, abuses aligned with colonial ideology: 'mission to civilise' White settlement and,	'Resolved and addressed' through decolonisation and 'end of empire' from the 20th century, imperial, distancing from and minimising of historical responsibilities, legacies, and actions of ex-slave owning imperial European powers	Legacy artefacts that are engrained in wider societal structures and entities, subtler and indirect forms of racism and discrimination, reverse settlement through post-colonial immigration and links to the 'metropole', contrasted with anti-immigration parities and policies

Source: Adapted from Fernando (2010, p. 8), the authors have added to identity and included sections on oppression and colonialism.

What is racial trauma and how does it manifest?

The term racial trauma, which is also classed as race-based stress, describes the unjust, and discriminatory experiences of racism. These are experienced internally, externally, and are systemically located (Comas-Díaz et al., 2019). Such experiences may involve first-hand or vicarious physical and psychological threat or injury, ranging from more 'subtle' forms of discrimination such as microaggressions and shaming, to violence and oppression. Racial trauma is not a one-time event. Rather, people are exposed to consistent, similar chronic traumas and new and developing forms, which may be specific to a particular racialised minority. Research has evidenced that chronic exposure to racism can have detrimental behavioural outcomes, because of its links to a range of health conditions. These include the activation of autoimmune disease/conditions, depression, anxiety, low self-esteem, and so on (Nkansa-Dwamena, 2023). In line with this, Geronimus (2023) coined the term 'weathering' to describe a process that encompasses the physiological effects of bearing the brunt of racial, ethnic, religious, and class discrimination. This demonstrates that continued stress damages cardiovascular, neuroendocrine, and metabolic systems thereby contributing to vulnerabilities that lead to people in these communities dying younger (Geronimus, 2023).

We also align with those who note that racial trauma is not just psychological but is embodied and can be transmitted epigenetically. For example, Collins (2023) conceptualised that racial trauma can result in, what she termed 'acting in' in which the individual internalises distress or 'acting out' in which they are projecting it outside. Examples of 'acting out' can include hostile behaviours such as being violent towards others or self-destructive behaviours, such as substance abuse, or repeatedly putting oneself in situations that could end in a repeat of experiencing racism. Lago and Charura (2015) reflected on the implication of epigenetic changes because of trauma, and the conceptualisations of transgenerational trauma. They informed their discussion following on from research by Dias and Ressler (2014) on how parental mice olfactory experiences influenced the behaviour and neural structure in subsequent mice generations. Dias and Ressler's (2014) study provided a framework for addressing how environmental information may be inherited transgenerationally at behavioural, neuroanatomical, and epigenetic levels. In this case, mice trained to associate an odour with an aversive electric shock transferred the acquired memory to their descendants and memory traces were evident even in their third generation. This study indicated that transgenerational, rather than intergenerational, inheritance mechanisms may be inherited (Dias &

Ressler, 2014). Moreover, Lago and Charura (2015) reflected on whether this happens not only in mice as noted by Dias and Ressler in their study, but whether experienced embodied trauma impacts humans, not only at an interpersonal, emotional, and behavioural level, but also at epigenetic levels.

We are therefore challenged here to further consider transcultural perspectives of working with racial trauma, its presentation and impact (Lago & Charura, 2015). The results of research and perspectives illuminates the impact of racial trauma upon the expression of distress, which has been typically viewed psychopathologically and medically, akin to post-traumatic stress disorder symptomatology (PTSD). However, such a direct equation of Racial trauma = PTSD has been likened to a 'psychiatric imperialism' (Fernando, 2010), because this omits the cultural-ethnic phenomenological identity of the individual, and firmly locates distress within the client and may homogenise and generalise the experience (and provenance) of trauma.

Whilst racial trauma can lead to PTSD, we acknowledge here that PTSD is, however, radically different to racial trauma: Due to the ongoing and pervasive nature of racial trauma(s), the idea of 'post' is challenged (Cénat, 2023). Racial traumas are constant and enduring, permeate and affect the community (Comas-Díaz et al., 2019). Additionally, these experiences damage the sense and consistency of identity and lifespan development and trajectory of the individual, through the internalisation of these harmful messages and experiences and subsequent external reinforcements to elicit intergenerational racial traumatisation, discussed later.

Critical race theory (CRT) as a base for racial trauma therapeutic work

The CRT movement began in the post-civil rights era as schools were being desegrated. CRT is based upon the critical theory of legal scholars and assesses how institutions, such as criminal justice, education, the housing market, health care, and labour market institutions, have unequal practices (Delgado & Stefancic, 2012). In this chapter, the application of CRT practice is being extended to critiquing inequality and therapeutic conceptualisations of racial trauma for people from ethnically diverse communities. We summarise and adapt some of the themes found in CRT and illustrate them with reference to Counselling Psychology and racial trauma sphere before outlining how racial trauma can be worked with (Delgado & Stefancic, 2012; Charura & Clyburn, 2023; McDowell & Jeris, 2004).

The summarised tenets of CRT:

1. Challenging the belief that racism is normal or ordinary and the argument that race is socially constructed and not biologically natural. Our intentionality as Counselling Psychologists should include a commitment to engage with and challenge systemic oppression that causes and perpetuates the myth that racial trauma is not a disorder but a 'normal reaction' to an 'abnormal situation' and oppressive system.

2. Focusing on what CRT scholars call 'interest convergence' or 'material determinism', the argument is that legal advances (or setbacks) for POC tend to serve the interests of dominant White groups. Thus, the racial *hierarchy* that characterises Western and European societies may be unaffected or even reinforced by *ostensible improvements* in the legal status of oppressed or exploited people. *As Counselling Psychologists, it is important to be awakened to the social injustice that can emerge even through so-called 'legal advances' as these can inadvertently perpetuate racism, and oppressive system and racial trauma.*

3. CRT values the notions of intersectionality and anti-essentialism, which argue that no individual can be adequately identified by membership in a single group. The person from the minoritised group presenting for therapy, for example, may also identify as a woman, heterosexual, having a faith, and so on.

4. The ultimate goal of CRT is social justice. This can be illustrated by challenging unfair outcomes for ethnic minorities in society and promoting awareness of racial trauma, and this should be seen as an ethical and moral position.

5. CRT critiques the perspective that racism is primarily an individual or psychological problem. Thus, systemic racism, discriminatory and racist practices, should be seen and challenged as contributory factors to racial trauma, rather than locating the trauma in the individual.

6. CRT argues that White supremacy and racism is so ingrained in our institutions and cultural practices and that it is often unrecognisable, creating an invisible norm against which all other races are measured. People from diverse communities have a unique voice in/on racial matters because of their socially minoritised position and experiences with racism oppression and microaggressions. Thus, CRT encourages the challenging of narratives that are White-dominated 'truth', and hearing counter-narratives and 'voice-of-colour' which is the competence by those from racialised groups to speak about race and racism (Delgado & Stefancic, 2012; McDowell & Jeris, 2004).

CRT therefore offers us a strong theoretical framework to build our practice on and to champion the importance of working therapeutically with racial trauma. There is a diversity of ways to work with racial trauma. However, due to the limitations in word count here in this chapter we have selected and suggested adaptations for power threat meaning framework as an overarching model that can be integrated in practice.

Working with racial trauma

In their research, Haeny et al. (2021) highlighted how The American Psychiatric Association formally apologised for its support of structural racism and called for the application of anti-racism framework in clinical research and practice. They noted that whilst anti-racism requires a multi-level approach, key components of this work include acknowledging the existence of racism and understanding how racism developed and evolved as well as its ongoing manifestations. In 2020, the British Psychological Society published on their website a statement on racial injustice, stating that 'The BPS stands in solidarity with all those who are feeling pain and expressing righteous anger about racial injustice and recommit to valuing diversity and fighting inequity' (BPS, 2020). Whilst we acknowledge these important statements, our critique is that these commitments have not been fully realised or translated into what this means for the profession and its practice (i.e., in relation to training, research, therapeutic work, and engaging with diverse communities).

Systemic racial oppressions: Power, threat, and meanings in clinical practice

Having thoroughly discussed the influence of racial trauma on individuals and communities, this section will discuss the phenomenological impact of systemic racism using the PTMF (Johnstone et al., 2018).

Systemic racism 'refers to the processes and outcomes of racial inequality and inequity in life opportunities and treatment' (Banaji et al., 2021, p. 2). This involves socially embedded racially discriminatory systems, structures, organisations, and policies, which permeate and influence across and within societal, community, and individual levels. Examples of systemic racism may (in)directly include discriminatory laws, attitudes, social programmes and initiatives, beliefs, values, educational, juridical, and organisational entities, in their application, or their omissions. This results in unfair practices, hindering opportunities, and outcomes for

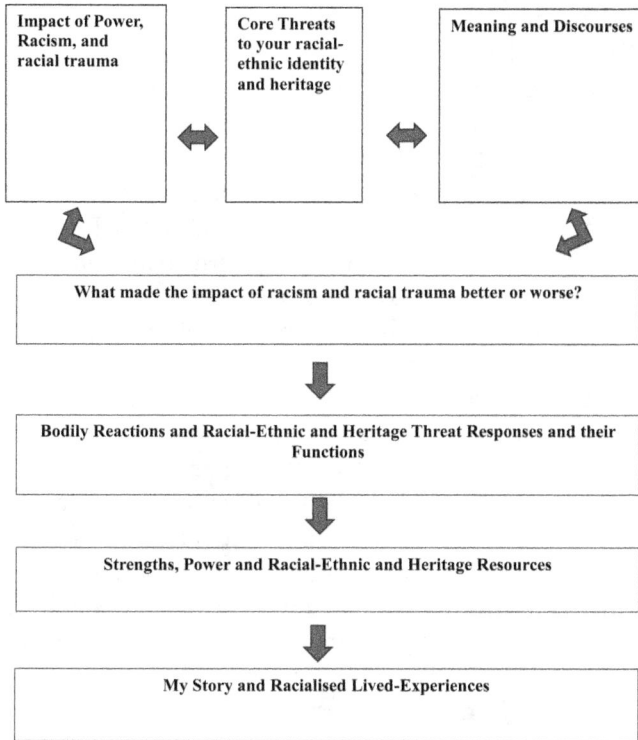

Figure 6.1 Racial trauma-informed PTM Framework (adapted from Johnstone et al., 2018)

racialised minorities. As a result of these prejudiced systems, those affected by these imposed, deliberate, or unintentional processes face a depletion and diminishment of access to resources, negatively affecting lifespan trajectories. The deprivation and severe restriction on these forms of capital: Economic, social, and cultural have well-evidenced consequences for health inequalities (Pinxten & Lievens, 2014). This leaves individuals, groups, and communities in an enduring state of threat, fear, and uncertainty, with profound consequences.

The PTMF (Figure 6.1) is a trauma-informed conceptualisation of mental distress, not asking what is 'wrong' with someone, but rather, 'what has happened?', offering a phenomenological narrative from which clients and therapists can work. This shifts and relocates the position of expertise and power towards the clients. It asks six fundamental questions (Johnstone et al., 2018), which are discussed in turn. We have adapted this framework to be, to explore and voice racial trauma and impacts of racial discrimination, violence, and oppression:

1. 'What has happened to you?'
    (How is Power and racism operating in your life?)
    Power in this question denotes accessibility or deprivation of resources and the affiliated 'capitals', or the discriminatory misuse of power against the individual, group, or community. This ranges from the biological, embodied, violence or coercion, socio-legal-economic, cultural, interpersonal, and ideological (Johnstone et al., 2018; Pinxten & Lievens, 2014). In this sense, power may be used against an individual/community from a racialised minority group; or they may not hold power or have access to less resources in a dysfunctional or discriminatory system.

2. 'How did racism affect you?'
    (What kind of Racialised Threats does this pose?)
    These are the perceived and actual threats and impacts of (in)access to power and or 'racist power against' rather than 'power with'. These consequences radiate from and to the individual, as well as from and to the systemic level. Examples of these effects are relational, emotional, social and community, economic and material, environmental, bodily, identity, values and knowledge, and phenomenological trauma, loss, degradation, and inconsistencies. Within this, some situations may have been able to mitigate certain racist threats or lessen their impact. This is the first aspect that considers positive resources and strengths that maintain a coherent racialised minority identity, both individually and as a community.

3. 'What sense did you make of the racism you have experienced?'
    (What is the Meaning of these racist situations and experiences to you?)
    This question refers to the phenomenological 'meaning-making' of those racist threats vis-à-vis the (core) beliefs, feelings and embodied physiological responses and reactions. Examples may include a sense of hopelessness, despair, anger, grief, mistrust, fear, or isolation, that may be both internalised by the individual or externalised and projected outwards to others and wider society (Comas-Díaz et al., 2019).

4. 'What did you have to do to survive such racism/endure this racial trauma?'
    (What kinds of Race-based Threat Response are you using?)
    This question asks about an individual's expressed physical, psychological, and behavioural (protective) responses to specific race-based threat they have faced, to meet their holistic needs. These may be both positive or negative or harmful to self or others. These are akin to the

symptomologies of mental and physical ill health, particularly the fight, flight, or freeze mechanisms in relation to PTSD (Cénat, 2023), the psychoanalytic and psychodynamic and relational defences (Fanon, 1952) and behavioural strategies of coping to maintain a sense of self and existence.

5. 'What are your strengths?'
(What access to power resources do you have?)
This question seeks to clarify and to begin building upon positive resources, influences, relationships, and aspects of the individual's racial and ethnic identity, coping mechanisms and helpful functioning, body, mind, and personality. These may also include interpersonal and intrapersonal resources, protective and productive beliefs, cultural practices, group and social memberships, and purposeful and meaningful identities and roles that contribute to intrapsychic stability.

6. 'What is your story and your lived experiences?'
(How does all this narrative fit together?)
This is perhaps the most specific, in beginning to map and express a client's racial-ethnic narrative, in their own words, as they have experienced and perceived their life, histories, traumas, experiences, hopes, goals, and strengths. It is from these questions that a rich and unique formulation can be collaboratively formed.

Conclusion

This chapter has reviewed and highlighted key issues of racial trauma and working therapeutically with affected clients. It is important to emphasise that racial trauma relates to damaging experiences that are either due to an impactful event/s, and/or chronic, enduring exposure to racially specific existential threats. This consequently creates responses within and external to those individuals. As authors, we have offered discussion and definition around terminology and language, and reflected upon our own identities and positionalities and we encourage you to do the same. The chapter reviewed CRT and the impacts of racism on individuals. The latter section focussed on an adapted racially sensitive PTM framework template to use therapeutically with clients, using a racial trauma-focussed approach. We conclude the chapter with several reflective questions for readers to consider and refer to, to prompt further thought and discussion, but more crucially, to act.

Chapter questions to provoke thoughts:

1. Which racial, ethnic and heritage identities do you hold and how have wider systems maintained, contributed to, and impacted these?
2. How visible/less visible were these identities in relation to your childhood, compared to now and what might that have meant for you, your family and local communities, back then and now? Is there a difference and, if so or not, how might you explain this?
3. Consider formulating a client who has experienced and been impacted by racial trauma using the framework we have adapted from the Power Threat Meaning Framework (Johnstone et al., 2018).
4. How can psychological therapy become more accessible, welcoming, and inclusive for clients who have experienced racial trauma and oppression?
5. In line with this, might the psychological models, frameworks that you use perpetuate the racial trauma? and how might you develop your anti-discriminatory, antiracist, and anti-oppressive clinical, supervisory, or teaching practice?

References

Banaji, M. R., Fiske, S. T., & Massey, D. S. (2021). Systemic racism: Individuals and interactions, institutions, and society. *Cognitive Research: Principles and Implications*, 6(1). https://doi.org/10.1186/s41235-021-00349-3

Blackburn, S. (2017). *Truth*. Profile Books.

British Psychological Society (BPS). (2020, June 2). BPS statement on racial injustice. https://www.bps.org.uk/news/bps-statement-racial-injustice

Cénat, J. M. (2023). Complex racial trauma: Evidence, theory, assessment, and treatment. *Perspectives on Psychological Science*, 18(3), 675–687. https://doi.org/10.1177/17456916221120428

Charura, D., & Clyburn, S. (2023). Critical race theory: A methodology for research in psychotherapy. In K. Tudor & J. Wyatt (Eds.), *Reflexive research for reflective practice: Qualitative research methodologies for psychotherapy.* (pp. 72–86). Routledge.

Charura, D., & Lago, C. (Eds.) (2021a). *Black identities + White therapies: Race, respect + diversity*. PCCS Books.

Collins, L. Y. (2023). Healing racial trauma from public school systems. *Journal of Research Initiatives*, 8(1), 3.

Comas-Díaz, L., Hall, G. N., & Neville, H. A. (2019). Racial trauma: Theory, research, and healing: Introduction to the special issue. *American Psychologist*, 74(1), 1–5. https://doi.org/10.1037/amp0000442

Delgado, R., & Stefancic, J. (2012). *Critical race theory* (2nd ed.). New York University Press.

Denyer, T., Wade, K., Whitney, M., Charura, D., & Proctor, G. (2022). 'Listen with love': Exploring anti-racism dialogue in psychotherapy and counselling training. *Psychotherapy & Politics International*, 20(1 & 2). https://doi.org/10.24135/ppi.v20i1and2.06

Dias, B. G., & Ressler, K. J. (2014). Parental olfactory experience influences behavior and neural structure in subsequent generations. *Nature Neuroscience, 17*(1), 89–96. https://doi.org/10.1038/nn.3594

Fanon, F. (1952). *Black skin, White masks*. Pluto Press.

Fernando, S. (2010). *Mental health, race and culture* (3rd ed.). Red Globe Press.

Geronimus, A. T. (2023). *Weathering*. Little Brown & Company.

Green, M. J., Matsebula, J., & Sonn, C. C. (2007). Reviewing Whiteness: Theory, research, and possibilities. *South African Journal of Psychology, 37*(3), 389–419. https://doi.org/10.1177/008124630703700301

Gunew, S. (2007). Rethinking Whiteness. *Feminist Theory, 8*(2), 141–147. https://doi.org/10.1177/1464700107078138

Haeny, A. M., Holmes, S. C., & Williams, M. T. (2021). Applying anti-racism to clinical care and research. *JAMA Psychiatry, 78*(11), 1187–1188. https://doi.org/10.1001/jamapsychiatry.2021.2329

Health & Care Professions Council (HCPC). (2023). *Standards of proficiency: Practitioner Psychologists*. https://www.hcpc-uk.org/globalassets/standards/standards-of-proficiency/reviewing/practitioner-psychologist—new-standards.p

Johnstone, L., Boyle, M., Cromby, J., Dillon, J., Harper, D., Kinderman, P., Longden, E., Pilgrim, D., & Read, J. (2018). *The power threat meaning framework: Overview*. British Psychological Society.

Lago, C., & Charura, D. (2015). Working with transgenerational/intergenerational trauma: The implication of epigenetic considerations and transcultural perspectives in psychotherapy. *The Psychotherapist*, (59), 23–25.

Maharaj, A. S., Bhatt, N. V., & Gentile, J. P. (2021). Bringing it in the room: Addressing the impact of racism on the therapeutic alliance. *Innovations in Clinical Neuroscience, 18*(7-9), 39–43.

McDowell, T., & Jeris, L. (2004). talking about race using critical race theory: Recent trends in the journal of marital and family therapy. *Journal of Marital and Family Therapy, 30*(1), 81–94. https://doi.org/10.1111/j.1752-0606.2004.tb01224.x

Nkansa-Dwamena, O. (2023). Attending to self, attending to others: The impact on the Black therapist of client presentations of racial trauma. In N. Zahid, & R. Cooke, (Eds.). *Therapists challenging racism and oppression*. (pp. 62–76)PCCS Books.

Owen, D. S. (2007). Towards a critical theory of whiteness. *Philosophy & Social Criticism, 33*(2), 203–222. https://doi.org/10.1177/0191453707074139

Pinxten, W., & Lievens, J. (2014). The importance of economic, social and cultural capital in understanding health inequalities: Using a Bourdieu-based approach in research on physical and mental health perceptions. *Sociology of Health & Illness, 36*(7), 1095–1110. https://doi.org/10.1111/1467-9566.12154

Saini, A. (2019). *Superior: The return of race science*. Beacon Press.

Smith, J. A., Flowers, P., & Larkin, M. (2022). *Interpretative phenomenological analysis: Theory, method and research* (2nd ed.). Sage.

Bias and diagnosis   7

Ranjot Bhogal and Neha Cattra

Overview

This chapter regarding Diagnosis intends to consider psychiatric diagnosis from the perspective of race, ethnicity, and culture, from a United Kingdom (UK) Counselling Psychology lens. The chapter will take readers through the history of these issues – the use a of socially constructed notion of race being utilised to oppress and discriminate against so-called 'inferior' groups, and resulting in very real racism, including in mental health. We discuss why examining these issues is important, given the failures of trainings to attend to this adequately – especially in the context of Health and Care Professions Council (HCPC, 2015) standards stating that practitioners' ought 'be aware of the impact of culture, equality and diversity on practice' and 'be able to practise in a non-discriminatory manner'. We explore whether diagnosis has a place in today's mental health systems, and whether attention to individuals' race, ethnicity, and culture can enhance our understanding and therefore treatment of the people and communities with whom we work. We discuss the current professional context – especially that of Counselling Psychology and we ponder possible future directions.

DOI: 10.4324/9781003415244-9

Introduction

This chapter explores psychiatric diagnosis from the perspective of race, ethnicity, and culture, and from a UK Counselling Psychology lens. Many of the arguments present here relate to other professions, particularly the wider psychological professions. The chapter will take the reader through the history of these issues, why this topic is important, the current professional context, and future directions.

Counselling Psychology in the UK came into being as a distinct specialism largely because of disillusionment with the medical model – see Hogan (2019) for an explanation of the history of this term, favouring Engel's (1977) 'Biopsychosocial' model as an alternative. It is important that we acknowledge the utility and importance of mental health diagnosis as for some this provides relief that their experiences are understood by others, and also starts to point clinicians in the direction of potential treatments.

The authors' positionality

Ranjot Bhogal is a UK-born chartered Counselling Psychologist of Indian ethnicity. It sadly came to light that Ranjot's paternal grandfather had fallen victim to the violence that erupted in India in the aftermath of Operation Bluestar in 1984. Following her grandfather's passing, some members of Ranjot's family began to experience fluctuations in mood and repeated somatic complaints with no organic pathology which were challenging to communicate in Punjabi to English-speaking healthcare professionals. Consequently, Ranjot developed a new culturally sensitive assessment measure for depression in the Punjabi language, titled the Punjabi Depression Inventory (PDI) (Bhogal, 2020).

Neha Cattra is a cisgendered British-Indian gay woman. Neha is a chartered Principal Counselling Psychologist and has worked clinically in adult mental health for most of her career. She also works as a lecturer on a Clinical Psychology doctoral training programme. With close family members in need of mental health treatment, she has had challenging experiences of navigating the same adult mental health systems she has worked in. She has spent much of her own life so far navigating various identities, at times assimilating and others pushing against the arbitrary barriers between them. Neha is married to a psychologically minded psychiatrist, with whom she has useful verbal sparring matches about the validity of diagnosis that have helped shape her views.

History and professional context

The historical connection between race and diagnosis is complex and deep-rooted. Historically, Psychologists and Psychiatrists have used racial categories to diagnose and treat mental health conditions. It is a human-made construct that Race confers upon some certain privileges and on others certain 'deficiencies'. This notion has often been utilised to support discriminatory practices and ideologies. For instance, the notion of 'drapetomania' (Cartwright, 1851), an alleged mental disorder attributing the tendency of slaves to escape their owners, was used in the 19th century to justify the enslavement of African Americans. Similarly, during the early 20th century, the concept of 'feeble-mindedness' was used to diagnose and institutionalise individuals who were considered intellectually inferior (Gould, 1981).

In the mid-20th century, there was a shift away from overt racism in psychological diagnosis. Both Psychiatry and Psychology grew in a post-European Enlightenment period, as Morrison (1990) put it – the heyday of slavery and colonialism, during which powerful myths about race were establishing themselves in the collective Western psyche. For example, the Diagnostic and Statistical Manual of Mental Disorders (DSM; American Psychiatric Association, 2022), was primarily based on the experiences of predominantly White, middle-class individuals (Maramba & Nagayama Hall, 2002). This has raised concerns that diagnostic criteria do not accurately capture the experiences of individuals from diverse racial, ethnic, and cultural backgrounds.[1]

As we examine bias with regards to race, we go beyond the visible differences of skin colour to consider a person's cultural identity – something that is fluid and dynamic – living and breathing. We draw upon the concept of cultural humility (Lekas et al., 2020) which encourages a process of continual development rather than cultural competence which is content driven – as something to attain. Adopting a White-Western-centric view of the typically marginalised global south, and assuming that one has reached a predetermined set of 'competencies' risks stereotyping and furthering discrimination.

Race and diagnosis in Counselling Psychology have become increasingly important issues. Diagnosis can be a key element of the therapy process, and it is essential that diagnoses are accurate, appropriate, and culturally sensitive. However, there are concerns that race and ethnicity may impact the diagnostic process, leading to misdiagnosis, underdiagnosis, or overdiagnosis of certain conditions.

The problem(s) with diagnosis

The ethos of Counselling Psychology in diagnosis is to view the person as a whole, rather than simply focusing on symptoms or behaviours

(Douglas, Woolfe, Strawbridge, Kasket and Gailbraith, 2016). Indeed, a non-pathologising approach is central to Counselling Psychology, where mental health issues are considered a communication of psychological distress. This approach is in contrast to traditional medical models, which tend to prioritise identifying and treating specific symptoms or diagnosing mental health disorders based on rigid criteria. Levy (1992), in his tongue-in-cheek essay intended to unmask the absurdity of diagnoses, proposes a category of 'Pervasive Labelling Disorder' for the DSM aimed at the institution of Psychiatry, which he conceptualises as prevalent in those who attain positions of power and is used to control others.

As Goldie's schema of para-medical professional stances (1977) notes, those working in systems where medical discourse is dominant may adopt and/or move between three stances – compliant, eclectic, or radically opposed. Newnes (2014) relates this to Clinical Psychology, though this may also apply to Counselling Psychologists in similar contexts. Compliance is construed as 'going along with' the dominant discourse, contributing to the legitimisation of diagnostic systems. Eclecticism is characterised by not directly challenging the dominant discourse, and offering talking therapies as adjuncts to medical treatment – perhaps the most familiar position to many – and is certainly the position both of the authors recognise adopting. Radical opposition is precisely that – the direct challenge to, or the fleeing from medically laden systems.

In the early 1900s Kraepelin reconceptualised emotional problems as having a biological aetiology – thus aligning with the medical model of disease. Indeed, the psychological professions have long rejected this notion, and opted for a non-biological treatment in the form of a talking therapy. Psychological distress is subjective and therefore categorisation is mired by the same subjectivity – whilst manuals such as the DSM have provided a shared language through symptom checklists, these are still constructs. There are currently no objective biological tests that definitively indicate that one person has what is known as Depression, or another person has what we term as 'Schizophrenia'.

There has also been a shift in the positive nature of suffering – where suffering was seen as purposeful, redemptive and had the possibility of leading to unexpected gains. As such, some pain has been seen as part of life and therefore growth. However, the medical model proliferates the notion that suffering is a fluke of biological misfortune, and therefore something to be remedied post haste as nothing can be gained from it. This can lead to decontextualisation of psychological distress what Whooley (2014) refers to as the tendency of the DSM, and psychiatric nosology generally, to fail to acknowledge the fundamental way in which mental distress—its distribution, manifestation, and meaning – are determined by and situated in social structures and cultural meaning-systems.

There is much written about the general pitfalls of a medical model of mental illness – for example in two volumes of *De-Medicalizing Misery* (Rapley et al., 2011; Speed et al., 2014). Further, in *A Prescription for Psychiatry*, Kinderman (2014) acknowledges the fact that what in the West are considered problematic hallucinations or voice-hearing, other cultures may respect and protect these experiences as spiritual or indeed, as an everyday tangible experience of the presence of God, or ancestors.

In James Davies book *Cracked – Why Psychiatry Is Doing More Harm Than Good* (2013), he refers to Psychiatric Imperialism and gives several examples of a 'Western' lens of mental health permeating a non-Western culture and shaping beliefs about mental health. His book challenges the notion that greater awareness or less secretiveness about mental health are the reasons for increased diagnoses in non-Western nations.

Psychiatry has played a role in shaping culture, it does not merely 'reveal' disorder but could actually increase their prevalence by highlighting their existence in an otherwise unprimed culture (Davies, 2013, discussions with Edward Shorter). The vehicle for this might be what Shorter refers to as a culturally moderated 'symptom pool' which legitimises expressions of distress. In other words, cultures dictate how distress can be expressed in a way that others can understand so that individuals are not ostracised. This suggests that individuals may adopt an unconscious embodiment of symptoms – likened to contagious yawning. This makes some anecdotal sense, for example in cultures where psychological distress is somatised – this becomes a 'legitimate' way for psychological distress to be embodied. We know from the psychological lexicon of studies of conformity that show just how much the need to be part of an in-group can alter our behaviour (Asch, 1951). As noted earlier with Goldie's schemata (1977) even Psychologists are not immune to social forces that might seem to outsiders to 'collude' with predominant models, despite purporting to acknowledge these culturally idiosyncratic understandings.

All of this leads us to understand that concepts of distress are cultural constructions borne out of the interplay of myriad influences as Loewenthal and Snell (2003) state from language (Lacan), the other and difference (Levinas), to power (Foucault), and more. More latterly, these concepts that have formed in a Western milieu are being exported in the form of the DSM and ICD to other nations, and the vehicle is often pharmaceutical companies (Davies, 2013). As Davies (2013) goes on to say, so called 'success stories' are seen where companies have understood and exploited the specific cultural meanings of where distress originates from. In the two examples provided, the socio-political zeitgeist is tapped into, and progressively altered using disease-laden terminology, to shape and ultimately subvert the prevailing cultural conceptualisation of depression. In so doing, we see that the location of 'the problem' causing distress is moved from wider systemic pressure located in society, to the internal world of individuals (Davies, 2013).

In the West, mental health disorders are viewed as treatable with medical and/or psychological interventions, but non-Western communities may use religious rituals for treatment instead. Religion as a coping mechanism has gained attention recently (Dein, 2020). Studies show that about 50% of the African population with mental health concerns consult traditional healers before seeking professional help (Burns & Tomita, 2015). Kleinman (1980) emphasised the importance of incorporating patients' beliefs into treatment plans for increased patient satisfaction. Khalifa et al. (2011) and Ofori-Atta et al. (2018) found benefits in combining religious rituals with formal psychiatric treatment. Therefore, approaching mental health in non-Western cultures requires cultural sensitivity, collaboration between mental health professionals and traditional healers, and a culturally informed approach that respects diverse perspectives.

Davies (2013) points to the facts that research has shown that despite this exportation of a Western model, the efficacy of anti-psychotics is questionable. Research has also shown that there are lower recovery rates, higher social impairments, and overall higher levels of medicalisation in the developed world in comparison to non-Western nations when anti-psychotics are used. One such reason for this is that there is often better community support for the emotionally and mentally distressed in other cultures which stands to reason when a shared aetiology is external to the individual and linked to societal forces others also experience and can therefore relate to.

Black and ethnic communities are more likely to be misdiagnosed and subjected to an inappropriate service-led approach (King, 2019). We also know that Black and ethnic communities are at more risk for a diagnosis of non-affective and affective psychoses (Halvorsrud et al., 2019), at increased risk of involuntary psychiatric care (Barnett et al., 2019), and that their symptoms may be expressed differently. This can lead to the under-reporting of symptoms due to the fear of potential consequences, historical experiences of discrimination, stigma and mistrust of healthcare systems. Black and ethnic communities are also more likely to be misdiagnosed as they present with cultural symptoms which are not accounted for in the DSM as it is based on a Western perspective. Diagnosis can also lead to stigmatisation and labelling, which can be harmful to individuals and impact their self-perception and relationships with others, including professionals and organisations.

To address these issues, Counselling Psychology promotes a person-centred, culturally sensitive, and collaborative approach to diagnosis, which considers the individual's unique experiences, social context, and cultural background. One might consider this the restoration of the inherent meaning made of experiences, given that Johnstone suggests that 'the single most damaging effect of psychiatric diagnosis is loss of meaning' (2018). There are increasing calls for the development of more culturally relevant assessment tools and criteria – such as the PDI (Bhogal, 2020). It is the view of the authors that diagnosis is not a problem per se, but how it is arrived at and then utilised – for example the DSM acts as a gatekeeping tool for access to treatment in a North American health insurance context.

Why race is important in considering diagnosis

Much of the research that has influenced psychiatry and psychology, are predominantly conducted primarily on Western, Educated, Industrialised, Rich, and Democratic (WEIRD) communities, which are unrepresentative of the world's population. Coined by Social Psychologist Joseph Henrich and his colleagues (Henrich et al., 2010), it is used to describe potential limitations of generalising research findings based on this narrow sample as their experiences may not accurately represent the experiences and needs of individuals from other racial and cultural backgrounds. Given this WEIRD sampling, it is not surprising that the implications for diagnosis in relation to race is being highlighted more and more in Counselling Psychology.

Given the increasing multicultural, multi-ethnic make-up of the UK, it is of utmost importance that our understanding of Mental Health and treatment of such encompasses nuanced cultural humility and curiosity in order to appropriately serve these diverse populations. As individuals from non-Western communities are underrepresented in clinical research studies, this compounds a lack of understanding of how mental health conditions may manifest differently in these populations. Disregarding the significance of race and culture can lead to erroneous assessments, diagnoses, and misinterpretation of symptoms. As such, the most appropriate treatment for that person may not be delivered, and further still – a culturally incongruent self-understanding may be perpetuated for the individual. For example, the diagnostic criteria for disorders such as depression and anxiety have been criticised for being based on Western conceptions of mental health and illness, which may not align with cultural beliefs and practices of other populations.

Individuals from diverse racial or ethnic backgrounds encounter distinct social and cultural factors such as discrimination, prejudice, systematic historical and intergenerational trauma, and acculturation challenges, among others, that impact on their psychological well-being. Race and culture understandably impacts constructions of mental illness- with some cultures perceiving mental illness to be a family matter rather than an individual concern, which may have an impact on the process of diagnosis. Lastly, incorporating culturally responsive practices, including considering race and ethnicity during diagnosis, fosters the development of cultural humility in Counselling Psychology. By acknowledging and embracing diverse perspectives and experiences, Counselling Psychologists can deliver interventions that are effective and culturally appropriate. Additionally, attending to race and culture ensures a more precise assessment of an individual's condition, promoting accuracy in understanding their experiences and needs. This approach promotes inclusivity and understanding, guides intervention planning, enhances treatment efficacy, and fosters collaboration among individuals.

Such a nuanced approach recognises that race and culture are a dynamic and integral part of an individual's life and should be considered in all aspects of therapy – from assessment and diagnosis to measuring outcomes. Griner and Smith's (2006) research demonstrated the benefits of tailoring mental health interventions to align with the cultural backgrounds of individuals, particularly when targeting specific racial or ethnic groups. It emphasises the clients' expertise in their own cultural experiences and encourages their active participation in the therapeutic process. These findings highlight the importance of studying the cultural construct of mental health and serves as encouragement for further research in this field.

In order to promote inclusivity, cultural sensitivity, and accurate assessments for individuals from diverse backgrounds, there has been a history of directly translating English mainstream measures into various languages. Researchers such as Lai and Surood (2008) have proposed that adapted mainstream assessments are suitable for culturally diverse populations as they are in a language familiar to them. However, challenges arise when attempting to translate a cultural idiom of distress into other languages, as there may not be an equivalent idiom in the target language. It is important to recognise that the relevance of a particular concept cannot be assumed to be the same across different cultures (Hilton & Skrutkowski, 2002).

Martín-Baró's (1996) Liberation Psychology also challenges traditional diagnostic practices by emphasising a contextual, empowering, and socially conscious approach to understanding and addressing psychological distress. Similarly, the Power Threat Meaning Framework (PTMF; Johnstone

& Boyle, 2018) offers an alternative to conventional psychiatric diagnoses. It refocuses on understanding an individual's life context, exploring the meaning of their distress, and identifying power and threat sources and attending to them. This empowers individuals and shifts towards a more person-centred approach that is aligned to their values.

To mitigate errors in attribution, judgemental heuristics, and diagnostic overshadowing, Sue and Sue (2012) suggest the implementation of cultural assessment tools in clinical practice with the aim of enhancing cultural attunement. The DSM-5 (2013) aimed to address some of the critique regarding a lack of cultural consideration by introducing the Cultural Formulation Interview (CFI) and aims to promote culturally competent practice by elucidating patients' perspectives on health, illness, and treatment. The CFI addresses domains like cultural identity, perceptions of the problem, causes, coping, help-seeking, and the relationship between the individual and the clinician. Used flexibly rather than verbatim, the goal is to broaden the clinician's understanding of the patient's experience, fostering shared decision-making and culturally sensitive care (Aggarwal & Lewis-Fernández, 2020). See Bredström (2017) for a fuller critique of the DSM-5's attempt to incorporate greater cultural sensitivity.

Whilst the CFI has gone some way to address culture, it remains a generic tool for all communities when applying what remains a Western-centric perspective of mental illness. The recent development of the PDI (Bhogal, 2020) represents a significant and foundational effort to explicitly incorporate a specific culture and community into clinical practice. The study was conducted to develop a new cultural measure that was intrinsically linked to and formulated in their native Punjabi language and culture. Unlike adaptations or translations of mainstream measures, this inventory was specifically created and tailored to detect depression in Punjabi-speaking individuals who now permanently reside in the UK, but originally migrated from India. It stands as an original and unique measure capable of identifying cultural aspects of depression within its target population, therefore being socially conscious as other models have indicated the importance of.

Recommendations

In light of the increasing recognition of the influence of race and ethnicity on mental health, and continued discrimination against those of minority groups, it has become more imperative to explore and address these factors in Counselling Psychology. Ensuring that these are not just 'warm words' and are inherent in the practice of Counselling Psychology involves taking intentional steps to decolonise curriculums (SOAS, 2018) and continued professional development (CPD), engage in courageous discussions and increase representation within the field. As training institutions, there is a pedagogical responsibility inherent to expose trainees to the very best of knowledge and opportunities for critique. In decolonising curricula that have for so long considered the 'best' knowledge to come from a narrow lens, this is becoming more possible.

First and foremost, there is a distinct lack of racial and cultural diversity in trainee-cohorts, teaching staff and the research and theories drawn upon in the curriculum. Enhancing the recruitment of Counselling Psychologists from diverse backgrounds is a crucial step towards fostering inclusivity and cultural humility within the field. Actively seeking out and attracting trainees from diverse racial and ethnic backgrounds is essential to creating a pipeline of Counselling Psychologists who are representative of diverse communities. This can be achieved by implementing targeted recruitment efforts, such as establishing partnerships with community organisations, attending career fairs in underrepresented communities, and offering scholarships or financial aid packages specifically for individuals from marginalised groups. In so doing, conversations about different cultural conceptualisations of mental illness can be brought forth for appropriate reflection and debate to cultivate cultural humility.

Additionally, it is essential to create a supportive and inclusive environment within these programmes, where trainees and trainers from diverse backgrounds feel valued, heard, and supported. This can be achieved by implementing mentorship programmes, providing culturally sensitive supervision, and fostering a curriculum that incorporates diverse perspectives and experiences. In time it is hoped that research is therefore also more inclusive and has the potential to highlight nuanced cultural understandings that supplement a diagnostic approach.

Given the core importance of self-reflexivity in Counselling Psychology, it is imperative that practitioners engage in ongoing supervision and CPD that fosters discussion of issues pertaining to the practitioners' and their clients' cultural and ethnic experiences. These spaces may allow for examination of their own values, beliefs, and assumptions, which may inadvertently shape their therapeutic approach. It is hoped that such opportunities can promote shared learning and adoption of best practice.

Collaborating with community leaders to develop community-based interventions for mental health support could also be a potentially vital step in addressing the mental well-being of the community. By engaging with local leaders, we can harness their deep understanding of the community's needs and dynamics to co-create initiatives that are culturally sensitive and relevant. Community leaders can also help identify key stakeholders, secure resources, and mobilise community members, ensuring that mental health treatments are not only accessible but also embraced by the community. These treatments can be more culturally tailored and accessible to underserved communities, addressing barriers to care.

Evaluating efforts to promote diversity in the field of Counselling Psychology is vital to assess the effectiveness and impact of these initiatives. Feedback from both professionals and clients can be gathered to gauge their perceptions and experiences regarding diversity and cultural humility in the field. Additionally, the examination of outcomes, such as client satisfaction, treatment outcomes, and cultural sensitivity in therapeutic practices, can provide valuable insights into the impact of efforts to increase cultural humility.

Conclusions

Throughout this chapter we have strived to present a constructive critique of diagnosis from the nuanced perspective of race, ethnicity, and culture. Psychiatric diagnoses constructed on the basis of Whiteness, and applied to those of other backgrounds are inherently flawed. The constructs of 'diagnosis', the disease laden field of Psychiatry and the dominant discourse of Whiteness all continue to oppress and control certain populations, if not ignore or assimilate them.

As we conclude this chapter, it is evident that there is still significant work to be done in incorporating race into the practice of Counselling Psychology and indeed Applied Psychology. This is a call to arms – more research is needed so as not to perpetuate the reductivist approach of utilising the CFI for all communities, such as the PDI (Bhogal, 2020). This extends to curriculum development and into recruitment processes for trainings. By promoting research and practice that actively incorporates race as a fundamental aspect of psychological assessment, intervention, and treatment, we can strive for a more equitable and inclusive Applied Psychology profession that meets the diverse needs of diverse communities and fosters positive mental health outcomes.

We are reminded that this is the work of all within the profession. Too often, the cognitive load of interrogating the implicit bias in conceptualisations of mental illness, falls to those who have been marginalised themselves – in this regard, those from non-White backgrounds. We encourage allyship, shared learning, constructive, and purposive dialogue in regard to how the profession can continue to develop cultural humility. For this, we need all of our colleagues to ensure that race, in relation to the core values of pursuing Social Justice, is very much at the core of working as Counselling Psychologists.

Chapter questions to provoke thoughts:

Our readers may come from a range of backgrounds themselves; they may be starting out or developed in their understanding of the issues we present here, nonetheless, we encourage all our readers to critically reflect on the following questions having now read the chapter:

1. Is diagnosis relevant in a racially, ethnically, and culturally sensitive mental health system?
2. What biases or stereotypes might impact the accuracy and/or utility of mental health diagnoses in different racial or ethnic groups?
3. How do we encourage and indeed embrace cultural humility and anti-discriminatory practice in relation to diagnosis?
4. How do we ensure that the constructs upon which diagnostic and treatment decisions are made are culturally appropriate?

Note

1. It is acknowledged that DSM-5 has attempted to address concerns around culture, racism, and discrimination. However, this does not mitigate its foundation nor its inherent exclusion of these factors.

References

Aggarwal, N. K., & Lewis-Fernández, R. (2020). An introduction to the cultural formulation interview. *Focus: The Journal of Lifelong Learning in Psychiatry, 18*(1), 77–82. https://doi.org/10.1176/appi.focus.18103

American Psychiatric Association. (2013). *Diagnostic and statistical manual of mental disorders* (5th ed.). https://doi.org/10.1176/appi.books.9780890425596

American Psychiatric Association. (2022). *Diagnostic and statistical manual of mental disorders* (5th ed., text rev.).

Asch, S. (1951). Effects of group pressure on the modification and distortion of judgments. In H. Guetzkow (Ed.), *Groups, leadership and men: Research in human relations* (pp. 177–190). Carnegie Press.

Barnett, P., MacKay, E., Mattews, H., Gate, R., Greenwood, H., Ariyo, K., Bhui, K., Halvorsrud, K., Pilling, S., & Smith, S. (2019). Ethnic variations in compulsory detention under the Mental Health Act: A systematic review and meta-analysis of international data. *The Lancet Psychiatry, 6*(4), 305–317.

Bhogal, R. (2020). Punjabi Depression Inventory: A culturally sensitive measure for Punjabi-speaking migrants residing in the UK. *Counselling Psychology Review, 35*(2), 22–29.

Bredström, A. (2017). Culture and context in mental health diagnosing: Scrutinizing the DSM-5 revision, *Journal of Medical Humanities, 40*, 347–363. https://doi.org/10.1007/s10912-017-9501-1

Burns, J. K., & Tomita, A. (2015). Traditional and religious healers in the pathway to care for people with mental disorders in Africa: A systematic review and meta-analysis. *Social Psychiatry and Psychiatric Epidemiology, 50*(6), 867–877.

Cartwright, S. (1851). Report on the diseases and physical peculiarities of the negro race. *New Orleans Medical and Surgical Journal, 7*(8), 706–716.

Davies, J. (2013). *Cracked: Why psychiatry is doing more harm than good.* Icon Books.

Dein, S. (2020). Religious healing and mental health. *Mental Health, Religion & Culture, 23*(8), 657–665.

Douglas, B., Woolfe, R., Strawbridge, S., Kasket, E., & Galbraith, V. (2016). *The handbook of counselling psychology.* Sage.

Engel, G. L. (1977). The need for A new medical model: A challenge for biomedicine. *Science, 196*(4286), 129–136. https://doi.org/10.1126/science.847460

Goldie, N. (1977). The division of labour among the mental health professions–a negotiated or an imposed order? In M. Stacey, M. Reid, C. Heath, & R. Dingwall (Eds.), *Health and the division of labour* (pp. 22–34). Croom Helm.

Gould, S. J. (1981). *The mismeasure of man.* W. W. Norton & Company.

Griner, D., & Smith, T. B. (2006). Culturally adapted mental health interventions: A meta-analytic review. *Psychotherapy: Theory, Research, Practice & Training, 43*, 531–548.

Halvorsrud, K., Nazroo, J., Otis, M., Hajdukova, E. B., & Bhui, K. (2019). Ethnic inequalities in the incidence of diagnosis of severe mental illness in England: A systemic review and new meta-analyses for non-affective and affective psychoses. *Social Psychiatry and Psychiatric Epidemiology, 54*(11), 1311–1323.

Health & Care Professions Council (HCPC). (2015). *Standards of proficiency: Practitioner Psychologists.* https://www.hcpc-uk.org/standards/standards-of-proficiency/practitioner-psychologists/

Henrich, J., Heine, S. J., & Norenzayan, A. (2010). The weirdest people in the world? *Behavioral and Brain Sciences, 33*(2/3), 1–75. https://www2.psych.ubc.ca/~henrich/pdfs/WeirdPeople.pdf

Hilton, A., & Skrutkowski, M. (2002). Translating instruments into other languages: Development and testing processes. *Journal of Cancer Nursing, 25*(1), 1–7.

Hogan, A. J. (2019). Social and medical models of disability and mental health: Evolution and renewal. *Canadian Medical Association Journal, 191*(1), E16–E18. https://doi.org/10.1503/cmaj.181008

Johnstone, L. (2018). Psychological formulation as an alternative to psychiatric diagnosis. *Journal of Humanistic Psychology, 58*(1), 30–46. https://doi.org/10.1177/0022167817722230

Johnstone, L., & Boyle, M. (2018). The power threat meaning framework: An alternative nondiagnostic conceptual system. *Journal of Humanistic Psychology.* https://doi.org/10.1177/0022167818793289

Khalifa, N., Hardie, T., Latif, S., Jamil, I., & Walker, D. M. (2011). Beliefs about jinn, Black magic and evil eye among Muslims: Age, gender and first language influences. *International Journal of Culture and Mental Health, 4*(1), 68–77.

Kinderman, P. (2014). *A prescription for psychiatry: Why we need a whole new approach to mental health and wellbeing.* Palgrave Macmillan.

King, C. (2019). Race, mental health, and the research gap. *The Lancet Psychiatry, 6*(5), 367–368.

Kleinman, A. (1980). *Patients and healers in the context of culture: An exploration of the border-land between anthropology, medicine, and psychiatry.* University of California Press.

Lai, D. W. L., & Surood, S. (2008). Socio-cultural variations in depressive symptoms of ageing South Asian Canadians. *Asian Journal of Gerontology & Geriatrics, 3,* 84–91.

Lekas, H. M., Pahl, K., & Fuller Lewis, C. (2020). Rethinking cultural competence: shifting to cultural humility. *Health Services Insights, 13. doi:10.1177/1178632920970580*

Levy, D. A. (1992). A proposed category for the diagnostic and statistical manual of mental disorders (DSM): Pervasive labelling disorder. *Journal of Humanistic Psychology, 32*(1), 121–125. Retrieved from: PLD.pdf (pepperdine.edu)

Loewenthal, D., & Snell, R. (2003). *Post-modernism for psychotherapists: A critical reader.* Routledge.

Maramba, G. G., & Nagayama Hall, G. C. (2002). Meta-analyses of ethnic match as a predictor of dropout, utilization, and level of functioning. *Cultural Diversity and Ethnic Minority Psychology, 8*(3), 290.

Martín-Baró, I. (1996). *Writings for a liberation psychology.* Harvard University Press.

Morrison, T. (1990). *Playing in the dark: Whiteness and the literary imagination.* Picador, Pan Macmillan.

Newnes, C. (2014). The diagnostic and statistical manual: A history of critiques of psychiatric classification systems. In E. Speed, J. Moncrieff, & M. Rapley, (Eds.), *De-medicalizing misery II: Society, politics and the mental health industry.* (pp. 190–209). Palgrave Macmillan.

Ofori-Atta, A., Attafuah, J., Jack, H., Baning, F., & Rosenheck, R., the Joining Forces Research Consortium (2018). Joining psychiatric care and faith healing in a prayer camp in Ghana: Randomised trial. *The British Journal of Psychiatry, 212*(1), 34–41.

Rapley, M., Moncrieff, J., & Dillon, J. (Eds.). (2011). *De-medicalizing misery: Psychiatry, psychology, and the human condition.* Palgrave Macmillan.

School of Oriental and African Studies – SOAS (2018, May). *Decolonising SOAS Learning and Teaching Toolkit. Decolonising SOAS.* https://blogs.soas.ac.uk/decolonisingsoas/learning-teaching/toolkit-for-programme-and-module-convenors/

Speed, E., Moncrieff, J., & Rapley, M. (Eds.). (2014). *De-medicalizing misery II: Society, politics and the mental health industry.* Palgrave Macmillan.

Sue, D., & Sue, D. (2012). *Counselling the culturally diverse: Theory and practice.* Wiley.

Whooley, O. (2014). Nosological reflections: The failure of DSM-5, the emergence of RDoC, and the decontextualization of mental distress. *Society and Mental Health, 4*(2), 92–110. https://doi.org/10.1177/2156869313519114

The impact of systemic racism   8

Adebayo Idowu

Overview

Racism is a prevalent problem in the UK, which unfortunately has a significant impact on the well-being of individuals from Black and ethnic communities. Counselling Psychology is at the forefront of addressing social justice issues in practice, research and professional development. Despite Counselling Psychology's commitment to addressing social issues, literature has shown that the discipline continues to perpetuate discriminatory actions and racial bias through its policies and practices.

This chapter will explore issues of race and systemic working within psychology with a Counselling Psychology lens. It will briefly explore the racist origins of psychology, its contribution to oppressive practices, and will shed some light into the systemic barriers to accessing psychological therapies that is encountered by clients from ethnic backgrounds. It will also look at how the issues of race and racism are thought about within the system, with particular focus on healthcare services.

The chapter also considers strategies for addressing these issues and aim to encourage the reader to move away from individual level strategy to an organisational strategy for addressing racism. There is a call for the integration of diversity into the field of Applied Psychology in the areas of training activities and research.

DOI: 10.4324/9781003415244-10

Systemic racism

Systemic racism is a longstanding social issue that continues to threaten the mental health of people from ethnic backgrounds and poses a barrier to change within Applied Psychology disciplines and the field of mental health (Pieterse et al., 2023). The origin of the discipline of psychology and psychiatry was largely racist, as many academics were determined to falsely use science as a driving tool to prove that White people were intellectually and morally superior to the racialised population (Guthrie, 2004; Hogarth, 2017). The American Psychiatric Association (APA) perpetuated these racist beliefs through their use of selective diagnostic criteria for mental illness to justify oppressive practices (Fernando, 2017). APA have since issued an apology to Black and ethnic communities for its contribution to systemic racism (APA, 2021).

The British Psychological Society (BPS) have not followed suit to offer an apology. Unfortunately, this only serves to purport the culture of silence and denial in addressing painful issues that ethnic communities have faced within the system that is supposed to improve their wellbeing. Hence, psychology continues to undermine the experience of individuals from ethnic backgrounds while professing to be an ally, even though their deafening silence suggests that systemic racism only matters to individuals directly affected by it. Black and ethnic communities should not hold the responsibility for creating a shift in the attitude and behaviours of individuals and systems that perpetuate systemic racism. Indeed, psychology has an ethical responsibility to acknowledge and dismantle dominant discourses of power that perpetuate racism and discrimination.

We must also consider the power dynamics that are present between Psychologists of Black and ethnic communities and White service users, White Psychologists with clients of Black and ethnic communities and between White practitioners and practitioners of Black and ethnic communities (Constantine & Sue, 2007). A systematic review carried out by FitzGerald and Hurst (2017) found that racism and prejudiced actions impact significantly on the psychological safety of clients from Black and ethnic communities. It is well documented that the manifestation of racism is changing, as it has become less overt to more covert prejudice. Consequentially, White Psychologists who tend not to personally experience racism, are likely to find it more difficult to perceive and recognise covert racism (Williams et al., 2022). A form of cover of racism emerges in microaggressions. Some researchers have reported connections between microaggressions and systemic racism (Friedlaender, 2018; Williams et al., 2020a). Furthermore, Skinner-Dorkeoo et al. (2021) found that microaggressions tend to reinforce established systems of oppression, and argued that when microaggressions become prevalent within the system, society may become more tolerant of racism.

Research has reported that microaggressions significantly impact on patients from Black and ethnic communities (Saleem et al., 2020; Williams et al., 2020b). They have become more recognised and understood within therapeutic settings in the past few decades, and therefore emphasising the importance of therapists from all backgrounds bringing this to their consciousness within their work. These microaggressions tend to come in different forms. It can be experienced when a White colleague asks a colleague from a racialised background "where are you really from?" "what are you?", questions that reinforce ideas that the person differs from their White counterpart and undeserving of equal treatment. Microaggressions may be in the form of a White Psychologist choosing not to validate or explore a Black patient's disclosure of distress associated to racism action, which may then result in therapeutic ruptures between the White therapist and patient from Black and ethnic communities. Another example could be a White Psychologist reporting that a female Black patient had been aggressive during a group intervention, even though they were in fact assertively expressing a viewpoint. Psychologists from Black and ethnic communities may also experience microaggression when their suggestions are disregarded or belittled by their White colleagues in meetings. It is important to note that while microaggressions are mostly explored at interpersonal level, they also contribute to the maintenance of systemic racism.

Racial disparity

The reality of racial disparities and discriminatory behaviour at the disadvantage of Black and ethnic communities within healthcare and how they can be addressed continues to perplex policymakers and healthcare practitioners. More so, there remains a prevalence of discrimination within the NHS despite the Equality Act (2010) prohibiting discriminatory behaviour based on the protected characteristics, including race. In response to the unequal access to career opportunities and unfair treatment of employees from Black and minority communities at the workplace, in 2014 the NHS Equality and Diversity Council made implementing NHS Workforce Race and Equality Standard (WRES) a requirement for NHS commissioners and NHS healthcare providers. The aim of WRES is to present detailed data analysis of strategies to address inequality and their impact. While the WRES report published in 2023 shows some improvement, there is evidence that racial inequality remains rife across the NHS (WRES, 2023).

Disproportionate numbers of employees from Black and minority communities experience discrimination from colleagues, the public and management. Staff from Black and minority backgrounds are more likely to experience harassment, bullying and abuse from patient and staff. They are also less likely to be given opportunity for continued professional development (CPD) and training in comparison with their White counterparts. Unfortunately, this impacts on their career progression. Furthermore, WRES (2023) report also demonstrate that employees from Black and minority backgrounds are more likely to enter formal disciplinary process compared with their compared colleagues. WRES (2023) report continues to emphasise the challenges faced in improving quality and inclusion in the NHS workplace, as opposed to focusing on the institutional Whiteness that the NHS continues to demonstrate.

It is generally purported that racial and ethnic disparities in health care may be a result of lack of cultural competence by health providers (Horner et al., 2004). Consequently, these disparities have been targeted with individual level education such as provision of cultural competence training to enhance knowledge of variety of cultural groups. It has been argued that these strategies have shown limited effectiveness in reducing racial and ethnic disparities in healthcare when they are not infused with more systemic strategies (King, 1996; Wyszewianski & Green, 2000). The idea that healthcare professionals can sufficiently learn and develop full understanding of cultures that are fundamentally different from their own has been criticised. It may indicate a disregard for the complexity of culture by assuming that one may simply become culturally competent by gathering information about other cultural groups. Hence, this may explain why racial and ethnic disparity remains problematic despite the provision of cultural competence training. It has been discussed that a systems change approach is necessary to address healthcare disparities as these disparities are rooted in institutional racism (Griffith et al., 2007). This idea aligns with the dismantling racism approach, a community organising model that incorporates elements of power, socio-political development, and empowerment theory, which assumes that everything is directly or indirectly connected to everything else, hence it is proposed that when there are complex organisational problems a multi-level systematic change is required (Midgley, 2006).

It is documented that there are insufficient number of Psychologists from Black and ethnic communities to address the unmet needs of patients from similar backgrounds (Stewart et al., 2017). A 2013 study by the Health & Social Care Information Centre found that only 9.6% of qualified Clinical Psychologists in England and Wales are of Black and ethnic background, this is despite 13% of the population being of Black and ethnic backgrounds

(Office of National Statistics, 2018). This is a result of a systemic structure and issues that marginalises aspiring Clinical Psychologists and qualified Psychologists from Black and ethnic communities. The demographic, theories and processes within Clinical Psychology is influenced by Whiteness, which is often demonstrated by DClinPsych applicants from Black and minority communities being less likely to be selected for training in comparison with their White counterparts (Turpin & Coleman, 2010). Similarly, it has been reported that they are less likely to be offered opportunities for career progression compared to their White colleagues (Rennalls et al., 2019). Qualified Clinical Psychologists from Black and ethnic communities tend to stand out as different within the profession, leading to feelings of isolation and alienation (Odusanya et al., 2018). These structural barriers and systemic issues that significantly impacts on applicants from Black and ethnic communities often result in them feeling disenfranchised, unwelcomed and exhausted, hence causing them to question pursuing a career in Clinical Psychology (Bawa et al., 2019; Meredith & Baker, 2007). Likewise, qualified Clinical Psychologists have reported feeling marginalised, hyper-visible, invisible, and undermined due to systemic issues held within Clinical Psychology (Paulraj, 2016).

Representation

The psychology discipline, including Counselling Psychology, remains very White middle class, therefore limiting the chance of clients from Black and ethnic communities working with Psychologists that are of similar background to them, whom they may be able to connect with culturally. Weekes' (2010) literature review found that there is a lack of consistency in the empirical support for the beneficial effect of racial matching within therapy. It must be highlighted that there is limited research on the relationship between racial matching and positive experience of psychological therapy, and the findings have been mixed. A number of studies have provided support for model of racial matching. (Johnson & Caldwell, 2011; Thompson & Alexander, 2006).

Farsimadan et al. (2007) found that race matching increased therapeutic alliance, therapist credibility, and therapy outcomes for Black African, Black Caribbean, South Asian, and Middle Eastern clients. Other researchers have reported that racial similarity does not have a significant impact on therapy outcomes (Behn et al., 2018; Flicker et al., 2008). The impact of racial matching on the experience of therapy requires continued research. However, it would make sense that cultural customs, attitudes and references relating to a client's experience may be better understood on an experiential level by a therapist they perceive to be of close cultural match to them. Conversely, I recognise that racial diversity within therapeutic relationship may also serve an important purpose in cross-racial understanding of experiences. It is important to note that the proposal that sameness equates to better therapeutic relationship does not take into account the complexity of racial identity, particularly in situations where the therapist or client is struggling with their identity development. Fundamentally, therapist sharing similarities with their client can be helpful when the issues explored in therapy are part of the sameness.

It is not shocking that 91.5% of the BPS members are of White origin (Bullen & Hacker Hughes, 2016). Unfortunately, this impacts greatly on the experience of Black and ethnic background patients within mental health services. A qualitative study by Memon et al. (2016) provided evidence for the lack of relatability ethnic minorities tend to experience within therapy, as they report feeling that their therapist is not able to relate or understand their experience. They report feeling frustrated as a result which consequently has an impact on the therapeutic relationship. Kalathil et al. (2011) also reported that majority of the female participants from Black and ethnic communities in their qualitative study felt that mental health services did not consider the impact of racism and discrimination on their experience of distress. For there to be a change in this there is a need for the training programmes to consider how to support Black and ethnic communities to get on the programmes to enable the increased possibility of racial match. Racial match refers to a culturally responsive care for reducing health disparities that matches clients and clinicians of similar ethnic backgrounds. Racial match has been associated to better engagement and favourable treatment outcomes (Flicker et al., 2008; Meyer & Zane, 2013).

Systemic care

It is important that the system of care considers ethnic minority cultural beliefs and values, and moves to provide services within the community and with the involvement of the community in all aspects of the system to enable cultural sensitivity and aptitude. This is very much aligned with the assertion by Stroul and Friedman (1996) that systems of care should provide services in a manner that is culturally competent, ensuring they are responsive to the cultural, racial and ethnic differences of the population they deliver services to. I am mindful that merely focusing on promoting cultural competence within a system of care may be quite simplistic, in that it ignores the complexity of race and culture by assuming that one may become culturally competent by gathering information about other cultural groups. Therefore, it may be more productive to consider systemic issues from both interpersonal level where the person seeks to understand themselves, their prejudice and bias and at a systemic level where systems of care promote cultural understanding and sensitivity. Clinical experiences alongside supervision of psychologists working with diverse clients is required in order to adequately integrate cultural competence awareness into training (e.g. Williams & La Torre, 2022). Cultural humility should drive changes in the way systems of care are designed and implemented, ensuring that appropriate changes are made that ensures the systemic culture and values are compatible with the population that they serve. It is imperative that efforts are made by systems of care and commissions to develop outreach process to identify participants who can serve as community partners.

Further, it is imperative to engage an empirical review of current practices in Applied Psychology training programmes that perpetuate discriminatory actions and racial bias through their policies and practices. This includes evaluating criteria inherent in current admission practices which contributes to limited representation of Psychologists and researchers from Black and ethnic communities. Once admitted, doctoral programmes must do more to cultivate environments that support trainees from Black and ethnic communities to thrive and have a sense of belonging. Also, majority of training programmes do not consider the value of assessing and treating the impact of racial trauma and systemic racism. On the whole, current training in the provision of culturally responsive research and clinical care is inadequate. Hence, it is important that training prepare Counselling Psychologists and Applied Psychologists to be equipped to address systems of racial oppression, and re-establish the field of Counselling Psychology as a relevant and responsive applied speciality area of psychology that is contributing to efforts that dismantle systemic racism (Thambinathan & Kinsella, 2021).

It has been noted that discourse around racism is often anxiety provoking for most psychologists and therapists (DiAngelo, 2018; Smith et al., 2021). Many people are often fearful of being perceived as racists by addressing the issue as they have been socialised to not talk about them (William, 2020). It is important that this discourse is encouraged within and beyond Counselling Psychology as it is only through this that we can enhance understanding, appreciation, and interaction with individuals of diverse cultures and belief systems, and may in turn result in the eradication of racial disparities (Lawton et al., 2021).

Nonetheless, the reliability of cultural competence training has been put into question, Bintley and George (2020) have argued that process-oriented models that facilitates understanding of oneself should take precedence over gaining knowledge of other people's culture. While healthcare professionals have responsibility to provide quality care irrespective of cultural differences, the eradication of the racial disparities must encompass interpersonal, institutional, and systemic levels. Psychologists must be willing to accept rather than avoid the uncomfortable feelings relating to the discourse of race, which would in turn allow them to become curious about the biases that arise and learn to manage them. A critical part of this process is to foster genuine reciprocal relationships with individuals from diverse cultures, hence enabling them to learn about the person and their culture, develop empathy, and improve their clinical practice (Okech & Champe, 2008). At the same time, Counselling Psychology training programmes need to develop clinical strategies that address issues relating to race and ethnic minority status when treating ethnic minority clients.

There is a need for accurate and well-balanced historical education around experience of racism, which may play a significant role in improving understanding and awareness of systemic racism and microaggressions that tend to aid racial discrimination. Nelson et al. (2013) argued that a lack of awareness of historical racism prevents people from recognising contemporary systemic racism. It is also essential to equip trainees with both clinical and research skills to address health disparities and provide culturally responsive care, recognising and changing Whiteness as a default in clinical research, conceptualising and contextualising race, and experience of racism when providing psychological assessments and treatments, hence addressing the biopsychosocial impacts of racial trauma and systemic racism. There should be an exploration of the impact of racial trauma on the mental well-being of minority clients as acknowledging and addressing such issues is likely to improve the quality of care. As previously indicated, Psychologists should embed the practice of exploring their clients' many identities and its importance to them in the assessment process, incorporating these contextual frames throughout the intervention.

Conclusion

While Counselling Psychology has made some progress in embracing multi-culturally relevant frameworks in the form of stronger commitment to issues relating to race and ethnicity, there is a need for the system to reflect and put action and change behind the discourse around commitment to addressing systemic racism. Full integration of diversity into the field of Counselling Psychology, applied psychologies and related activities are yet to be realised, such as training activities, curriculum, and research on areas relevant to the ethnic minorities (Pieterse et al., 2023). For Psychologists to effectively engage in addressing racism, it is important that we move focus beyond individual racial attitudes, with more emphasis on the systemic structures that promotes racial bias and discriminatory actions. It may be beneficial to conduct more research that focus on the Black and minority populations, who tend to experience significant forms of marginalisation. Pieterse et al. (2023) also argued that given the complexity of racism and discriminatory practice, it is imperative to create new measures for describing and understanding the realities of systemic racism and represent how it impacts Black and ethnic communities.

In order to capture the complex experiences of racism, it may be beneficial to consider developing psychometric measures and undertake qualitative research which captures nuanced experience of racism, hence opening the door for more research on the racism within systemic structures, including healthcare services and hopefully work towards intervention and prevention. While this chapter has largely focused on systemic racism in psychology with particular focus on health care services, it is acknowledged that racism is also prevalent in other systems including education, criminal justice, social services, and in employment.

Chapter questions to provoke thoughts:

I would like to encourage the readers to ask the following questions as a starting point for reflexivity about issues of race and systemic working within psychology:

1. How do I racially define myself and how is this represented within a system of care?
2. What perceptions and assumptions do I have that are informed by race and inform my practice?
3. How does my race impact on my interaction with clients and professionals of another ethnic background?
4. What does it mean to be culturally competent within a system of care and is this achievable?
5. How can psychology address systemic racism considering the profession's White supremacy culture?

References

American Psychiatric Association (APA). (2021). Historical Addendum to APA's apology to Black, indigenous and people of colour for its support of structural racism in psychiatry. https://www.psychiatry.org/newsroom/historical-addendum-to-apa-apology (accessed July 6, 2023).

Bawa, H., Gooden, S., Maleque, F., Naseem, S., Naz, S., Obi Oriaku, E., Thomas, R. S., Vipulananthan, V., Bains, M., & Shiel, L. (2019). The journey of BME aspiring psychologists into clinical psychology training: Barriers and ideas to inclusive change. *Clinical Psychology Forum*, *323*, 3–13.

Behn, A., Davanzo, A., & Errázuriz, P. (2018). Client and therapist match on gender, age, and income: Does match within the therapeutic dyad predict early growth in the therapeutic alliance? *Journal of Clinical Psychology*, *74*(9), 1403–1421.

Bintley, H., & George, R. E. (2020). Teaching diversity in healthcare education: Conceptual clarity and the need for an intersectional transdisciplinary approach. In D. Nestel, G. Reedy, L. McKenna, & S. Gough (Eds.), *Clinical education for the health professions: Theory and practice* (pp. 1–19). Springer.

Bullen, K., & Hacker Hughes, J. (2016). Achieving representation in psychology. *The Psychologist*, *29*, 246–255.

Constantine, M. G., & Sue, D. W. (2007). Perceptions of racial microaggressions among black supervisees in cross-racial dyads. *Journal of Counselling Psychology*, *54*, 142.

DiAngelo, R. (2018). *White fragility: Why it's so hard for White people to talk about racism*. Beacon Press.

Equality Act 2010. (2010). https://www.legislation.gov.uk/ukpga/2010/15/contents (accessed September 18, 2023).

Farsimadan, F., Draghi-Lorenz, R., & Ellis, J. (2007). Process and outcome of therapy in ethnically similar and dissimilar therapeutic dyads. *Psychotherapy Research*, *17*, 567–575.

Fernando, S. (2017). *Institutional racism in psychiatry and clinical psychology*. Palgrave Macmillan.

FitzGerald, C., & Hurst, S. (2017). Implicit bias in healthcare professionals: A systematic review. *BMC Medical Ethics*, *18*, 1–18.

Flicker, S. M., Waldron, H. B., Turner, C. W., Brody, J. L., & Hops, H. (2008). Ethnic matching and treatment outcome with Hispanic and Anglo substance-abusing adolescents in family therapy. *Journal of Family Psychology*, *22*, 439–447.

Friedlaender, C. (2018). On microaggressions: Cumulative harm and individual responsibility. *Hypatia*, *33*(1), 5–21.

Griffith, D. M., Mason, M., Yonad, M., Eng, E., Jefries, V., Plihcik, S., & Parks, B. (2007). Dismantling institutional racism: Theory an action. *American Journal of Community Psychology*, *39*, 381–392.

Guthrie, R. V. (2004). *Even the rat was White. A historical view of psychology*. Allyn and Bacon.

Hogarth, R. A. (2017). *Medicalizing Blackness: Making racial difference in the Atlantic World, 1780–1840*. UNC Press Books.

Horner, R. D., Salazar, W., Geiger, H. J., Bullock, K., Corbie-Smith, G., Cornog, M., & Flores, G. (2004). Changing healthcare professionals' behaviours to eliminate disparities in healthcare: What do we know? How might we proceed?. *The American Journal of Managed Care*, *10*, SP12-9.

Johnson, L. A., & Caldwell, B. E. (2011). Race, gender, and therapist confidence: Effects on satisfaction with the therapeutic relationship in MFT. *The American Journal of Family Therapy*, *39*(4), 307–324.

Kalathil, J., Collier, B., Bhakta, R., Daniel, O., Joseph, D., & Trivedi, P. (2011). *Recovery and resilience: African, African-Caribbean and South Asian Women's narratives of recovering from mental distress*. Mental Health Foundation.

King, G. (1996). Institutional racism and the medical/health complex: A conceptual analysis. *Ethnicity and Disease*, 6(1–2), 30–46.

Lawton, L., McRae, M., & Gordon, L. (2021). Frontline yet at the back of the queue – Improving access and adaptations to CBT for Black African and Caribbean communities. *The Cognitive Behaviour Therapist*, 14(30), 1–9.

Memon, A., Taylor, K., Mohebati, L. M., Sundin, J., Cooper, M., Scanlon, T., & de Visser, R. (2016). Perceived barriers to accessing mental health services among Black and minority ethnic (BME) communities: A qualitative study in Southeast England. *British Medical Journal Open*, 6(11), e012337–e012337 https://doi.org/10.1136/bmjopen-2016-012337

Meredith, E., & Baker, M. (2007). Factors associated with choosing a career in clinical psychology—Undergraduate minority ethnic perspectives. *Clinical Psychology & Psychotherapy: An International Journal of Theory & Practice*, 14(6), 475–487.

Meyer, O. L., & Zane, N. (2013). The influence of race and ethnicity in clients' experiences of mental health treatment. *Journal of Community Psychology*, 41(7), 884–901.

Midgley, G. (2006). Systemic intervention for public health. *American Journal of Public Health*, 96(3), 466–472.

Nelson, J. C., Adams, G., & Salter, P. S. (2013). The Marley hypothesis: Denial of racism reflects ignorance of history. *Psychological Science*, 24(2), 213–218.

NHS England's Work Race Equality Standards (WRES) 2022 data analysis report for NHS trusts. (2023). https://www.england.nhs.uk/long-read/nhs-workforce-race-equality-standard-wres2022-data-analysis-report-for-nhs-trusts/ (accessed on October 14, 2023).

Odusanya, S. O. E., Winter, D., Nolte, L., & Shah, S. (2018). The experience of being a qualified female BME clinical psychologist in a national health service: An interpretative phenomenological and repertory grid analysis. *Journal of Constructivist Psychology*, 31(3), 273–291.

Office of National Statistics. (2018). *Ethnicity and national identity in England and Wales 2018*. Gov.uk. Crown Copyright. https://www.ethnicity-facts-figures.service.gov.uk/uk-population-by-ethnicity/national-and-regionalpopulations/population-of-england-and-wales/latest

Okech, J. E. A., & Champe, J. (2008). Informing culturally competent practice through cross-racial friendships. *International Journal for the Advancement of Counselling*, 30, 104–115.

Paulraj, P. S. (2016). *How do Black Trainees Make Sense of Their 'Identities' in the Context of Clinical Psychology Training?* Doctoral dissertation, University of East London.

Pieterse, A. L., Lewis, J. A., & Miller, M. J. (2023). Dismantling and eradicating anti-Blackness and systemic racism. *American Psychological Association*, 70(3), 235–243.

Rennalls, S., Baah, J., & Alcock, A. (2019). "People didn't quite see me": Addressing ethnic disparities in clinical psychology by enhancing facilitators and minimising barriers into training. *Group of Trainers in Clinical Psychology Conference*, Liverpool.

Saleem, F. T., Anderson, R. E., & Williams, M. (2020). Addressing the 'myth' of racial trauma: Developmental and ecological considerations for youth of colour. *Clinical Child and Family Psychology Review*, 23, 1–14.

Skinner-Dorkeoo, A. L., Sarmal, A., Andre, C. L., & Rogbeer, K. G. (2021). How microaggressions reinforce and perpetuate systemic racism in the United States. *Perspectives on Psychological Science*, 16(5), 903–925.

Smith, L., Proctor, G., & Akondo, D. (2021). Confronting racism in counselling and therapy training – Three experiences of a seminar on racism and Whiteness. *Psychotherapy and Politics International, 19*. https://doi.org/10.1002/ppi.1579

Stewart, C. E., Lee, S. Y., Hogstrom, A., & Williams, M. (2017). Diversify and conquer: A call to promote minority representation in clinical psychology. *The Behavior Therapist, 40*, 74–79.

Stroul, B. A., & Friedman, R. M. (1996). The system of care concept and philosophy. In B. Stroul (Ed.), *Children's mental health. Creating systems of care in a changing society* (pp. 1–22). Paul H. Brookes Publishing Co., Inc.

Thambinathan, V., & Kinsella, E. A. (2021). Decolonizing methodologies in qualitative research: Creating spaces for transformative praxis. *International Journal of Qualitative Methods, 20*, 1–9.

Thompson, V. L. S., & Alexander, H. (2006). Therapist' race and African American clients' reactions to therapy. *Psychotherapy: Theory, Research, Practice, Training, 43*(1), 99–110.

Turpin, G., & Coleman, G. (2010). Clinical psychology and diversity: Progress and continuing challenges. *Psychology Learning & Teaching, 9*(2), 17–27.

Weekes, J. C. (2010). Race-matching in psychotherapy: Findings, inconsistences and future directions. *Graduate Student Journal of Psychology, 12*, 8–13.

Williams, M. T. (2020). *Managing microaggressions: Addressing everyday racism in therapeutic spaces.* Oxford University Press.

Williams, M. T., Faber, S. C., & Duniya, C. (2022). Being an anti-racist clinician. *The Cognitive Behaviour Therapist, 15*, 1–22.

Williams, M. T., Kanter, J. W., Pena, A., Ching, T. H., & Oshin, L. (2020a). Reducing microaggressions and promoting interracial connection: The racial harmony workshop. *Journal of Contextual Behavioral Science, 16*, 153–161.

Williams, M. T., & La Torre, J. (2022). Clinical Supervision in Delivering Cognitive Behaviour Therapy Across Race, Ethnicity, and Culture. In E. A. Storch, J. S. Abramowitz, & D. McKay (Eds.), *Training and Supervision in Specialized Cognitive Behaviour Therapy: Methods, Settings, and Populations* (pp. 265–288). American Psychological Association.

Williams, M. T., Skinta, M. D., Kanter, J. W., Martin-Willett, R., Mier-Chairez, J., Debreaux, M., & Rosen, D. C. (2020b). A qualitative study of microaggressions against African Americans on predominantly White campuses. *BMC psychology, 8*(1), 111. https://doi.org/10.1186/s40359-020-00472-8

Wyszewianski, L., & Green, L. A. (2000). Strategies for changing clinicians' practice patterns. A new perspective. *Journal of Family Practice, 49*(5), 461–464.

Race and politics   **9**

Dominique Fray-Aitken

Overview

This chapter explores 'race' as political and embedded within the very fabric of psychology. The chapter asks four questions about 'racism' for the readers to reflect upon. I begin with exploring how 'racism' has shaped the very foundations of academic knowledge, excluding or marginalising students with alternative psychologies. Systemic 'racism' is so prevalent that even academic knowledge is shaped by power and social norms.

The chapter then moves on to explain how 'racism' is hidden and, therefore, difficult to challenge. A thoughtful and socially aware approach is needed in addressing 'racism', with emphasis placed on a willingness to explore and understand the struggles created by 'race' as well as the burdens marginalised people face both with mental health and with accessing effective treatment. The chapter then moves onto social positioning, social privilege, tokenism, and what racism truly means.

For the purposes of this chapter, 'race' will be placed in quotation marks as it is seen to be actively constructed through social conversations and interactions. The term 'racism' is used to show the dynamic and constantly shifting nature of 'racism'. In addition, the terms 'therapist' and 'psychologist' will be used interchangeably.

DOI: 10.4324/9781003415244-11

All clients' names and their identities have been altered for confidentiality purposes.

How is applied psychology impacted by the politics of 'race'?

In practice, psychology is very limited by cultural imperialism, which has been based on a European, and later, a western definition of what it means to be a person in the world. We now have decolonised perspectives of psychology. Grosfoguel (2007), for example, said that 'racism' has shaped knowledge. Western psychology has been seen to be universal, but this very individual way of seeing the world is not universal. We know from books like Things Fall Apart (Achebe, 1959) that when community identity is threatened, mental health suffers. Yet, psychology caters to a largely Western, male identity.

Despite the Diagnostic Statistical Manual of Mental Disorders (DSM, 2013) not taking culture into account when discussing trauma (albeit attempts at addressing racism, culture, and discrimination have been made), I have worked with people who experienced social traumas like 'racism'. In a well-known and even quite shocking example, the rape trial of the ex-South African president Jacob Zuma used Western psychological testing on an African woman and then used this test to make assumptions about her mental health. Such assumptions did not apply to her definition of reality or to her underlying philosophy of the world. This shows the extent of cultural imperialism within psychology and the harm it can cause.

In my private practice, I have seen women who have faced traumas and struggles mislabelled by professionals within the National Health Service (NHS). Often their 'treatment' was to manage their symptoms, but such symptoms did not consider fully the difficult experiences they had been through. Our healthcare system and the biomedical perspective it takes on mental health denied these women's social sufferings and stigmatised them with further labels which created mistrust. My female clients were told that they were faulted, that their mistrust (based on 'racial' discrimination) was paranoia, and that they should adjust to oppression.

In Black Skin, White Masks, Fanon (2008) said the colonised will only be heard when they turn *White*, and in my practice, this is still evident. Women who reported microaggressions or 'racial' discrimination were told that they were imagining it. One woman shared her experience of when she tried to report her son being bullied at school because of his hair, she was given feedback that 'it wasn't "racism"; he has a very strong personality which challenged the other children'. The spaces we navigate everyday are shaped by 'racial' inequalities which are very often denied (Bhaba, 1994), but it determines how people are treated daily.

As discussed earlier, these 'racisms' shape psychology, too. They can be difficult to challenge. In many psychology courses, *Black* students are often chosen last and are often the first to drop out. Even in countries such as South Africa where *Black* students could be in the majority, academics such as Lesiba Baloyi (2008) argued that African students, uncomfortable with course material, are either forced to adjust or drop out. Baloyi (2008) stated that there is a very real need to challenge what he called the 'epistemicide' present in psychology, which only recognised a Western culture. If students cannot share who they are within psychology or add to psychological research, it is very unlikely that Psychologists will understand social injustices and its impact on mental health because the discipline will remain dominate to privileged perspectives. During the writing of my doctoral thesis, I was told by a supervisor that my insights as a deaf, *Black* woman should be bracketed or set aside, rather than being allowed to shape my insights into challenges faced by clients with multiple identities within a therapeutic context. My thesis drew on interpretative phenomenology and Heidegger (1927) argued that we cannot separate our experiences from our theories.

I came across an example by Brown (2003) who described how 19th century Psychiatrists would diagnose slaves as suffering from 'drapetomania' or the desire to run away. Social perspectives shape psychological knowledge, and these insights should not be bracketed or swept aside. We need to hear and acknowledge marginalised perspectives to understand the psychological impacts of social injustice; we also need to recognise cultural diversity and the many ways of seeing the world. Fanon's (2008) argument throughout his text that the Black man remains unseen behind the assumptions and anecdotes of the coloniser is appropriately apt and shows how the 'psy' disciplines have been (and are) used to uphold social norms.

How does an ignorance of social structures impact your clients?

When people ignore the systemic impacts of 'racisms', it makes it easier to deny the material impacts on others. This means that struggles become invisible, and people are imagined existing on an equal playing field. Many of my clients who struggle with structural 'racism' are often stigmatised further because they are expected to 'try harder'. To illustrate, one of my clients was told that she could achieve if she 'just set her mind to it', which ignored the fact that she was a single mother in an abusive relationship and faced structural barriers because of 'race'. She was viewed as an outsider in her community because of 'race', her immigrant status meant she struggled to access both social and financial support for her son who was also being bullied at school. For her, this led to feelings of powerlessness and anger because she battled to feel heard while trying to navigate a difficult situation. These are the same feelings that the UK Mental Health Taskforce have found to be common for *Black* women, who struggle with higher rates of anxiety and depression, with an average of 30% of *Black* women experiencing mental health challenges, when compared to 23% of *White* women. The Taskforce identified that along with the risks of violence or poverty, isolation, gender-based violence, postnatal depression, and other traumas impacted women's mental health.

For the mother who was told to 'just set her mind to it', there was more to her struggle, but she did not have the opportunity to discuss it or to be heard. As Davis and Steyn (2012) noted, it can be difficult for people with 'race' privilege to set aside previously held beliefs for long enough to listen.

Erasmus (2010) reported that we can only work towards change when we acknowledge the structural, dynamic, and constantly evolving nature of 'racism'. Without acknowledging, for example, that 'racism' can manifest in xenophobic narratives of threat to culture, or in the maintenance of a limited definition of human psychology, we are unable to challenge this. If we see 'racism' as personal prejudice alone, we are unable to see the challenges people experience.

Studies have shown that when people try to reduce personal prejudice by bringing people together to see a common humanity, we might be able to reduce personal prejudice, but deeper structural 'racisms' remain hidden (Zuma, 2014). Goldberg (2004) advised that when people focus on a common humanity alone, it leaves 'racist' structures hidden, and the material impacts of 'race' remain disguised. Therefore, 'racism' becomes more deeply entrenched (Federico, 2013).

From personal experience, it can be hard to get even empathic people to see and understand structural 'racism'. Without personal experience of 'racism', or the ability to walk the path of discrimination, many people simply do not believe it exists. These denials impact others who are torn between frustration and self-doubt.

One of the biggest struggles for clients is the idea of colour-blindness, or the belief all people are equal beings. While it is helpful for individuals to deny stereotypes and actively embrace each other as a unique human being, colour-blindness often means that we ignore the struggles people face because of systemic 'racism'. Goldberg (2004) spoke of the weight of 'race', or the struggles of convincing others that 'racism' does exist, and that people do experience systemic injustices or prejudices. Comments such as 'poor people are lazy' not only deny suffering but create stigma (Foster, 1991). Seeing 'race' as individualistic might mean that psychotherapy helps people to adjust to an oppressive system (Ahmed & Pretorius-Heuchert, 2001).

Thinking through these challenges

The question which would naturally arise is the following: If people do not see systemic injustice and it goes unchallenged, how do we move forward? Noting injustices is particularly important for Psychologists, who might risk either ascribing clinical reasons for social problems or encouraging clients to adjust to oppressive circumstances. Bogle et al. (2021) argued for cultural humility rather than cultural competence while practicing psychology. As discussed earlier, Psychologists are shaped by their knowledge, culture, and beliefs. We can take a blind approach to oppression, or, as marginalised therapists, we can internalise oppression and struggle to assist our clients with recognising injustice. Humility means being willing to listen and learn from another person's experiences or insights. It is also about giving yourself space to properly address any questions you might have or thoughts you might have pushed away. Davis and Steyn (2012) reported that exploring social justice is about uncovering questions or doubts that may be unconscious but are already present. Alan Kaplan (2002) said that when we listen and explore together, we can deepen and widen our understanding of a situation.

Sacks (2017) provided an example of exploring old questions in her Ted Talk Rethinking Home and the Art of Changing One's Mindset. She shared the questions she asked about 'racism' and injustice while growing up in apartheid South Africa. Her questions included wondering why servants were forced to eat from tin plates in the yard while her family ate from China plates, in the dining room. These questions haunted a five-year-old Sacks and focused on the rituals and beliefs underpinning social divides through the eyes of a child. Likewise, Steyn (2001) provided an example of a man uncovering his deep love for the nanny who had nurtured him as a little boy, a love which had been mocked and derided because it was for a woman of different (and, said to be inferior) 'race'. Uncovering these emotions and challenging current social beliefs enable people to see the unjust hierarchies which exist, both for themselves and for 'other' people. This process may produce initial resistance but a long-term motivation to work towards social transformation and change (Davis & Steyn, 2012).

Ultimately, we are all a part of a system which exploits others, and which, in some way, has exploited us, whether through age, gender, 'race', nationality, sexuality, or religion. None of us are independent, and we are all influenced or wounded by beliefs which harm us (Smith, 2013). Growth moves us towards new awareness, but this can be painful, making us feel as though the world as we once knew it has been knocked down.

Taking up a passport of consciousness and engaging critically with society can help Psychologists to make space for clients to explore the struggles their clients face because of 'racism'. It can also mean assisting clients to understand 'racism' and to use activism to search for better treatment.

How does racism and social marginalisation impact mental health – The need for a transformed understanding?

One of my clients, a young and exceptionally talented young woman, struggled with depression. She had been offered a scholarship to a distinguished school during her adolescence but had felt excluded because of 'race'. The other girls had seen her as an outsider and had asked her lots of questions about her life. She had been asked to braid the other girls' hair, had people touch her own hair, and had been told that she was hard to identify outside of school because she looked just like 'everyone else' from her 'race' group. Adolescence is a time of belonging, and my client felt as though she just could not fit in. Her knowledge in the classroom surprised her classmates, and people constantly showed surprise at her English ability. She was told by a past counsellor that her feelings of anxiety were related to 'over-sensitivity', leaving her reluctant to seek psychological help this time. It was only when her anxiety became unbearable that she sought out assistance.

She is not alone in her mental health struggles. As mentioned earlier, The U.K. Department of Social Development Taskforce (Sweeney et al., 2018) found that *Black* women had the highest rate of mental health struggles, with 29% reporting difficulties when compared to 23% of White women (Sweeney et al., 2018). While the Taskforce (Sweeney et al., 2018) highlighted the need for ethnic communities to have access to mental health services and effective treatment, this has been somewhat difficult in practice. Many of my clients have come to me after bouncing around from therapist to therapist within the NHS, often with a range of different diagnoses which confused them and desperately seeking to manage symptoms which are decontextualised. My clients have often experienced a great deal of trauma, a normal reaction to an abnormal situation, but they have been further stigmatised in their search for healing and inner peace. Their experiences have been the opposite of empowering.

'Racism' and social injustice means that my clients have faced layer upon layer of social stigma, which sometimes resulted on them being described as having an 'unstable personality' due to struggles with identity, something which Singh and Burns (2006) described as a normal reaction to 'racial' injustices. When people are told repeatedly that they are inherently inferior due to 'race', it is normal to struggle with forming a positive self-identity. Layers of stigma and self-doubt then reduce a person's confidence to speak out and seek justice (Brown, 2003). If you have an unstable personality, after all, could you trust yourself to leave an abusive relationship? As Herman (2015) pointed out, political injustices have a private impact, creating mistrust and a tendency to withdraw. It is no wonder then that the Mental Health Taskforce found that women struggled to ask for help with their anxiety or depression.

My clients have been judged because of the 'racisms' and oppressions they have experienced, but their responses to oppression are entirely normal. 'Racial' injustices, prejudices, and stereotypes produce humiliation, fatigue, anxiety, powerless, invisibility, and marginalisation (Erasmus, 2010). Indeed, as Steele (2011) shows, 'racial' stereotypes are so oppressive and so constantly present that a young *Black* man felt the need to whistle Vivaldi to show that he was not a threat to other people on the street. Continual experiences of disrespect, social stereotypes, police harassment, being overlooked for employment opportunities, and poor service in shops were regular experiences for marginalised 'racial' groups (Williams, 2018). These microaggressions, in combination with systemic injustices, mean that marginalised groups experience higher levels of stress and increased risks to mental health.

Goldberg (2004) explained that not only do people experience 'racial' struggles, but they then battle, as my clients do, to have these struggles recognised. Essentially, my clients have run into a wall of denial and disbelief which makes them wonder if they are faulted, if they are simply oversensitive, if they are overlooked because they might not have made a good impression, or if they are in fact unstable and not simply furious at being mistreated. Denial by a therapist is particularly painful because the therapist is seen to have power and insight into the client's mental health, and this authority is often trusted by clients. Sadly, Doucette (2011) found that unless in an advanced stage of social awareness, *White* therapists often could not understand that 'racialised' microaggressions were 'racially' motivated.

It is, therefore, vital to bring 'race' into the therapy room. Without understanding how 'racism' works, alongside the impacts of 'race', therapists risk further wounding their clients (Lee & Boykins, 2022). Morgan (2018) and Garner (2003) stated that clients from ethnic communities often experience 'racism' both while trying to access psychotherapy and while trying to work on their struggles within therapy. This often resulted in ethnic communities dropping out of therapy prematurely. Although the current psychotherapy practice struggles to attract and maintain connections with members of ethnic minority communities (Morgan, 2021), the opportunity for safe psychotherapy cannot exist without social justice.

As therapists, it is also vital not to privilege certain aspects of identity while ignoring others. This was a topic which was discussed in my doctoral thesis on Deaf identities, where a single aspect of identity could take full attention within a therapeutic setting, while other aspects of identity could be ignored. When exploring identity and mental health, Collins (2013) emphasised the importance of taking into consideration all aspects of identity, rather than favouring single aspects of identity over others. This is because identity is complex and intertwined. A person with class privilege might still experience 'racism', even though they have financial power. However, a person struggling with multiple layers of social injustice or inequality (such as the injustices created by disability, class inequality, sexism, or xenophobia) will face further complexities. To effectively understand a person's social struggle, a Psychologist would need to explore all elements of identity.

What are some important points to understand while creating a passport of awareness?

Rachel, a *Black* woman struggled with postpartum depression and anxiety. She needed employment to bring in income. Her employer kept calling her 'lazy' and had threatened to replace her with a *White* woman.

Rachel found it hard to leave her baby son in the mornings. He would cling to her and cry as she left. She believed she was easily replaceable at work and was trying to do her best to stay employed, but she would often come to work tired after looking after her small baby throughout the night. Her husband worked shifts and could not help her. She often brought her work home with her in the evenings. She felt pressured and felt as though she was neither an effective mother nor an efficient worker.

Social positioning

Rachel struggled because she felt disempowered. Various aspects of her identity, such as 'race', class, and gender intertwined new motherhood, leaving her feeling vulnerable and disempowered. To understand the politics of 'race', it is important to look at how a person has been positioned and how this limits choices or makes it more difficult to achieve goals (Rose, 1990), as well as impacts the power they have within their lives to access resources (Harley et al., 2002). Rachel knew she would struggle to find employment as a new mother, and her identity as a poor, *Black* woman limited her ability to fight for her rights. To understand how people navigate the world, their social roots, and the routes open to them, an understanding of social positioning is crucial (Steyn, 2001). Social positioning means understanding that power or oppression is related to identity (Harley et al., 2002).

As in Rachel's story, 'racial' identity can combine with other areas of social marginalisation, such as religion, sexual identity, national identity, class, disability, gender identity, or rural identity to increase or decrease social power (Collins, 2013). These intersectional identities increase the visibility of a person by marking out 'differences' and increasing the person's risk of experiencing microaggressions, social stressors, and discrimination. While some aspects of identity may be hidden or invisible, such as sexuality, 'racial' identity is mostly very visible (largely due to facial features, hair texture, and skin tone) and has massive implications on all levels of society, from education to health and employment opportunities (Steele, 2011).

Social privilege

Social privilege can be blinding because it means that people with privilege can be 'blind' or oblivious to the challenges faced by 'race' (Smith, 2013). Privilege includes experiences a person has not had, such as racial discrimination or humiliation. In White, for example, the author, Dyer (2017) argues that he is less likely to be stopped by the police or followed by a security guard based on social privilege. He can dress in a casual manner, or with torn jeans, without being seen as poor. While representing his company, he is not going to be seen as a token staff member while attending a conference or giving a presentation. This means that social stressors are lower for those with privilege, and pathways or routes open more easily based on social roots (Morrow & Weisser, 2012).

Tokenism

Anita was disheartened and angered. She came to psychotherapy because she was struggling with her doctorate. Despite having a master's degree and being very talented at her work, she had been told that, as a *Black* immigrant woman, she had been given her doctorate position because she helped to fill the quota. 'As a White woman, I struggled to get into the program', one of her colleagues said to her. 'You just walked right in. You didn't have to do all the work I had to do'.

Tokenism means being seen as a representative of a group, rather than a person who has inherent value. While at university, I was aware that *Black* students were seen to be token candidates in prestigious university positions, despite working incredibly hard, and facing a great deal of discrimination to get there. Indeed, as mentioned earlier, *Black* students are often chosen last for psychology courses and might struggle most with the coursework. While some students do benefit from social equity policies which aim to restore the exclusions of the past, this doesn't mean that the person awarded a job or position lacks talent or ability. Quite the opposite. It means that a person is fighting for a limited number of positions (R. Vettivelu & K. Acton, personal communication, 2021).

As mentioned earlier, psychological knowledge has been widely limited because it has been constructed through a privileged and largely male lens. This is true in many different fields, and Tim Brown (2009) has focused on how important it is to include marginalised knowledge when working towards a compassionate society. Increasing the insights shared by marginalised groups can help to create a just or safe society. People who have felt marginalised can explain why and how to ensure a safe and more efficient society. This means that marginalised ethnic groups bring great value; however, this value is often not recognised when people talk about 'token' identities.

Being seen as a token (rather than as a valued and insightful member of the community) has an impact on mental health, as it exposes people to microaggressions such as 'those people are stealing our jobs', being spoken down to or treated as inferior within a workplace or academic environment (R. Vettivelu & K. Acton, personal communication, 2021). As therapists, we benefit by seeing the value of a diverse and inclusive workforce, as well as the struggles people face because of being called 'tokens' (Brown, 2009).

'Racism'

'Racism' was created during the time of the enlightenment and has been a means of declaring people to be intrinsically different based on skin tone and hair type (Erasmus, 2010). Although 'racism' was a social construction, it was used to create a structural hierarchy which has material and psychological impacts (Erasmus, 2010). People faced both social marginalisation and microaggressions because of 'race' (Vettivelu & Acton, 2021).

'Racism' permeates every aspect of society, from the knowledge which has been created, to the material opportunities available to people. Marginalised people distrust a society which has been disempowering or exploitative, and this makes it even more difficult to find effective health care, including mental health care. 'Racism' is constantly changing and reconstructing itself, disguising itself to remain concealed (Erasmus, 2010). It is necessary to understand how 'racism' works to both dismantle it and to understand the struggles of navigating a 'racist' world. Without understanding 'racism', Psychologists cannot help clients untangle identity struggles or marginalisation, and assist them to use agency or activism to achieve their goals or improve their social circumstance (Smail, 1994).

Chapter questions to provoke thoughts:

To move forward into a passport of awareness, it is therefore helpful to reflect on the following questions:

1. How does racism shape Applied Psychology?
2. How is 'racism' maintained by remaining hidden (or unacknowledged), and what are the political impacts of ignorance?
3. How does social marginalisation impact mental health?
4. Which concepts help with a passport to awareness?

This will help to create a passport of awareness to navigate systemic 'racism' and the impact this has on clients.

References

Achebe, C. (1959). *Things fall apart*. Fawcett Crest.
Ahmed, R., & Pretorius-Heuchert, J.W. (2001). Community psychology: Past, present, and future. In M. Seedat, N. Duncan, & S. Lazarus, (Eds.). *Community psychology: Theory, method and practice* (pp. 79–80). Cape Town: Oxford University Press.
American Psychiatric Association. (2013). *Diagnostic and statistical manual of mental disorders* (5th ed.). https://doi.org/10.1176/appi.books.9780890425596
Baloyi, L. (2008). *Psychology and psychotherapy redefined from the viewpoint of the African experience* (Unpublished doctoral dissertation). University of South Africa.
Bhaba, H. (1994). *The location of culture*. Routledge.
Bogle, A., Rhodes, P., & Hunt, C. (2021). Cultural humility and decolonial practice: Narratives of therapists' lives. *Clinical Psychologist, 25*(1), 36–43.
Brown, T. (2009). *Change by design: How design thinking transforms organizations and inspires innovation*. Harper Business.
Brown, T. N. (2003). Critical race theory speaks to the sociology of mental health: Mental health problems produced by racial stratification. *Journal of Health and Social Behaviour, 44*(3), 292–301. https://doi.org/10.2307/1519780

Collins, P. H. (2013). Truth-telling and intellectual activism. *Contexts, 12*(1), 36–41.

Davis, D., & Steyn, M. (2012). Teaching social justice: Reframing some common pedagogical assumptions. *Perspectives in Education, 30*(4), 29–38.

Doucette, D. M. (2011). *Trainees' beliefs of racial microaggressions in cross-cultural psychotherapy dyads* (Doctoral dissertation). Roosevelt University.

Dyer, R. (2017). *White.* Routledge.

Erasmus, Z. (2010). Contact theory: Too timid for 'race' and racism. *Journal of Social Issues, 66*(2), 387–400.

Fanon, F. (2008). *Black skin, White masks.* Grove / Atlantic, Inc.

Federico C. M. (2013). The social context of racism. In Golec A., Zavala de, Cichocka A. (Eds.), *Social psychology of social problems: The intergroup context* (pp. 30–56). Chippenham, UK: Palgrave Macmillan.

Foster, D. (1991). Social influence I: Ideology. In D. Foster, & J. Louw-Potgieter (Eds.), *Social psychology in South Africa* (pp. 345–391). Lexicon Publishers.

Garner, L. H. (2003). Making connections: Developing racially and culturally sensitive psychoanalytic psychotherapy in NHS psychotherapy departments. *British Journal of Psychotherapy, 19*(4), 503–514.

Goldberg, D. T. (2004). The end (s) of race. *Postcolonial Studies, 7*(2), 211–230.

Grosfoguel, R. (2007). The epistemic decolonial turn: Beyond political-economy paradigms. *Cultural Studies, 21*(2–3), 211–223.

Harley, D. A., Jolivette, K., McCormick, K., & Tice, K. (2002). Race, class, and gender: A constellation of positionalities with implications for counseling. *Journal of Multicultural Counseling and Development, 30*(4), 216–238.

Heidegger, M. (1927). *Being and time.* (J. Macquarrie & E. Robinson, Trans. in 1962). Harper and Row.

Herman, J. L. (2015). *Trauma and recovery: The aftermath of violence – From domestic abuse to political terror.* Hachette.

Kaplan, A. (2002). *Development practitioners and social process: Artists of the invisible.* Pluto Press.

Lee, C. C., & Boykins, M. (2022). Racism as a mental health challenge: An antiracist counselling perspective. *Canadian Psychology/Psychologie Canadienne, 63*(4), 471.

Morgan, H. (2018). Between fear and blindness: The White therapist and the Black patient. In Lowe, F. (Ed). *Thinking space* (pp. 56–74). Routledge.

Morgan, H. (2021). Decolonising psychotherapy. Racism and the psychoanalytic profession. *Psychoanalytic Psychotherapy, 35*(4), 412–428.

Morrow, M. & Weisser, J. (2012). Towards a social justice framework of mental health recovery. *Studies in Social Justice 6* (1):27–43.

Rose, N. (1990). *Governing the soul: The shaping of the private self.* Taylor & Frances / Routledge.

Sacks, S. (2017, October). Rethinking 'home' and the art of changing one's mind-set. TED Conferences. https:// www.ted.com/talks/professor_shelley_sacks_rethinking_home_ and_the_art_of_changing_one_s_mind_set

Singh, S. P., & Burns, T. (2006). Race and mental health: There is more to race than racism. *British Medical Journal, 333*(7569), 648–651.

Smail, D. (1994). Community psychology and politics. *Journal of Community & Applied Social Psychology, 4*(1), 3–10. https://doi.org/10.1002/casp.2450040103.

Smith, A. (2013, August 14). *The problem with 'privilege'.* Andrea Smith's Blog. Retrieved from https://andrea366.wordpress.com/2013/08/14/the-problem-with-privilege-by-andrea-smith/

Steele, C. M. (2011). *Whistling Vivaldi: How stereotypes affect us and what we can do.* WW Norton & Company.

Steyn, M. (2001). *Whiteness just isn't what it used to be: White identity in a changing South Africa.* Suny Press.

Sweeney, A., Filson, B., Kennedy, A., Collinson, L., & Gillard, S. (2018). A paradigm shift: Relationships in trauma-informed mental health services. *British Journal of Psychiatry Advances, 24*(5), 319–333.

Williams, D. R. (2018). Stress and the mental health of populations of color: Advancing our understanding of race-related stressors. *Journal of Health and Social Behavior, 59*(4), 466–485.

Zuma, B. (2014). Contact theory and the concept of prejudice: Metaphysical and moral explorations and an epistemological question. *Theory & Psychology, 24*(1), 40–57.

PART 3
PERSPECTIVES IN PRACTICE

The role of intergenerational trauma and adultification in children and young people

10

Raisa Kumaga

Overview

This chapter addresses the disparities in mental health care for children and young people of colour in the United Kingdom, providing a critical examination of the knowledge base and revealing the heightened impact of racial inequalities on community well-being. Acknowledging the imperative outlined by the World Health Organisation (WHO) in 2023, the chapter underscores the necessity for mental health care to navigate the intricate web of social, political, economic, and environmental factors influencing families.

Within the UK context, the hostile environment, exemplified by incidents like the Windrush scandal and the destitution faced by migrant families, significantly contributes to the psychological distress experienced by racialised communities. However, the enduring colonial legacies and perpetuation of othering in the UK highlight a deeper intergenerational challenge, with families grappling with systemic racism, resulting in persistent disparities in accessing care and facing mental health difficulties.

The chapter commences by emphasising the transmission of parental trauma to the next generation, creating a compelling case for examining mental health within the broader familial context. Advancing, the narrative navigates the intersection of acculturation and belonging, challenging

DOI: 10.4324/9781003415244-13

conventional perspectives on the acculturation processes of racialised families in the United Kingdom. The exploration extends to societal and institutional forces shaping adultification and responsibility in racialised children. It underscores how systemic racism propels a premature assumption of adult roles, resulting in heightened responsibility and systemic survivor guilt with mental health consequences.

Concluding, the chapter advocates for healing trauma and strengthening relationships through resistance. It underscores the importance of storytelling and culturally and anti-racist informed therapies in promoting family well-being, challenging colonial legacies, and restoring agency within families through a nuanced understanding of non-Western traditions. The chapter calls for an inclusive understanding of children and young people's distress that incorporates systemic racism into mental health frameworks to effectively support the well-being of racialised families and their children in academic and clinical settings.

Introduction

In the United Kingdom, there is a strong commitment to developing integrated mental health care for children and young people, as highlighted in governmental documents like Transforming children's and young people's mental health provision (Government, 2017) and Children and Young people's mental health coalition strategy (Rainer & Abdinasir, 2023). This commitment is especially critical given recent 2022 findings, indicating increased distressed levels among children aged 7–16 (1 in 6) and young people aged (1 in 4) due to the COVID-19 Pandemic (NHS Digital, 2022).

The amplified distress brought about by the pandemic has exacerbated pre-existing racial inequalities for children, young people, and their families (Morris & Fisher, 2022). These disparities act as barriers to accessing essential support, underscoring the limitations of mental health systems in addressing the complex web of social, political, economic, and environmental factors (WHO, 2023). The WHO (2023) emphasises the need for governments to address the root causes of mental distress, which include issues like racism, xenophobia, social disadvantage, inadequate housing, and other psychosocial factors. Research conducted by Wallace et al. (2016) and Stopforth et al. (2022) has shown that Structural Racism in the United Kingdom underlies health inequalities (Hamed et al., 2020; Stopforth et al., 2022; Wallace et al., 2016) with its enduring effects manifesting through lower income and poorer health over time, a phenomenon known as "weathering" for racialised individuals. In 2021, the Mayor of London acknowledged the challenges faced by racialised children and young people in having their mental health needs met, recognising a deep-seated mistrust and lack of confidence in public institutions, and an experience of structural racism (Mayor of London, 2021).

Addressing the specific needs of racialised children and young people is crucial. There are many things that can be discussed to address the social conditions in relation to neurodiversity and disproportionate rate of over and underdiagnosing, specific psychological developmental models, intersectionality, and other themes however due to the scope of the chapter this will not be addressed but can be found elsewhere in Alleyne (2015), Turner (2021), and Roman-Urrestarazu et al. (2021).

In this chapter, the influence of systemic racism on racialised children, young people, and their families is examined, exploring intergenerational trauma and adultification. Highlighting the interconnectedness of heightened responsibility and systemic survivor guilt with these psychological processes, the chapter posits that these aspects play pivotal roles in shaping experiences of intergenerational trauma and adultification. The exploration begins by elucidating the dynamics within families and their implications for child well-being, followed by an examination of acculturation and belonging to contextualise adultification and intergenerational trauma. Concluding the chapter, the importance of recognising the restorative power and resistance inherent in the experiences of racialised children and young people is underscored.

Racial injustice and its impact on family dynamics and child well-being

Racism affects family relationships, increases parenting stress, and influences parental practices and coping strategies. In the United States, numerous research studies and systematic reviews have highlighted the impact of caregiver depression on parenting practices and racism mediating the relationship between poor child health and behavioural outcomes (Condon et al., 2022; Stern et al., 2023). In the United Kingdom, mothers' experiences of racism are linked to early child health and development (Kelly et al., 2013). In Europe, children of parents with mental health disorders often grapple with comprehending their parents' vulnerability and may form assumptions and behaviours, such as concealing their mental health concerns to evade stigma (Murphy et al., 2016). They may also hold certain perceptions about their parents and mental health in general, such as viewing their parents as fragile (Simpson-Adkins & Daiches, 2018). Studies have found that the effects of parental traumas and mental health can be transmitted to the next generation (Sangalang & Vang, 2017; van IJzendoorn et al., 2003).

Before we explore intergenerational trauma, it is necessary to understand what the challenges are of perceiving childhood as centred by the West. Childhood is a social phenomenon created and shaped through social interactions, time, space, and language thus influencing our perception and interaction with children as well as our psychological understanding of their experiences. Hence, the views of children and young people have changed and are influenced by historical, cultural, and political narratives. Consequently, contemporary developmental models and preferred methods and practices may be guided by outdated perceptions and warrants a dynamic view on childhood (Balagopalan, 2018).

Children and young people are confronted by another social environment that is a micro-reflection of society. Given the widespread negative attitudes towards individuals with a different skin colour, which often prevail in media, political, and civil institutions and in numerous activity domains within the United Kingdom, and through their interaction with peers and teachers these attitudes may also be transmitted to children and their behaviour (Kumaga, 2016; Modood, 1997). These perceptions of childhood are based on political and social systems and racial ideology that can shape children and young people's views on their racial identity and observed emotion regulation (Kumaga, 2016). Furthermore, racialised groups experiencing a multitude of injustices and therefore oppression inscribe their sense of self through internalising discourses and public expectations about their capabilities, and future possibilities (Onken et al., 2007). Children acquire beliefs and self-schemas on their racial and ethnic identity through socialisation processes. Racial socialisation is a process through which individuals, particularly children develop an understanding of the social meaning and significance of race. It involves the transmission of values, attitudes, beliefs, and behaviours related to race within a specific cultural and societal context. Racial socialisation plays a significant role in shaping how children perceive themselves, how they interact with others, and how they navigate the world (Hughes et al., 2006).

Several factors contribute to psychological well-being of children and young people, however, a perceived sense of belongingness with other people is said to be a predictor for self-esteem and perceived sense of mental well-being as well as greater overall satisfaction with life (Baumeister & Leary, 1995). Franceschelli et al. (2017) found that Black British Caribbean adults retrospectively found strength and resilience through their parents' preparation for future life chances in a racialised society due to the disadvantage in education and employment. This use of the relational bond with their history and identity was employed for restorative, progressive, and preventive purposes due to the acknowledgement of racism and the effects this will have on their children. Therefore, racial socialisation can support children's sense of belongingness, cultural pride, and resilience in the face of racial challenges.

On the other hand, negative racial socialisation may involve messages that devalue and downplay the impact of racism which leads children to a negative racial narrative, confusion, conflict, and alienation. In the United Kingdom, negative racial socialisation is also compounded by British colonial and migration patterns. The UK's history of immigration and its colonial past has had a profound impact on the racial landscape of the country. The experiences of racial discrimination and inequality faced by communities of colour, particularly those with historical ties to former British colonies, have shaped the socialisation experiences of children from these backgrounds. This is because these racial dynamics provide a blueprint to how children perceive power, privilege and the legacies of colonial injustice. For example, the superiority of Whiteness and equating Whiteness within the differential treatment of migrants coming into Europe with goodness and innocence are internalised and become the foundation of children and young people's racial identity. It is therefore important to unpack how the problems come about through the historical context and because of present-day systemic racial injustices in the United Kingdom.

There are some examples in the forced migration literature in the United Kingdom with children and young people that highlight the impact of migration and seeking asylum as mediating factors for post-traumatic stress but fail to recognise the policing of borders in the United Kingdom (Batista-Pinto Wiese, 2010). For example, former child soldiers are primarily seen as conflict victims (Doná & Veal, 2011). Yet, a disconnect emerges between this global perception and how national-level systems in the global North view them, particularly when seeking refugee status, sometimes considering them as potential threats (Doná & Veal, 2011). Adolescent forced migrants grapple with this tension too because the hostile environment towards migrants leads to over-scrutinising and a devalue of their sense of self (Alrababa'h et al., 2021; Wroe, 2018). The persistent racial structural disadvantage over time and across generations leads to social defeat and erodes the self-worth of racialised families (Fernando, 2017; Keating & Robertson, 2004; Southby et al., 2021). Considering oppression as a determinant of childhood development and mental ill health in such situations introduces the possibility that the individual's experiences encompass pain, anger, and grief arising from feelings of oppression. Paying attention to oppression as a determinant of mental ill health, as well as acknowledging the mental and

emotional toll of exposure to exploitation, marginalisation, disempowerment, cultural imperialism, and violence, creates additional pathways for
understanding, and promoting healing.

The intersection of acculturation and belonging

The differential treatment of migrant families and association with
Whiteness being perceived as good may influence the acculturation
processes of migrant families. Migrant families are expected to assimilate into their new environment, and different acculturation strategies are
believed to influence their mental health and parenting practices. Berry and
Hou (2017) discovered that individuals adopting marginalisation strategies
were most affected by discrimination, followed by those with an integration strategy, despite reporting increased life satisfaction. Acculturation
has been perceived as an important predictor in psychological well-being
and acculturation gaps within family relationships (Berry & Hou, 2017;
Bornstein & Cote, 2006; Lincoln et al., 2016; Mohamed & Yusuf, 2012).
The lens through which acculturation is viewed may carry racial connota-
tion emphasising that certain acculturation strategies should be achieved in
order to be accepted by the host society. In contrast, emphasising acculturation perpetuates a distinction between those deemed integrated and those
who are not, with blurred lines defining membership in a White-dominated
society (Schwartz et al., 2010). Such conditions for membership may vary
and can change within certain contexts, and spaces – for example – based on
the family's status and achievements.

The way racialised children and young people acculturate may be
influenced by other overarching identities. Given that, these identities
should not be viewed as fixed labels (Fernando, 2012). In addition, the process of acculturation is influenced by the racialised experience and the sense
of "othering". This can lead to emotional experiences such as confusion and
a persistent feeling of not belonging. These emotions arise from the constant questioning of one's existence, resulting from feelings of alienation
and identity insecurity (Alleyne, 2015; Layder, 2004). The racial challenges
that families face result in social suffering that affects the entire family unit.
This is exemplified by processes such as social defeat and social weathering.
Social defeat, originally a concept from animal studies, refers to the psychological consequences of sustained domination and subjugation (Björkqvist,
2001). In human subjects, it has been found that social defeat plays a significant role in the development of psychological distress, particularly among
racialised communities who experience chronic subjugation and outsider

status (Hall, 2024). Importantly, these experiences of social defeat and social weathering profoundly influence family dynamics and witnessing this or experiencing it directly while going through the acculturation processes may contribute to the perceived sense of belonging.

Societal and institutional forces shaping adultification and responsibility in racialised children

Racialised children in the United Kingdom encounter postcolonial processes of anti-blackness and othering ingrained in British society. These post-colonial dynamics contribute to adultification, systemic survivor guilt, and an inflated sense of responsibility among these children (Kumaga, 2023). Adultification, originally referring to the premature perception, treatment, or expectation of a child taking on adult roles within the family network (Burton, 2007), is nuanced and contested (Perillo et al., 2023). The concept of adultification highlights instances when the actions of these children seem out of sync with prevailing social and institutional expectations of childhood (Burton, 2007; Goff et al., 2014). In racially minoritised children, it manifests as others perceiving them as more mature, resilient, and responsible than their White counterparts (Goff et al., 2014), denying them the protection afforded by their human rights. The process of adultification appears to reflect the injustice and oppression of broader societal norms that dictate that racially diverse children must mature prematurely and conform to adult standards at an early age, a phenomenon deeply rooted in systemic racism. For example, the death of child C in the United Kingdom (Davis & Marsh, 2020).

The complexity of adultification lies in the intricate psychological processes that could impact the well-being of racialised children. Under oppressive conditions, racialised children and young individuals may be unfairly perceived as more responsible for their actions, driven by racialised notions of childhood that neglect their inherent vulnerability and need for protection. This heightened sense of responsibility may also be exacerbated when their family members experience systemic racism, compelling the second generation to assume a supportive role (Kumaga, 2023).

Responsibility in psychological terms is often related to the inflated perceptions of responsibility, closely tied to assessments of potential harm to oneself and others, including family members (Rachman, 1976). This heightened responsibility, marked by increased vigilance, intrusive thoughts, and self-blame (Mathieu et al., 2020), becomes a significant aspect for the second generation. As they take on caregiving roles to support their families, this responsibility at the same time serves as a vital connection to their familial, communal, and cultural roots (Markus & Kitayama, 1991; Singelis, 1994).

Additionally, adultification, can be observed as a protective feature. Leon and Rosen (2023) deduct this in their study on unaccompanied migrant children indebted relationships which may be a social protection mechanism that external observers may perceive as harmful. There is a potential conflict between the moral obligation to support their family and individual aspirations as well as pressure and fears of failing (Chase & Allsopp, 2020). Furthermore, other authors found that this process of adultification can support migrant families through language brokering (Crafter & Iqbal, 2020). However, the pervasive influence of systemic racism is a driving force behind the premature assumption of adult roles and responsibilities by racialised children even if it can be supportive for some families, it can also lead to pressure. Consequently, the weight of these expectations takes a considerable toll on their mental and emotional well-being. This complexity underscores the nuanced nature of adultification, echoing earlier discussions on the harm of perpetuating exclusionary and Eurocentric childhood narratives.

It is essential to emphasise that these dynamics extend beyond unaccompanied children to encompass racialised children in general, given the hostile and systemic racism experienced by them and their families in the United Kingdom. The interconnectedness of heightened responsibility and adultification presents multifaceted challenges for the second generation as they navigate familial, cultural, and societal expectations within the context of systemic racism invoking various emotions and beliefs.

Intergenerational trauma, systemic survivor guilt, and adultification: Racial oppression on families of colour

The hostile environment towards migrants and othering in British society means that daily stressors such as racism, immigration policies, and separation of family's economic hardship and other losses of resources may play an equally critical role in triggering attachment-related trauma and post-traumatic reactions in the parents which can affect the relationship with their children and consequently their well-being (Betancourt et al., 2015; Kumaga, 2023). For example (Kumaga, 2023) found in their study on Somali migrant families that the second generation presented with systemic survivor guilt. Systemic survivor guilt refers to the psychological distress experienced by individuals who belong to immigrant families, where they feel a deep sense of responsibility to enhance their families' position due to the struggles and traumas endured by their parents or ancestors. Although this may be a helpful strength as some of the participants thrived in education, it can also become a source of pressure, provoke heightened anxiety, and maintain the survival mode impacting their mental health.

Due to systemic racism, the oppression and suffering experienced by parents will also affect the conscious or unconscious actions of families. Racialised parents, grappling with the absence of a nurturing and protective environment within a racially biased system, are compelled to equip their children with the necessary tools to survive. These psychological responses are seen as adaptive survival mechanisms for racialised individuals in White-dominated and hostile societies.

In the realm of racialised children and young people, societal factors contribute to the emergence of systemic survivor guilt, given the absence of a supportive environment, presenting a challenge for parents striving to establish safety (Applegate, 2013; Fonagy et al., 2022; Kumaga, 2023). As a consequence, racialised children and young individuals may grapple with an inherent desire to alleviate their parents' distress, sparking a psychological conflict between self-reliance and vulnerability (Kumaga, 2023; Nielsen et al., 2018). These strategies for regulating emotions could serve as embodied responses to societal oppression. In this specific context, parents not only navigate their own survival but also shoulder the responsibility of ensuring their children's well-being in an environment that often lacks the necessary support and opportunities for their growth and development.

In summary, the interplay of societal pressures, adultification, and systemic survivor guilt creates a complex dynamic within racialised families, emphasising the multifaceted challenges they face in striving for survival, support, and the well-being of both parents and children.

Healing trauma and strengthening relationships through resistance

The systemic racism that induces the detrimental social defeat and suffering in racialised family benefits from narratives around systemic change and empowerment of families through resistance and amplifying their voices. Colonial legacies appear to have left an enduring mark, robbing individuals, families, and communities of agency and identity (Bhui et al., 2018; DeGruy Leary, 2017). Storytelling in Africana phenomenology plays a vital role in transmitting ancestral knowledge, preserving cultural heritage, and resisting the erasure of African histories (Gordon, 2008; Henry, 2005). To promote family well-being, it is essential to critically examine and address narratives contributing to trauma through community organisations and African-inspired therapies or adaptations of existing therapies such as culturally based systemic therapy. This process empowers individuals to reclaim their self-perception and agency, fostering personal growth, and strengthening family bonds. Contemporary psychology's ethnocentric bias overlooks the psychological wisdom in non-Western traditions (Fernando, 2017; Moodley & West, 2005). Recognising the impact of colonial legacies and cultural beliefs allows families to embark on a journey of cultural healing, enriching their self-concept, and heritage (Williams et al., 2023). Identity development, influenced by historical narratives and cultural contexts, shapes our understanding of ourselves and our relationships. However, these narratives have often silenced African voices and perpetuated stereotypes. Challenging these narratives can restore agency and genuine connections within families as well as recognising this wisdom and the strength of liberation and resistance is essential for supporting the well-being of children and young people (Afuape, 2011; Steve Biko as cited in Hook, 2012).

Nurturing empowerment and shared understanding for children and young people of colour

A young person called Jemma aged 15 has been observed as withdrawing in school and at home since a few months ago. Jemma is in private school and her father is from Nigeria and her mother is Jamaican. She has two younger siblings. Her parents are divorced but are both co-parenting. Jemma has shared with her mother in the past that she wishes that she was lighter skin as most of her peers were White or mixed heritage.

More recently, the head of year noticed that her grades are declining and that she misses lessons. Her parents report that she is irritable and fixed on how things are organised at home and in her room, she becomes worried about symmetry and orderliness which significantly impact daily life. This obsession extends to personal appearance, schoolwork, and the arrangement of items in their environment. The fear of something bad happening if things are not perfectly aligned creates persistent anxiety. This happened after an incident in school where a group of people were bullying her online and she was subsequently bullied about her physical appearance and sexual innuendos were made whereas other girls were praised about their physical features. Consequently, she shared negative self-beliefs about her racial features and identity. Her parents reported that they tried to discuss the racial dynamics and bullying with school, school indicated that it has an anti-bullying policy and will discuss this with the class. However, the parents felt that the racial undertones in the bullying were not addressed. Jemma was sent to counselling at school where they addressed her obsessive and compulsive behaviours, but these continued after counselling.

Chapter questions to provoke thoughts:

1. What are the possible intersecting processes of oppression that are affecting Jemma's well-being.
2. What type of initiatives can be supported in school to establish a more anti-racist and affirming atmosphere for young people's growth and development.
3. What in the family can be highlighted to empower the young people and their family that may be minimised in society?

There is a risk in conceptualising children and young people's distress solely under their internal and emotional distress such as with Jemma. At first glance, it appears that Jemma has obsessive and compulsive behaviours that can be addressed with therapies such as cognitive behavioural therapy. However, Jemma's distress may also be rooted within (1) the anti-blackness she has faced in her life whereby she wanted to be lighter – it is likely she witnessed the privilege her white counterparts' experiences, (2) the abuse due to her features.

Furthermore, the hypersexualisation in the bullying is rooted in the adultification of Black girls. In the realm of children and young people's mental health, it is widely recognised that effective interventions may necessitate directing attention towards the parent. This approach is rooted in the understanding that solely focusing on the individual child runs the risk of reintegrating them into an unchanged environment, thereby retriggering the same challenges that were addressed during therapy.

References

Afuape, T. (2011). *Power, resistance and liberation in counselling and psychotherapy*. Routledge.

Alleyne, A. (2015). *From Intergenerational Trauma to Intergenerational Healing*. Confer Online Module. https://www.confer.uk.com/module/module-intergenerational.html

Alrababa'h, A., Dillon, A., Williamson, S., Hainmueller, J., Hangartner, D., & Weinstein, J. (2021). Attitudes toward migrants in a highly impacted economy: Evidence from the Syrian refugee crisis in Jordan. *Comparative Political Studies*, *54*(1), 33–76. https://doi.org/10.1177/0010414020919910

Applegate, J. (2013). The erosion of the sociopolitical holding environment and the collapse of the potential space for creative repair. In E. Ruderman & C. Tosone (Eds.), *Contemporary clinical practice: The holding environment under assault* (pp. 19–29). Springer.

Balagopalan, S. (2018). Redeploying "Multiple childhoods". In S. Spyrou, R. Rosen, & D. T. Cook (Eds.), *Reimagining childhood studies* (pp. 23–39). Bloomsbury Academic.

Baumeister, R. F., & Leary, M. R. (1995). The need to belong: Desire for interpersonal attachments as a fundamental human motivation. *Psychological Bulletin, 117*(3), 497–529.

Berry, J. W., & Hou, F. (2017). Acculturation, discrimination, and wellbeing among second generation of immigrants in Canada. *International Journal of Intercultural Relations, 61*, 29–39. https://doi.org/10.1016/j.ijintrel.2017.08.003

Betancourt, T. S., Abdi, S., Ito, B. S., Lilienthal, G. M., Agalab, N., & Ellis, H. (2015). We left one war and came to another: Resource loss, acculturative stress, and caregiver child relationships in Somali refugee families. *Cultural Diversity and Ethnic Minority Psychology, 21*(1), 114–125. https://doi.org/10.1037/a0037538

Bhui, K., Nazroo, J., Francis, J., Halvorsrud, K., & Rhode, J. (2018). The impact of racism on mental health. *The Synergi Collaborative Centre.* http://www.synergicollaborativecentre.co.uk

Björkqvist, K. (2001). Social defeat as a stressor in humans. *Physiology & Behavior, 73*(3), 435–442. https://doi.org/10.1016/S0031-9384(01)00490-5

Bornstein, M. H., & Cote, L. R. (Eds.). (2006). *Acculturation and parent-child relationships: Measurement and development* (1st ed.). Routledge. https://doi.org/10.4324/9780415963589

Burton, L. (2007). Childhood adultification in economically disadvantaged families: A conceptual model. *Family Relations, 56*(4), 329–345. http://www.jstor.org/stable/4541675

Chase, E., & Allsopp, J. (2020). *Youth migration and the politics of wellbeing: Stories of life in transition.* Bristol University Press.

Condon, E. M., Barcelona, V., Ibrahim, B. B., Crusto, C. A., & Taylor, J. Y. (2022). Racial discrimination, mental health, and parenting among African American mothers of preschool-aged children. *Journal of the American Academy of Child and Adolescent Psychiatry, 61*(3), 402–412. https://doi.org/10.1016/j.jaac.2021.05.023

Crafter, S., & Iqbal, H. (2020). The contact zone and dialogical positionalities in "Non-normative" childhoods: How children who language broker manage conflict. *Review of General Psychology, 24*(1), 31–42. https://doi.org/10.1177/1089268019896354

Davis, J., & Marsh, N. (2020). Boys to men: The cost of 'adultification' in safeguarding responses to Black boys. *Critical and Radical Social Work, 8*(2), 255–259.

DeGruy, J. (2017). *Post traumatic slave syndrome: America's legacy of enduring injury and healing* (2nd ed.). Joy DeGruy Publications Inc.

Doná, G., & Veale, A. (2011). Divergent discourses, children and forced migration. *Journal of Ethnic and Migration Studies, 37*(8), 1273–1289. https://doi.org/10.1080/1369183X.2011.590929

Fernando, S. (2012). Race and culture issues in mental health and some thoughts on ethnic identity. *Counselling Psychology Quarterly, 25*(2), 113–123. https://doi.org/10.1080/09515070.2012.674299

Fernando, S. (2017). *Institutional racism in psychiatry and clinical psychology (vol. 17517893).* Palgrave Macmillan.

Fonagy, P., Campbell, C., Constantinou, M., Higgitt, A., Allison, E., & Luyten, P. (2022). Culture and psychopathology: An attempt at reconsidering the role of social learning. *Development and Psychopathology, 34*(4), 1205–1220. https://doi.org/10.1017/S0954579421000092

Franceschelli, M., Schoon, I., & Evans, K. (2017). 'your past makes you who you are': Retrospective parenting and relational resilience among Black Caribbean British young people. *Sociological Research Online, 22*(4), 48–65. https://doi.org/10.1177/1360780417726957

Goff, P. A., Jackson, M., Di Leone, B., Culotta, C., & Ditomasso, N. (2014). The essence of innocence: Consequences of dehumanizing Black children. *Journal of Personality and Social Psychology, 106*(4), 526–545.

Gordon, L. (2008). *An introduction to Africana philosophy.* Cambridge University Press.

Government. (2017). *Transforming Children and Young People's Mental Health Provision: A Green Paper.* Presented to Parliament by the Secretary of State for Health and Secretary of State for Education by Command of Her Majesty.

Hall, H. (2024). Dissociation and misdiagnosis of schizophrenia in populations experiencing chronic discrimination and social defeat. *Journal of Trauma & Dissociation, 25*(3), 334–348.

Hamed, S., Thapar-Björkert, S., Bradby, H., & Ahlberg, B. M. (2020). Racism in European health care: Structural violence and beyond. *Qualitative Health Research, 30*(11), 1662–1673.

Henry, P. (2005). Africana phenomenology: Its philosophical implications. *The CLR James Journal, 11*(1), 79–112. https://doi.org/10.5840/clrjames20051113

Hook, D. (2012). *A critical psychology of the postcolonial.* Routledge.

Hughes, D., Rodriguez, J., Smith, E. P., Johnson, D. J., Stevenson, H. C., & Spicer, P. (2006). Parents' ethnic-racial socialization practices: A review of research and directions for future study. *Developmental Psychology, 42*(5), 747–770.

Keating, F., & Robertson, D. (2004). Fear, Black people and mental illness: A vicious circle? *Health & Social Care in the Community, 12*, 439–447. https://doi.org/10.1111/j.1365-2524.2004.00506.x

Kelly, Y., Becares, L., & Nazroo, J. (2013). Associations between maternal experiences of racism and early child health and development: Findings from the UK millennium cohort study. *Journal of Epidemiology and Community Health (1979-), 67*(1), 35–41. http://www.jstor.org/stable/43281469

Kumaga, R. (2016). *Behavioural and emotional difficulties of children: The importance of ethnic and racial identity in primary school* [Doctoral dissertation, University of Cambridge]. https://doi.org/10.13140/RG.2.2.26469.63208

Kumaga, R. (2023). The psychological experience of second-generation Somalis whose parents were forced to migrate during the civil war in the '90s. [Doctoral dissertation, University of East London School of Psychology]. https://doi.org/10.15123/uel.8wq49

Layder, D. (2004). *Social and personal identity: Understanding yourself.* Sage.

Leon, L., & Rosen, R. (2023). Unaccompanied migrant children and indebted relations: Weaponizing safeguarding. *Child & Family Social Work, 28*(4), 1056–1065. https://doi.org/10.1111/cfs.13025

Lincoln, A. K., Lazarevic, V., White, M. T., & Ellis, H. (2016). The impact of acculturation style and acculturative hassles on the mental health of Somali adolescent refugees. *Journal of Immigrant and Minority Health, 18*(4), 771–778. https://doi.org/10.1007/s10903-015-0232-y

Markus, H. R., & Kitayama, S. (1991). Culture and the self: Implications for cognition, emotion, and motivation. *Psychological Review, 98*(2), 224–253. https://doi.org/10.1037/0033-295X.98.2.224

Mathieu, S. L., Conlon, E. G., Waters, A. M., McKenzie, M. L., & Farrell, L. J. (2020). Inflated responsibility beliefs in paediatric OCD: Exploring the role of parental rearing and child age. *Child Psychiatry and Human Development, 51*(4), 552–562. https://doi.org/10.1007/s10578-019-00938-w

Mayor of London. (2021). *Health Inequalities Strategy Implementation Plan 2021–24.* Greater London Authority. Retrieved February 12, 2024, from https://www.london.gov.uk/publications/health-inequalities-strategy-implementation-plan-2021-24

Modood, T. (1997). Introduction: The politics of multiculturalism in the new Europe. In T. Modood & P. Werbner (Eds.), *The politics of multiculturalism in the new Europe* (pp. 1–25). Zed Books.

Mohamed, A., & Yusuf, A. M. (2012). Somali Parent-child conflict in the Western world: Some brief reflections. *Bildhaan: An International Journal of Somali Studies, 11*(1), 17.

Moodley, R., & West, W. (2005). *Integrating traditional healing practices into counseling and psychotherapy.* SAGE Publications.

Morris, J., & Fisher, E. (2022). *Growing problems: What has been the impact of COVID-19 on health care for children and young people in England.* Nuffield Trust.

Murphy, G., Peters, K., Wilkes, L. M., & Jackson, D. (2016). Adult children of parents with mental illness: Losing oneself. Who am I? *Issues in Mental Health Nursing, 37*(9), 668–673. https://doi.org/10.1080/01612840.2016.1178359

NHS Digital. (2022). Mental Health of Children and Young People in England: 2022 Follow-up to the 2017 Survey. Retrieved February 12, 2024, from https://digital.nhs.uk/data-and-information/publications/statistical/mental-health-of-children-and-young-people-in-england/2022-follow-up-to-the-2017-survey/introduction

Nielsen, D. S., Minet, L., Zeraig, L., Rasmussen, D. N., & Sodemann, M. (2018). "Caught in a generation gap": A generation perspective on refugees getting old in Denmark—A qualitative study. *Journal of Transcultural Nursing, 29*(3), 265–273. https://doi.org/10.1177/1043659617718064

Onken, S. J., Craig, C. M., Ridgway, P., Ralph, R. O., & Cook, J. A. (2007). An analysis of the definitions and elements of recovery: A review of the literature. *Psychiatric Rehabilitation Journal, 31*(1), 9–22. https://doi.org/10.2975/31.1.2007.9.22

Perillo, J. T., Sykes, R. B., Bennett, S. A., & Reardon, M. C. (2023). Examining the consequences of dehumanization and adultification in justification of police use of force against Black girls and boys. *Law and Human Behavior, 47*(1), 36–52. https://doi.org/10.1037/lhb0000521

Rachman, S. (1976). Obsessional compulsive checking. *Behaviour Research and Therapy, 14*(4), 269–277.

Rainer, C., & Abdinasir, K. (2023). Children and young people's mental health. An independent review into policy success and challenges over the last decade. *Children & Young People's Mental Health Coalition.* https://cypmhc.org.uk/wp-content/uploads/2023/06/Review-of-CYP-Mental-Health-Policy-Final-Report.-2023.pdf

Roman-Urrestarazu, A., van Kessel, R., Allison, C., Matthews, F. E., Brayne, C., & Baron-Cohen, S. (2021). Association of Race/Ethnicity and social disadvantage with autism prevalence in 7 million school children in England. *JAMA Pediatrics, 175*(6), e210054. https://doi.org/10.1001/jamapediatrics.2021.0054

Sangalang, C. C., & Vang, C. (2017). Intergenerational trauma in refugee families: A systematic review. *Immigration Minority Health, 19*(3), 745–754. https://doi.org/10.1007/s10903-016-0499-7

Schwartz, S. J., Unger, J. B., Zamboanga, B. L., & Szapocznik, J. (2010). Rethinking the concept of acculturation: Implications for theory and research. *The American Psychologist, 65*(4), 237–251. https://doi.org/10.1037/a0019330

Simpson-Adkins, G. J., & Daiches, A. (2018). How do children make sense of their Parent's mental health difficulties: A meta-synthesis. *Journal of Child and Family Studies, 27*(9), 2705–2716. https://doi.org/10.1007/s10826-018-1112-6

Singelis, T. M. (1994). The measurement of independent and interdependent self-construals. *Personality and Social Psychology Bulletin, 20*(5), 580–591.

Southby, K., Keating, F., & Joseph, S. (2021). The meanings of mental health recovery for African and Caribbean men in the UK: An intersectionalities approach. *International Journal of Mental Health Systems, 4*(1), 83–95. https://doi.org/10.22374/ijmsch.v4i1.53

Stern, J. A., Dunbar, A. S., & Cassidy, J. (2023). Pathways to emotion regulation in young Black children: An attachment perspective, *Advances in Child Development and Behavior, 64,* 163–188. https://doi.org/10.1016/bs.acdb.2022.10.001

Stopforth, S., Kapadia, D., Nazroo, J., & Bécares, L. (2022). The enduring effects of racism on health: Understanding direct and indirect effects over time, *SSM – Population Health, 19,* 101217. https://doi.org/10.1016/j.ssmph.2022.101217

Turner, D. (2021). *Intersections of privilege and otherness in counselling and psychotherapy: Mockingbird.* Routledge.

van IJzendoorn, M. H., Bakermans-Kranenburg, M. J., & Sagi-Schwartz, A. (2003). Are children of holocaust survivors less well-adapted? A meta-analytic investigation of secondary traumatization. *Journal of Traumatic Stress, 16*(5), 459–469. https://doi.org/10.1023/A:1025706427300

Wallace, S., Nazroo, J., & Bécares, L. (2016). Cumulative effect of racial discrimination on the mental health of ethnic minorities in the United Kingdom. *Public Health, 106,* 1294–1300. https://doi.org/10.2105/AJPH.2016.303121

Wiese, E. B.-P. (2010). Culture and migration: Psychological trauma in children and adolescents. *Traumatology, 16*(4), 142–152. https://doi.org/10.1177/1534765610388304

Williams, M. T., Holmes, S., Zare, M., Haeny, A., & Faber, S. (2023). An evidence-based approach for treating stress and trauma due to racism. *Cognitive and Behavioral Practice, 30*(4), 565–588. https://doi.org/10.1016/j.cbpra.2022.07.001

World Health Organisation & United Nations. Office of the High Commissioner for Human Rights. (2023). *Mental health, human rights and legislation: guidance and practice.* https://www.who.int/publications/i/item/9789240080737

Wroe, L. E. (2018). 'It really is about telling people who asylum seekers really are, because we are human like anybody else': Negotiating victimhood in refugee advocacy work. *Discourse & Society, 29*(3), 324–343. https://doi.org/10.1177/0957926517734664

Rethinking the way we work with Black men   **11**

Melissa Butler

Overview

The chapter explores why we (society) need to rethink the way we conceptualise and work with Black men. It will consider how historical, social, and cultural factors interweave with racial discrimination to shape the experiences of Black men within the United Kingdom. Throughout, this piece will draw upon research and contextual examples to offer a critical analysis of the structural mechanisms that are employed to maintain the unacceptable treatment of Black men. Discussions will hone in on particular sectors (such as health care and policing) where there are clear racial disparities to explore how practices are utilised to the detriment of Black men and their well-being. This chapter will go beyond just stating the issues and instead will offer practical tools and principles that can be used in order to effectively enhance our engagement of and work with Black men. These suggestions are universally applicable, in order to support the reader in developing effective strategies for how they might introduce changes within their respective sectors. The reader is encouraged to consider this chapter as a call to action.

DOI: 10.4324/9781003415244-14

Introduction

Jones (2000) reminds us that race does not represent a biological difference between individuals, but rather is a social construct to highlight the impact of racism. Therefore, without tirelessly scrutinising the way we understand and work with Black men, we run the risk of becoming blind to this inequality and accepting it as a fixture within society. This chapter challenges the dominant narratives about Black men's relationship with seeking help, and also offer practical tools for society and Black men themselves to consider. These ideas will be drawn from a wide variety of sources, including my own experiences of working with Black men as a practicing psychologist. This chapter is for anyone who wants to incorporate more effective ways of working with Black men, as well as those who want to learn more about the damaging effects of inequality towards them.

A note on terminology

In order to meaningfully write this chapter, I move away from using homogenised terms that create a sense of vagueness about what is being said. Instead, I will use specific terminology when referring to a particular ethnic group. For example, when using the term Black men, I am referring to men from the African and Caribbean diaspora.

I acknowledge that within and between Black men there is vast heterogeneity. This chapter is not to group them into one, but rather to offer the reader an insight into how racial discrimination affects the way we, as a society, approach engaging with Black men.

My position

I (a Black female psychologist) am writing this piece to try and unpick some of the complex psychological inequalities that Black men experience within their respective ecosystems.

This is not my attempt at trying to offer a complete account of what it is like to be a Black man. I cannot do that. Instead, I want to give voice to the Black man's reality. I will contextually underpin how society positions Black men and offer a critical analysis about the consequences of this, with considerations around mental health specifically. I encourage you, the reader, to go deeper in your reflections, and see yourselves as agents of change.

Dehumanisation of Black men

History reminds us of the horrific dehumanisation Black people have been subjected to. Dehumanisation is the process of "perceiving a person or group as lacking humanness" (Haslam & Loughnan, 2014, p. 401). Oh (2020) describes a two-layered approach to dehumanisation. The first part involves the individual or group being stripped of their human qualities, such as emotions and basic needs. They are then positioned as possessing animalistic qualities, which equates to them being perceived as less than human. Unfortunately, this appalling treatment is not resigned to history. For instance, in sporting events when spectators mimic actions or sounds synonymous with those of monkeys, or when items such as bananas are thrown on football pitches. Both of these examples are a form of dehumanisation in the portrayal of Black people.

Through the process of stripping away their human attributes, Black men are seen as possessing superhuman qualities (Waytz et al., 2015). For example, Black men were perceived as being physically larger and stronger when compared to White men of the same size (Wilson et al., 2017). Depictions of superhumanised Black men can be found within the sporting industry, for example, 'Iron Mike'. Discursively, this popular nickname for American boxer Mike Tyson suggests that he is made out of an enduring metal, which gives the impression of indestructability. Historically, British boxer Lennox Lewis had the nickname, 'The Lion' – this creates connotations of a predator who will seek out and devour his prey. Further instances of superhumanisation can be found within the television industry. In the popular British game show, 'The Chase', quizmaster Shaun Wallace is often referred to by his nickname, 'The Dark Destroyer' – this constructs a discourse of mystery, but also of someone who can obliterate his opponents.

Are Black men beyond human affliction?

Arguably, these examples of superhumanisation could be described as harmless and even endearing ways of referring to Black men. On the other hand, there could be insidious consequences. For instance, if Black men are perceived as having beyond human strength, then it becomes logical to believe that they do not experience the same emotions as regular people would. Additionally, through society perpetually maintaining discourses about Black men being objects to fear and avoid, we are actively reinforcing unsafe and harmful realities for them. Therefore, raising questions about who the ones at risk are; as health care, law enforcement, and employment trends appear to place Black men as being at a marked disadvantage compared to their White counterparts.

By constantly positioning Black men as being violent deviants, society has decided that he begins from a place of defending himself. As a result, this creates an environment of rigidity, which could make it difficult for him to bring his whole self to spaces, because he has been presumed as not possessing attributes akin to sensitivity or vulnerability. It would be bizarre to query whether Black men experience fear and unease – as everyone else can. Yet, as a society we seem slow to consider the way our treatment of Black men might negatively affect how safe it feels for him to share parts of his being, that cannot be exemplified through his physicality. There appears to be a societal hypervigilance when it comes to honing in on acts that fit with the negative constructions surrounding Black men. Yet, these constructions often bypass his need for safety and the diversity of his emotional experience. It could be claimed that the onus is therefore on Black men to show more of their sensitivity in order to change society's perception of them. However, it feels as if society first needs to redress the dehumanising tactics employed to restrict how Black men express themselves. So rather than society having a predetermination of what to expect, it is important for Black men's voices to be welcomed, so that they can share what a safe space represents for them (Bernard, 2019).

Additionally, there appears to be physical consequences in superhumanising. Recent statistics show that Black men aged 18–34 experience the highest rates of force used by the police in the United Kingdom (Home Office, 2022). This dataset also notes that the police were four times more likely to use a taser for incidents involving Black people (in comparison to White people). Further statistics present a damning picture, with Black people nearly five times as likely to be detained under the Mental Health Act (1983) in comparison to their White counterparts (Department of Health, 2023). With Black men more likely to be detained compulsorily using harsher treatment measures, such as restraint and being placed in seclusion (Darko, 2021; Kapadia et al., 2022).

When considering the idea of superhumanisation from a law enforcement lens, it is possible to offer a contextualised hypothesis to these findings. If Black men are revered and simultaneously differentiated as a result of their physical prowess, it could be deemed necessary to incorporate the use of excessive and disproportionate force in order to overpower them. Through the perpetuation of this beyond-human narrative, we can become socialised to consider Black men as being above regular human affliction, which might then distort the manner in which they are perceived and treated by others. It could therefore be erroneously rationalised as acceptable for excessive force to be used against Black men. Tragically, there is evidence to support this hypothesis. The Mental Health Units (Use of Force) Act 2018, also known as Seni's Law, was introduced after a young Black man named Olaseni Lewis died as a result of severe and prolonged restraint by 11 police officers in 2010. The fact that Black men are disproportionately affected by the use of force suggests that there is a level of subjectivity when it comes to assessing who force is used with, and to what extent. Whether it is unconscious bias or an intentional decision, there needs to be greater awareness around how racial prejudices can be weaponised to appropriate the mistreatment of Black men.

Influencing change

The disproportionate rate of Black males being involuntarily detained appears to have influenced the '300 Voices' project, which was piloted in the West Midlands in 2014 (Time to Change, 2016). This project was a local partnership between the NHS, police, the Council and young Black men living in the area. A key aspect of this programme involved encouraging the men to consider a 'golden moment' that represented a positive experience they had when engaging with mental health services. It supported the move from a solely problem-focussed narrative, to one which highlighted opportunities to create systemic change. Promisingly, a thorough toolkit for organisations to deliver the '300 Voices' programme has been made publicly available online (https://www.mind.org.uk/media-a/4301/time-to-change-300-voices-toolkit-comp.pdf). Since the initial pilots however, there is little indication that this project has been widely utilised elsewhere. If so, this could represent a missed opportunity in support of Black men shaping mental health offerings, by utilising their lived experiences to steer change in their respective communities.

It would be amiss not to further highlight the power Black men have to influence real changes for one another, by reconstructing how they are positioned in the community. Through drawing upon their nuanced personal experiences, they are in a prime position to offer insights beyond what the media and society have decided about the mindset and dispositions of Black men. In doing so, they are able to reclaim the right to create their own narratives by deciding how they are presented both individually and collectively. That being said, there is a level of responsibility that comes with this reconstruction, because it becomes something greater than the individual man. Through seeing himself as a positive role model for those coming up, he is no longer objectified as one to be feared, but he can be a mentor or inspiration for someone else. For so long in the United Kingdom and further afield, Black men have been berated and mistreated. My concern is that some of these unjust ideas may have seeped into his inner being, thus affecting not only how he considers his own worth, but also the value placed upon what he can bring to the world around him. I would argue that in society there is at least some awareness of the power contained within Black men. For example, the sheer persistence of the fear discourse that surrounds them suggests that society considers this an apt representation, possibly due to a perception of great capability. Therefore, perhaps the fearful narrative continues because there is an implicit understanding of further potential within him. Therefore, in Black men utilising this influence by supporting today's Black boys, they become active agents in re-writing the misleading narratives that have been placed over them. I am by no means suggesting that this is a simple path to navigate, but rather through Black men seeing themselves as key to this process, we move closer to actualised change.

Conceptualising help seeking

There are many societal, cultural, and historical factors that appear to be influential in shaping how Black men assign meaning to the idea of seeking support. What follows is a brief exploration around how culture and masculinity can be instrumental in shaping the attitudes and beliefs of some Black men towards mental health.

Culture

Historically, African and Caribbean diasporan discourses about mental health difficulties have predominantly either minimised their existence or attributed it to a higher power. For instance, common mental health issues, such as depression and anxiety might not be deemed as requiring any particular intervention to manage (Dare et al., 2023). Whereas, when it comes to severe mental illnesses (such as psychosis), they might be considered to arise from some type of spiritual attack, which require divine interventions to treat (Dare et al., 2023). This way of constructing mental health appears to suggest that there is little need to seek support unless the symptomology is considered severe enough. This creates a discourse of rarity when it comes to requiring support, which appears to be evidenced through the lack of mental health investment in much of the Caribbean and Africa (Liverpool et al., 2023; Nicholas et al., 2022).

Further implications of support being viewed as unessential is that Black communities might wait longer before accessing help, which might exacerbate their presenting difficulties, and therefore extend the course treatment. This reflection might also feed into the sentiment that Black people appear to remain in the mental health system for longer periods of time in comparison to other groups. Another important consideration regarding Black men in the United Kingdom is that they may have acquired conflicting ideas about how mental health is conceptualised – through them trying to integrate influences from their ancestral homeland, and western narratives. This might affect not only their help-seeking beliefs but also the credibility they assign to their own mental health experiences. For example, if they believe that only serious mental health concerns warrant attention, then if he is affected by a milder complaint, he may not think this is worthy of seeking treatment. This could potentially influence how comfortable he feels sharing any mental health concerns. Furthermore, research has found that some Black people were reticent about acquiring mental health support due to concerns about stigmatisation from members of their community (Ogueji & Okoloba, 2022).

Since training as a Counselling Psychologist, I have become acutely aware of how damaging it can be to deny the concept of mental health. For example, whilst not with the same intention and extent as described previously, there are nonetheless dehumanising consequences associated with devaluing another's emotional experience. As if an innate part of our humanness is buried, it can be experienced as overwhelming when an emotionally taxing situation arises. In this respect, the act of denial itself can actually exacerbate mental ill health. I would therefore suggest that further work is needed within Black communities around exploring what continues to fuel the stigma surrounding mental health. Part of this might involve the dissemination of accurate and accessible information in order to challenge some inaccurate beliefs that might still be upheld. Additionally, I strongly advocate for Black families to continue working towards embracing conversations and expressions of mental health, regardless of whether it is considered comfortable or familiar.

Over recent years further work has been done to highlight the importance of Black men's mental health at home and within the community. For example, mental health charity 'Mind' launched 'Up My Street' in 2016 to equip young Black men with the skills needed to speak to one another and their families about mental health. Additionally, in 2019 Mind launched the three-year, 'Young Black Men's Programme' to challenge the stigma around mental health, foster peer support and also encourage them to access timely help.

Black masculinity

For some Black men it appears as though there are external influences that have an impact in shaping what masculinity represents to them. Prior to adulthood, there is a process of adultification that Black boys experience in many settings, including education and law enforcement (Hines et al., 2021). Anecdotally, this seems to happen in the home as well, for instance if there is a need to care for younger siblings or if he is placed in a position of authority. In these contexts, adultification is another form of dehumanisation for Black males because they are perceived and treated as being older than they are, which interrupts their experience as children. One of the many consequences of adultification for Black male children is that they are forced to step into manhood early; with this comes the need for them to learn what that entails. For some, this involves creating a shield of protection, in the form of toughness. The difficulty with this construction is that Black males might be particularly susceptible to toxic ideas around masculinity, which conveys emotional regulation as a sign of weakness (Hines et al., 2021). Therefore, we see how even as boys, Black men might have absorbed negative messages about acknowledging their emotional well-being.

Poussaint (1966) details how a Black man's sense of identity was projected unto him through oppressive Eurocentric narratives. According to Hooks (2004) part of the racists' agenda is to ensure that Black men feel belittled and therefore have a distorted sense of their masculinity. This serves to diminish Black men's autonomy and thus reinforces the oppression they experience. Additionally, it creates a warped societal expectation around how a Black man should be, and how others will experience him. A further contraindication of placing Black men within a Eurocentric masculinity narrative is that it negates the contextual experiences that they most likely have had to navigate, such as discrimination, deprivation, and generational trauma. Therefore, it is important we remain respectful of the subjectivities associated with how masculinity is defined and personified by Black men

Behind the caricature

I grew up in Tottenham, North London, where I was amongst many others of the African and Caribbean diasporan. Not only did this act as somewhat of a buffer against the racist rhetoric placed upon Black men, but I also had the opportunity to form meaningful relationships with them. The love, care, sensitivity, and protection I got to experience from Black men is an enduring reminder that he is more than the caricature he has been depicted as.

In writing this chapter, it felt important not just to present psychological research and scholarly texts; I needed to engage with Black men about their varied experiences. I was not barraged with narratives that fed into an aggressive or criminal inclination. Rather, Black men who were willing and able to share their joys, triumphs, battles, and distresses. Interestingly, they were neither hard to reach or difficult to engage. I would contend that traditional ways of conceptualising Black males' attitude towards seeking help is an insidious means of maintaining the narrative that Black men do not want to discuss mental health matters or are harder to engage. Not only could this have the effect of making support more inaccessible for Black men. It also absolves services and professionals of their responsibility to address the discriminative practices that hinder the provision of equitable care for the communities they serve.

Embedding change

I will now outline some principles and practical recommendations that can be implemented to help enrich the way we engage with and support Black men. The purpose of these strategies is to offer applicable ideas to help enhance current ways of working to empower, consider and care for Black men. The following proposals are universal, meaning that individuals from a range of sectors can incorporate them into their practice and learning objectives.

1. *It takes a village …*
    To create real change for Black men within society, it feels apt to draw upon a meaningful African proverb. The proverb 'it takes a village to raise a child', conveys the need for multiple people and systems to support the healthy development of a child (Reupert et al., 2022). I would argue that 'it takes a village to eradicate racial inequality'. In this sense, we are all the 'village', because we are the loved ones, employers, community leaders, policymakers, educators, and professionals who can help each other to flourish (Reupert et al., 2022). Through working in partnership, we can all be drivers of change. We therefore each hold some responsibility for not only the way we treat others, but also the need to hold other members of our 'village' accountable.
    The 'Shifting the Dial' programme in Birmingham appears to be an example of such partnership working. Commissioned in 2018, this three-year pilot aimed to support the mental health of young Black men (Abdinasir & Carty, 2021). An evaluation of the programme offers support for such initiatives, finding that attendees experienced increases

in skills, confidence, and their well-being (Harris & Abdinasir, 2022). This project appears to highlight the need for consistent and long-term funding opportunities in order to deliver lasting change.

2. *Empowering Black men*

Until we appreciate the intersectionality of what it means for him to be Black and a male, we cannot meet him where he is (Franklin, 1999). This might raise queries about what this could look like in practice. Below are some tools and reflections to guide further thinking.

He leads:

When it comes to sharing his experience as a Black man, empower him to be in control over how much, or how little he shares. At the same time, remain engaged with whatever he decides. Asking him what he would find helpful could be one of the most liberating gestures you could offer.

Build an alliance:

Much of my work as a psychologist is contingent upon how I relate to my clients, and how they relate to me. In the therapy space, whilst my knowledge of theory and skill is imperative, this is not the cornerstone of my practice. In other words, I do not approach therapy from a position of insight simply because of my training. Instead, I endeavour to meet the other where they are, and we embark upon their journey from that starting point. This oversimplified way of considering my practice is offered in order to highlight how the way we consider ourselves (and therefore others), can affect what we are able to achieve together.

Reconstructing the construction:

Unfortunately, some reductionistic constructions assigned to us can permeate into our being, to the point where we start to believe (and possibly enact) what has been spoken onto us. Instead of aligning their thinking to these biases, the following questions are designed to help Black men delve deeper into their personal experiences:

Where has this (negative/problematic) thought come from?

How does this make me feels emotionally and/or physically?

In what way does my reality (as a Black man) differ from the way I am being portrayed?

Whilst these questions are useful for Black men to ask of themselves when critically interrogating what society has said about who they are. They can also be adapted and used by others to explore the impact of discrimination on Black men.

3. *Cultural humility*

Sometimes we overestimate how much we know, which can serve as a barrier to working alongside Black men (and anyone really). We can be so fixed on confirming our own hypotheses that we become blind to the person before us. For these reasons adopting a position of cultural humility can help when working with Black men. Tervalon and Murray-García (1998) defined cultural humility as "a lifelong commitment to self-evaluation and self-critique" with the intention of rectifying power imbalances and working in partnership with others (p. 117). This involves learning about the culture of others but starting from a place of examining one's own beliefs and values. Through adopting a cultural humility framework, the individual recognises that sustaining change is an ongoing process, which draws upon their enduring commitment to learning about themselves and others (Tervalon & Murray-García, 1998). In practice, it is important that we constantly seek to understand the individual through clarification, and not let prior experience or expectation interfere with the work that needs to be done. Essentially, the key here is to act from a position of humility, which might be a shift of position from 'I know what to do' to asking him 'can we think together about what to do?' A way to help services develop familiarity with this practice is to offer spaces for skills acquisition and refining, such as clinical supervision and reflective practice.

4. *Innovative investing*

I call on the government and community leaders to provide sufficient investment for tailored and culturally responsive mental health support for Black men. This is to include national campaigns targeted at raising awareness of Black men's mental health and increased treatment options available. One such offering is the 'Young Black Men and Mental Health' programme, launched in 2022 by Islington Council and partnering organisations. One aspect of this three-year project includes training staff at selected barbershops in the borough to recognise if a customer might be struggling with his mental health and signpost him to appropriate support. I consider this to be a good example of responsive investing in areas of influence for Black men. Anecdotally, my understanding is that the barbershop can be a place of great significance to a Black man, with some prepared to travel far and wide to be seen by his chosen barber. I believe this is because the barber/customer relationship is one that is built on trust and loyalty, which can continue over many years. Through the development of this alliance, the customer may offer the barber insights into his internal world, which might give way to emotional well-being issues being voiced. If the barber feels equipped to offer support, this may help his customer feel more comfortable and develop greater confidence in discussing mental health concerns. This in turn may not only support the emotional well-being of Black men, but it could also go some way towards rewriting the narrative about Black men's aptitude in relation to exploring their mental health and well-being.

These guiding principles speak to the point that there is still work to do in the quest for equitable treatment for Black men. In the book Black Fatigue, Winters (2020) defines this concept as "repeated variations of stress that results in extreme exhaustion and causes mental, physical and spiritual maladies that are passed down from generation to generation" (p. 1). This definition is a reminder for us all that racial discrimination has a cumulative effect on Black men (and Black people as a whole), because they already bear the scars of racist abuse. Therefore, rather than trying to mitigate, minimise or meander racism, it is necessary to realise that we all have a part to play in rectifying this injustice.

Chapter questions to provoke thoughts:

1. How do you respond when you witness racial discrimination?
2. What biases or beliefs do you hold about Black men?
3. In your community, what practices are currently hindering racial equity for Black men?
4. How have others (e.g. people you know, the media and society) impacted the way you perceive Black men?
5. What can you do to promote racial equity for Black men?

References

Abdinasir, K., & Carty, S. (2021). *Young Black men's mental health during COVID-19. Experiences from the shifting the dial project.* Centre for Mental Health. https://www.centreformentalhealth.org.uk/sites/default/files/publication/download/CentreforMentalHealth_ShiftingTheDial_YBM_Covid_0.pdf

Bernard, J. (2019). Treddin' on thin ice. In D. Owusu (Ed.), *Safe* (pp. 71–80). Trapeze.

Dare, O., Jidong, D. E., & Premkumar, P. (2023). Conceptualising mental illness among university students of African, Caribbean and similar ethnic heritage in the United Kingdom. *Ethnicity & Health, 28*(4), 522–543.

Darko, J. (2021). How can general practice improve the mental health care experience of Black men in the UK? *British Journal of General Practice, 71*(704), 124–125.

Department of Health. (1983). *Mental Health Act.* https://www.legislation.gov.uk/ukpga/1983/20

Department of Health. (2023). *Detentions under the Mental Health Act.* https://www.ethnicity-facts-figures.service.gov.uk/health/mental-health/detentions-under-the-mental-health-act/6.0

Franklin, A. J. (1999). Invisibility syndrome and racial identity development in psychotherapy and counseling African American men. *The Counseling Psychologist, 27*(6), 761–793.

Harris, P., & Abdinasir, K. (2022). *Shifting the dial: Evaluating a community programme to promote young Black men's mental health.* Centre for Mental Health. https://www.centreformentalhealth.org.uk/sites/default/files/publication/download/CentreforMentalHealth_ShiftingTheDial_PDF.pdf

Haslam, N., & Loughnan, S. (2014). Dehumanization and infrahumanization. *Annual Review of Psychology, 65,* 399–423.

Hines, E. M., Fletcher, E. C. Jr, Ford, D. Y., & Moore, J. L. III (2021). Preserving innocence: Ending perceived adultification and toxic masculinity toward Black boys. *Journal of Family Strengths, 21*(1), 1.

Home Office. (2022). *Police use of force statistics, England and Wales: April 2021 to March 2022.* https://www.gov.uk/government/statistics/police-use-of-force-statistics-england-and-wales-april-2021-to-march-2022/police-use-of-force-statistics-england-and-wales-april-2021-to-march-2022#use-of-force-incidents-and-tactics

Hooks, B. (2004). *We real cool: Black men and masculinity.* Routledge.

Jones, C. P. (2000). Levels of racism: A theoretic framework and A gardener's tale. *American Journal of Public Health, 90*(8), 1212.

Kapadia, D., Zhang, J., Salway, S., Nazroo, J., Booth, A., Villarroel-Williams, N., Becares, L., & Esmail, A. (2022). *Ethnic inequalities in healthcare: A rapid review.* NHS Race & Health Observatory. https://www.nhsrho.org/wp-content/uploads/2022/02/RHO-Rapid-Review-Final-Report_v.7.pdf

Liverpool, S., Prescod, J., Pereira, B., & Trotman, C. (2023). Prevalence of mental health and behaviour problems among adolescents in the English-speaking Caribbean: Systematic review and meta-analysis. *Discover Mental Health, 3*(1), 11.

Nicholas, A., Joshua, O., & Elizabeth, O. (2022). Accessing mental health services in Africa: Current state, efforts, challenges and recommendation. *Annals of Medicine and Surgery, 81,* 104421.

Ogueji, I. A., & Okoloba, M. M. (2022). Seeking professional help for mental illness: A mixed-methods study of Black family members in the UK and Nigeria. *Psychological Studies, 67,* 164–177.

Oh, R. (2020). Black citizenship, dehumanization, and the Fourteenth Amendment. *Law Faculty Articles and Essays,* 1202. https://engagedscholarship.csuohio.edu/fac_articles/1202

Poussaint, A. F. (1966). The negro American: His self-image and integration. *Journal of the National Medical Association, 58*(6), 419.

Reupert, A., Straussner, S. L., Weimand, B., & Maybery, D. (2022). It takes a village to raise a child: Understanding and expanding the concept of the "village". *Frontiers in Public Health, 10,* 424.

Tervalon, M., & Murray-García, J. (1998). Cultural humility versus cultural competence: A critical distinction in defining physician training outcomes in multicultural education. *Journal of Health Care for the Poor and Underserved, 9,* 117–125.

Time to Change. (2016). *300 Voices Toolkit. Better must come: Towards hope.* https://www.mind.org.uk/media-a/4301/time-to-change-300-voices-toolkit-comp.pdf

Waytz, A., Hoffman, K. M., & Trawalter, S. (2015). A superhumanization bias in Whites' perceptions of Blacks. *Social Psychological and Personality Science, 6*(3), 352–359.

Wilson, J. P., Hugenberg, K., & Rule, N. O. (2017). Racial bias in judgments of physical size and formidability: From size to threat. *Journal of Personality and Social Psychology, 113*(1), 59.

Winters, M. F. (2020). *Black fatigue: How racism erodes the mind, body, and spirit.* Berrett-Koehler Publishers.

Working with women of colour

12

Mou Sultana

Overview

This chapter aims to discuss some of the major clinical considerations when working therapeutically with "women of colour" (WOC). First, there needs to be a discussion on what do we really mean by WOC and how do we define this term? The chapter will then highlight some considerations on guiding documents when entering this field; provide some guidance on theoretical lens most appropriate to this field as well as suggest practical points to be mindful of.

The chapter then provides a snapshot of the most common difficulties and barriers experienced by WOC that add to the layers of complexities to unpack in therapy. Towards the end, there is a short case study positioned to illustrate the major messages of the chapter in practice. Finally, the chapter highlights some of the major risks to be considered when working with WOC that make them one of the most vulnerable populations.

Defining "women of colour"

The term "women of colour" is meant to be an inclusive and broad descriptor that refers to women who belong to racial or ethnic groups that are non-white or primarily of European descent. It is a term used to

DOI: 10.4324/9781003415244-15

acknowledge and highlight the diversity of women from various non-white racial and ethnic backgrounds. "Women of colour" or WOC is defined by the European Network Against Racism (2017) in the following way:

> Women of colour is a term used to describe women of racial, ethnic and religious minority backgrounds; women who are not white; or women who experience racism. The term "woman" is used here to include all those self-identifying as women and is deliberately inclusive of members of the non-binary and transgender communities. (p. 3)

There are some major issues in this definition. Consider the following questions. By writing "… women who are not white" is this definition suggesting that the phrase WOC does not refer to "White Women"? If so, why did the definition not write "white women are not WOC"? Is that too blunt? Too triggering for some? Is White not a colour? Many would argue it is.

In American standards and in most western countries it is a common perspective to hold for many women who are White, that colour does not exist. They may consider themselves as colour blind. For them, race is not an issue and a White person, or a person of colour may seem the same. While this type of thinking may come from a seemingly good place or a place of "justice and equality for all", colour-blindness however is a highly problematic phenomenon for several reasons. Only a few are mentioned here within the context of this discussion.

This view ignores the obstacles on the way for a woman of colour to achieve the same (or even close enough) as their White counterpart. Meaning, historic, and contextual inequalities are not acknowledged or understood appropriately through these lenses. This comes with the risk of disproportionate prioritising of personal accountability/responsibility and minimising/ignoring systemic oppression. Moreover, colour-blindness often comes from a place of and highlights, privilege. Privilege is when one can afford to ignore or minimise or deny a problem, mainly because one is not personally effected by the problem. Especially in the world of therapy, this becomes a major issue. There is nothing more painful for WOC than to experience their White therapist as someone who does not see colour at all due to their own privilege. There is nothing more discouraging for WOC clients than to experience a therapist who is colour-blind because they are not able to put themselves in the client's shoes enough to even consider that their colour may be a problem. WOC are more likely to refuse to go to therapy or ignore the sufferings they are experiencing, and there are more barriers for them to overcome before they end up in front of a therapist (Jiménez, 2023; Kant et al., 2023; Nelson et al., 2020; Richards, 2021; Smalls, 2022; Smith et al., 2023). It is our ethical duty as Counselling Psychologists, Applied Psychologists and therapists to create an encouraging and inviting place for WOC. However, just a seemingly "good intention" such as "I don't see colour" or a slight internal struggle with the mention of the term "white women" may hinder our therapeutic alliance.

Although many well-meaning people who are not persons of colour will believe that the world is a level playing field and everyone has a fair game, in reality, WOC and White women do not experience the world in the same way. Any therapist who operates from a position of colour-blindness will struggle to build therapeutic alliance with their WOC clients. But that leads us to another question. Is "white women" a phrase that has the potential to trigger those who are White and women? After all, in recent times, author Saira Rao's account was deactivated by the social media company LinkedIn apparently for using the phrase "white women", which is also the title of her New York Times best-selling book published by Penguin and co-authored by Regina Jackson (Brownlee, 2022). The Forbes article on this issue clarified the following (Brownlee, 2022):

> While many will say it's not the phrase itself that's problematic; it's the context, is it really? Or is there something particularly triggering about simply naming white women as a particular group of people as we would any other people – single moms, older Americans, finance professionals, wealthy Republicans, Black fathers, Asian teachers, Catholic youth, heterosexual men, Italian immigrants, Asian women or Jewish faith leaders for example?

Let's add "Black women", "Chinese women", "Arabic women" to that list. Many White women are comfortable saying these terms but being called a "white women" may leave them with an uncomfortable feeling. For a therapist it is essential that they question themselves and monitor their own reaction to the phrase "white women". If this chapter is about working with WOC, then it is crucial to consider our own response to the phrase "white women", especially if we are White, because we are not WOC. Yet the definition did not use this phrase. Notice the subtle struggle to be inclusive continues in the next piece of the definition, "… or women who experience racism". What does that mean? Are we referring to those who experience racism due to their religion or ethnic minority background? Can that be a white woman? Can white women experience racism? If they can, do they become WOC? If they can't become WOC just because they experience racism, and we agree that racism is only experienced by WOC, then why this seeming hesitation in this definition to ignore the term "white women" and an apparent attempt to fit everyone in this definition despite their race? It is important that we note these difficulties and discomfort even in the literature that is meant to help us understand these subtle nuances. Hence, as therapists and Applied Psychologists working with WOC, we must first and foremost observe our own internal and external reactions to this division and the type of labelling such as WOC and "white women".

Women of colour can encompass a wide range of identities, including but not limited to African American, Latina, Native American, Asian American, Pacific Islander, Middle Eastern, and multiracial women, among others. Please note that the term WOC is not limited to any specific culture or ethnicity and is used as a way to promote inclusivity and recognise the shared experiences of women from diverse racial and ethnic backgrounds. The term is often used in discussions related to social justice, intersectionality, and feminism to emphasise the unique experiences and challenges faced by women who belong to marginalised racial or ethnic groups. Professor Loretta Ross (Womenofcolour.org.au, 2023) explained the following:

> Women of Colour is not a biological designation. It is a solidarity definition. A commitment to work in collaboration with other oppressed women of colour who have been minoritized. It is a term that has a lot of power.

This term goes beyond the biological destination. Being Black, Asian, African American, Caribbean can be one's choice of identity based on their "biology". Professor Ross (Womenofcolour.org.au, 2023) clarified that this is "primitive ethnic claiming". Whereas WOC refers to a "political designation" (Womenofcolour.org.au, 2023). Professor Ross did so by focussing on the following aspect (Womenofcolour.org.au, 2023):

> … when you choose to work with other people who are minoritised by oppression, you've lifted yourself out of that basic identity into another political being and another political space.

However, individual preferences for this terminology do vary. This is why it is always good practice to be respectful and use the language preferred by the individuals or groups you are addressing when discussing issues related to race and identity.

Where do we start learning?

At present, there is no formal guideline for working with WOC. The American Psychological Association (APA) in 2018 published Guidelines for Psychological Practice with Girls and Women. Then in 2019, the APA published Guidelines on Race and Ethnicity in Psychology. The combined content of these documents intersects in some areas providing some insight into WOC's mental health needs. However, they are inadequate. Prior to these publications, the European Network Against Racism (ENAR) in 2017 published a toolkit titled "Women of Colour in the Workplace" at the nineth European Equal@Work Seminar. This official document seems to have researched the topic of WOC in-depth from a non-psychological aspect. There are plenty of literature available exploring and critiquing sociological perspectives of WOC's existence and experience (Collins-Hill, 1990; Mirza, 1997; Rothenberg, 2000; Spivak, 1999; Tizard & Phoenix, 1993; Young, 1994). When it comes to the discipline of Counselling Psychology, one needs to go beyond the formal documents, engage with cross-disciplinary literature, and start learning about the historical and sociological context that are sometimes highly nuanced and invisible. Working with WOC requires engaging with literature that are written by experts by experience (Brah & Phoenix, 2004; Mirza 2015, 2022; Smiet, 2020). Voices that are otherwise discarded should be the major source for any Applied Psychologist trying to understand WOC's needs. Only when we begin to pay attention to this topic in this way, will it slowly become clearer that there is not just gender or race to be considered here, but rather sexuality, class, age, ability, religion, and number of other factors that interplay.

Working with intersectionality in mind

Gender, sexuality, race, class, religion are not topics that fit into distinct boxes, they are not separate experiences, rather they are problematically interconnected, contradictory at times, and produces conflicting results both in the intrapersonal and the interpersonal sphere. This is the realm of intersectionality. The concept of intersectionality is a good place to start from when thinking about positioning oneself in relation to this topic.

When considering intersectionality, the following needs to be spelled out:

> When race and gender are conceptualised as separate and independent from each other there is a tendency for the most powerful members of marginalised groups, in this case, White women and Black men – to universalise themselves and their particular experiences and position themselves as the only legitimate representatives of the group as a whole.
>
> (Christoffersen & Emejulu, 2023, p. 632)

The above is meant to be a reminder that research on intersectionality often does not capture experiences of WOC especially because there seems to be a generalised division in thinking of marginalisation as "white women" and "black men". Intersectionality research especially conducted by white feminist scholars and researchers tend to reflect intersectionality as "powerful academic appropriation", as part of "white feminist theory" (Christoffersen & Emejulu, 2023). The construct of "women" in intersectional research is often already "white". In the UK, majority of issues that are addressed in intersectional research and projects are often conducted by those influenced by white feminist theories. They tend to mainly focus on disabled women or Lesbian, Gay, Bisexual, Transgender (LGBT) women (Christoffersen & Emejulu, 2022). The following is an excerpt of one of the most powerful speech in human rights delivered by Isabella Baumfree in 1851 (NPS.gov, 2024). It captures the blatant fact that black women aren't treated equally compared to white women, as if they are "less" women. A discrimination that still exists today in 2024 in several degrees across the globe in forms of stereotypes of "black angry woman" or "strong black woman".

> That man over there says that women need to be helped into carriages, and lifted over ditches, and to have the best place everywhere. Nobody ever helps me into carriages, or over mud-puddles, or gives me any best place! And ain't I a woman? Look at me! Look at my arm! I have ploughed and planted, and gathered into barns, and no man could head me! And ain't I a woman? I could work as much and eat as much as a man – when I could get it – and bear the lash as well! And ain't I a woman? I have borne thirteen children, and seen most all sold off to slavery, and when I cried out with my mother's grief, none but Jesus heard me! And ain't I a woman?

The question of racism mixed with sexism, creates a unique marginalised position of oppression for WOC. The existence of inequal institutional structures and other barriers are often missed by those who are not WOC. Applying intersectionality to the therapeutic setting is essential because it allows the therapist to recognise this aspect of WOC's experience that otherwise gets omitted.

Extra layers of complexities

There are several reasons why WOC would attend therapy and each client has a different unique reason for seeking support. Moreover, each session with each client can be different as they may reveal distinct aspects of their stories and struggles. Uniqueness of human subjectivity is one of the major factors that makes it impossible to ever identify a one-size-fits-all step-by-step guide to delivering therapy. WOC are no exception. Every WOC has a unique story to tell, and they experience the world uniquely. Hence, it is impossible to provide a standard framework that will fit the needs of every WOC. However, systematically approaching the goals in hand may help us understand the major factors that one needs to consider when providing therapy. In other words, identifying the major issues that most WOC attend therapy to resolve may help us recognise the most common barriers they experience that contribute to their difficulties and misery.

Let's begin with outlining some of the major reasons why WOC may seek therapy: Mild to moderate mental health difficulties such as symptoms of anxiety and depression, diagnosis of PTSD, mood disorders, personality disorders, neurodiverse diagnosis, eating disorder, phobia, trauma and substance abuse, mood regulation, anger management, grief and loss, personal development and growth related difficulties, confidence, identity, time management, life stages transition, parenting, ageing, family related issues, relationship difficulties, work or career related issues, stress management, and many more.

Anyone experiencing the above difficulties will have their own set of personal, historical, circumstantial, environmental, and some level of systemic barriers. But WOC experiencing these issues will have further barriers and layers of complexities that require intersectional approaches to understand them. As a rule of thumb, when working with WOC the therapist must be mindful of the following five major pointers.

1. The whole picture: Within the context of therapy, the biggest barriers experienced by WOC are not just personal, circumstantial, and environmental but predominantly their barriers have a larger historical context: Systemic and institutional oppression and inequalities.
2. Invisible barriers: In most cases, these barriers may not seem visible from the outset like they would in the cases of other clients. This is because systemic and institutional contributing elements remain invisible unless one knows where to look.
3. Sociologically informed: Power operates stronger when invisible. One needs to be aware of the invisible power that is in operation or the lack of it when working with WOC. Power that has deprived WOC of privileges that others who are not WOC are not deprived of. Cross-disciplinary theories of power are needed here to conceptualise this

phenomenon. For example, using the Foucauldian theory of power one can argue that biopower and disciplinary power are less visible and more powerful than sovereign power. Power that are in operation and that contribute to the felt sense of disempowerment of WOC, may remain invisible to the naked eye unless one uses the intersectionality lenses, and they are sociologically informed.

4. Willingness to learn from the client: Intersectional perspective and sociological awareness may help the therapist understand the most common barriers that contribute to the struggles of WOC. However, the majority of the barriers that a WOC face on a regular basis in their social, occupational, domestic sphere, and in their internal world will require more than intersectional lenses and sociologically informed therapy. The most important prerequisite to understand and recognise these barriers is the therapist's willingness to learn from the client about the phenomena of being a woman of colour and how they experience the world, even when the psychologist is themselves a woman of colour. The psychologist's sense of humility to accept that they do not know the whole story even though it may seem familiar. That no matter how similar these barriers may seem, there are always going to be extra layers of unique subjective complexities adding to the WOC's difficulties.

5. Awareness of own limitation: On the other hand, the psychologist's willingness to be aware of their own limitation is another prerequisite. For them to be humble enough to acknowledge that this is about sufferings and experiences that they themselves may never have and never will be able to understand completely because they are not WOC themselves. Hence, what is needed the most in a therapeutic setting is the therapist's intention to want to learn and to not assume that they know what it means to be, to function and to survive as a WOC.

Perils

While there is a higher risk of experiencing mental health difficulties for WOC, they are also less likely to seek help or mental health care in comparison to their White counterparts. The following section outlines the most common risk factors, stressors, barriers that WOC can experience with the aim to provide a picture of their journey before, during and after therapy.

Throughout a WOC's life including childhood and teenage years they experience microaggressions. According to the APA Dictionary (n.d), microaggression is described as:

> …commonly occurring, brief, verbal or nonverbal, behavioural, and environmental indignities that communicate derogatory attitudes or notions toward a different "other." Microaggressions may be intentional or unintentional, and the perpetrators may possibly be unaware of their behaviour. Microaggressions can cause recipients to feel that they are abnormal, inferior, invisible, powerless, or untrustworthy, and can accumulate over time and lead to severe harm.

Experiencing microaggressions throughout their life can make some of them become almost numb to criticism, becoming stronger and tougher! Which is another stereotype that black women may experience on a regular basis – strong black woman! Strong black woman encompassing someone who absorbs all pain, protects, shields, continues on despite everything, self-sufficient, internalising a sense of responsibility for others. Strong black woman is also expected to be a nurturer, carer, and an endless provider of love. However, if they are too strong, they may be labelled as the "angry black woman". If they are too tolerant, they face the risk of being seen as "weak". So, while they may experience frustration much more so than White women due to these added expectations and microaggressions, they also have to manage their emotions internally a lot more because of the judgements. The expectations from family and culture tend to pigeonhole them (Pappas, 2021).

WOC are expected to strike a balance between predetermined conflicting and contradictory gender roles. This is a recipe for experiencing burnout, exhaustion, stress, guilt, shame, feeling of inadequacy, fear of not getting it right, and anxiety. At the same time, WOC also tend to be sexualised and objectified early on in life, especially young black girls. This adds to the construction of a negative self-perception and experiencing internal shame among several other detrimental effects on their mental health, making them more susceptible to have a history of trauma, abuse, and neglect.

There is a general lack of representations of WOC in mostly every field of life. Hence, there is a lack of role model for WOC to look up to. Those who dare to dream have to also be fortunate to get access to education, lack of access to education is a major barrier for WOC. If after all these they manage to get qualifications, WOC may become very aware that they have unequal access to the labour market. This is on top of managing their household duties, childcare, eldercare, and other culture and gender specific expectations. Some WOC may try to mitigate this by achieving excellence in education and training. Immigrant WOC may need to retrain in their new country as their previous qualification may not seem "enough". This leads to over qualifications, which may then be used against them, and they miss out on opportunities further. Many WOC accept roles that are under-paid, accepting de-skilling, and most of the times accepting significant pay-gaps. They experience racism, sexism, gender-bias, and classism. If they are young and excelling at their roles, they experience microaggression rooted in ageism on top of sexism and racism. If the WOC is a less able-bodied person then add ableism to that list of their experience.

Case study

Faduma is a 28-year-old Black female lawyer seeking therapy. Her presenting symptom is anxiety. She is 1 of 4 children, born in Somalia and immigrated to the UK at age 15. She attended secondary school and went on to study law. She currently works as a lawyer and is training to be a barrister. In expanding her reasons for seeking therapy, Faduma said she needed to learn coping strategies to manage the overwhelming sense of anxiety and a feeling of "I am not good enough". These presenting issues may indicate that Faduma needs a type of therapy or therapeutic approach that is aimed at helping her build resilience and boost her confidence.

Therapies such as cognitive behavioural therapy (CBT), mindfulness-based cognitive therapy (MBCT), and acceptance and commitment therapy (ACT) might seem appropriate in this case. While these approaches may certainly help with confidence boosting, the major rationale behind these theories may be interpreted in the following way:

1. There may be a lack of evidence that Faduma's fear or anxiety arose from external factors.
2. There may not be actual evidence of Faduma being perceived as "not good enough". Hence, these feelings may be arising due to Faduma's distorted sense of reality.
3. Faduma's perceived reality is not reflective of actual reality.

On the basis of these interpretations, the goal may thus be to work on cognitive distortions and inner beliefs to make them aligned with Faduma's external reality.

A therapist operating from the above position will have a partial view of the situation. In that case, the therapist is not on the same page as Faduma.

This will act as a barrier in building therapeutic alliance. This is because it is not just a question of cognitive distortion or reality check. "Reality" for the therapist will be quite different to Faduma's, especially if the therapist is a White female or even a Black male.

In reality, every room that Faduma has ever entered, her credibility and worth have been immediately questioned. She has experienced microaggressions at every junction of her life and in between. At the beginning, she perhaps did not comprehend that her value as a human may drop immediately due to the colour of her skin, the texture of her hair, the sound of her accent, or anything else. But the invisible and sometimes not so subtle dynamics around her, has taught her otherwise over time.

Each room she enters now, she prepares for a fall. She makes sure that she excels in everything she works on just to avoid any added factors that can put her credibility up for questioning. She has worked three times harder than her white counterpart just to get the minimal respect that a human deserves, a place where her worth is not up for questioning as soon as she enters a room. But it does not work. She cannot fight the reactions or ideas that people have to/about her even before she walks in the room – the stereotypes and the biases. The sound of her name is enough to trigger them. A lot of decisions about her in this way are often made "unofficially" before she even gets the chance to walk in the room. Whether it is school, college, job interviews, internships, entry exam, law training, or barrister exam. Faduma has internalised how she is not good enough in some people's eyes, sometimes even before they have seen or heard her. This is not a cognitive distortion. This is her reality! The barriers that she faces are racism, sexism, gender bias, stereotype bias, microaggression, inequalities, less opportunities than her white counterpart, and many more. These barriers are not going to disappear with reality testing. But the therapist's willingness to recognise these struggles, explore these experiences and wish to learn about these invisible dynamics may help Faduma be seen and heard for who she is – perhaps for the first time.

The biggest barrier for Faduma in therapy will be if her therapist does not know how to manage their own anxiety while Faduma tells her story and describes her distress. In particular, and in the absence of the therapist exploring their own positioning in relation to the terms "white women" and/or "white folks", they may react defensively to Faduma if she uses these terms. Hence, therapists willing to ethically practice with WOC need to attend regular supervision and personal therapy where they will be given the chance to open up and understand their own position and biases.

Conclusion

It is hoped that the world of therapy will become more welcoming and aligned to the needs of WOC clients in the recent future. Representation matters and hence more WOC therapists need to be involved in both service delivery and planning. Despite all the progress we have made as a human race, stigma still remains one of the biggest barriers. One can only hope that more engagement, partnership, and open dialogue with the WOC community will help address this issue. Above all, we remain hopeful of a brighter future where white women and WOC will be treated equally as women unlike Sojourner's experience captured in her speech from 1851.

Chapter questions to provoke thoughts:

1. Does the term "white women" elicit discomfort for you?
2. "I am already familiar with psychological research literature, I am well informed, but have I considered the accounts of experts by experience?". Are current published psychological articles enough to inform the practice of work with WOC?
3. Is intersectional thinking enough in informing the work with WOC?
4. How do you tell and interpret the stories WOC share with you?

References

American Psychological Association. (n.d.). Microaggressions. In *APA dictionary of psychology.* Retrieved April 15, 2024, from https://dictionary.apa.org/just-world-hypothesis.

Brah, A., & Phoenix, A. (2004). Ain't I a woman? Revisiting intersectionality. *Journal of International Women Studies, 5*(3), 75–86.

Brownlee, D. (2022, December 27). Why is the phrase "White Women" triggering for many White women? *Forbes.* https://www.forbes.com/sites/danabrownlee/2022/12/27/why-is-the-phrase-white-women-triggering-for-many-white-women/

Christoffersen, A., & Emejulu, A. (2023). "Diversity within": The problems with "Intersectional" White feminism in practice. *Social Politics: International Studies in Gender, State & Society, 30*(2), 630–653. https://doi.org/10.1093/sp/jxac044

Collins-Hill, P. (1990). *Black feminist thought.* Unwin Hyam.

European Network Against Racism. (2017). Women of colour in the workplace. https://www.enar-eu.org/wp-content/uploads/20112_equal_work_2018_lr.pdf

Jiménez, N. (2023, January 30). Is Irish psychotherapy falling short of racial and ethnic inclusion? *The Irish Times.* https://www.irishtimes.com/health/your-wellness/2023/01/30/is-irish-psychotherapy-falling-short-of-racial-and-ethnic-inclusion/

Kant, T., Sorkhou, M., De La Cruz, G., Katz, J. L., Sharif-Razi, M., & George, T. P. (2023, July 5). Mental health care for women of color: Risk factors, barriers, and clinical recommendations. *Psychiatric Times.* https://www.psychiatrictimes.com/view/mental-health-care-for-women-of-color-risk-factors-barriers-and-clinical-recommendations

Mirza, S. (1997). *Black British feminism*. Routledge.

Nelson, T., Shahid, N. N., & Cardemil, E. V. (2020). Do I really need to go and see somebody? Black women's perceptions of help-seeking for depression. *Journal of Black Psychology*, 46(4), 263–286. https://doi.org/10.1177/0095798420931644

NPS.Gov. (2024). Sojourner truth: Ain't I A woman? (U.S. National Park Service). https://www.nps.gov/articles/sojourner-truth.htm

Pappas, S. (2021). *Effective therapy with Black women. Monitor.* American Psychological Association. https://www.apa.org/monitor/2021/11/ce-therapy-black-women

Richards, E. (2021, September 23). The state of mental health of Black women: Clinical considerations. *Psychiatric Times*, 38(9), 14–15.

Rothenberg, P. (2000). *Invisible privilege*. University of Kansas Press.

Smalls, K. (2022). *African American women's perspectives on mental health (thesis)*. Philadelphia College of Osteopathic Medicine Psychology Dissertations, 588.

Smiet, K. (2020). *Sojourner truth and intersectionality: Traveling truths in feminist scholarship* (1st ed.). Routledge.

Smith, L. D., Minton, C. A., Taylor, L., & Price, E. W. (2023). Seeking counseling services: A phenomenological study of African American women. *Journal of African American Studies*, 27(3), 251–267. https://doi.org/10.1007/s12111-023-09631-8

Spivak, G. C. (1999). *A critique of postcolonial reason: Towards a history of vanishing present*. Harvard University Press.

Tizard, B., & Phoenix, A. (1993). *Black, White or mixed race?: Race and racism in the lives of young people of mixed parentage* (2nd ed.). Routledge.

Womenofcolour.org.au. (2023). *Women of colour phrase origin*. https://womenofcolour.org.au/the-origin-of-the-phrase-women-of-color/

Young, L. (1994). *Fear of the dark*. Routledge.

Working with older adults of colour 13

Natalie V. Bailey

Overview

This chapter, grounded in Counselling Psychology, offers an insightful exploration into the mental health experiences of older Black Caribbean adults in the United Kingdom. As one of the largest and longest-established ethnic minority groups in the country, their narratives are rich and multifaceted, yet often underrepresented in mainstream discourse. Although this chapter is centred on older Black Caribbean adults, the insights offered may resonate with other older adults of colour, each navigating their individual cultural and historical contexts.

The chapter's narrative is shaped using Interpretative Phenomenological Analysis (Smith et al., 2009), which delves into personal stories that reveal not only the challenges but also the often-unspoken psychological impacts of ageing in an adopted land. Throughout the chapter, reflective questions are strategically embedded in the narrative, inviting readers to engage deeply with the content. These questions are designed to prompt critical thoughts and to consider the broader implications for Counselling Psychology practice and research. This chapter is not merely about understanding the experiences of these individuals; it is an empathetic journey into their complex realities, aiming to contribute valuable perspectives and insights to learners, practitioners, and researchers in the field of mental health.

DOI: 10.4324/9781003415244-16

Meryl's story: Resilience and struggle in diaspora

Our exploration begins with the story of Meryl (Figure 13.1), who at 72, carries the wisdom of her years with grace. Her story, like a tapestry, is interwoven with vibrant threads of joy, resilience, and silent struggles. Born under the warm Caribbean sun, Meryl's life took a dramatic turn when she arrived in London in her late teens. This wasn't merely a change in geography; it was a journey into a world where every step was a negotiation between her past and an unfamiliar present.

"In the Caribbean, our struggles were like the heat – ever-present but seldom spoken of," Meryl recalls, her voice, a blend of warmth, and sorrow.

"Depression and mental struggles were like a persistent mist over London streets, quiet and unnoticed, yet ever-present in our lives." Meryl's journey through life in the United Kingdom was marked not just by the struggle to adapt but also by the silent battles against the invisible weight of unspoken mental health challenges.

Meryl's narrative is a window into the soul of the older Black Caribbean community in the United Kingdom. Her transition from the vibrant landscapes of the Caribbean to the bustling, often grey streets of London was a testament to her resilience. "We wore masks," she explains, "masks woven from our strength and resilience, hiding our inner turmoil as we tried to fit into this new world." Her story echoes the experiences of many in her community – a narrative of adaptation, survival, and the constant juggle between cultural identity and adaptation.

Figure 13.1 "Meryl"

As she aged, the complexity of maintaining her cultural identity in a land that still felt foreign grew. Meryl speaks of the challenges faced by her generation – the longing for the familiar, the sense of displacement, and the resilience required to forge a life in a society vastly different from the one they left behind.

Meryl's journey is not just her own, but a reflection of a larger story shared by many older Black Caribbean adults. It sheds light on the crucial role mental health professionals play in recognising and addressing the unique needs of this community. "Our stories are not just about the struggles but also about the undying spirit of a community that has much to teach about resilience, adaptation, and the human experience," Meryl shares, her eyes shining with the wisdom of her years.

Meryl's story, enriched with personal experiences and emotional depth, invites readers to walk in her shoes, to feel the warmth of her Caribbean roots, and to understand the complexity of her life in the United Kingdom. It's a narrative that not only highlights the challenges but also celebrates the strength and spirit of older Black Caribbean adults, providing valuable insights for those working in the field of mental health.

Questions to provoke thoughts:

1. How do Meryl's experiences and coping mechanisms reflect the broader experiences of diaspora communities?
2. What role can mental health professionals play in understanding and addressing the impacts of migration on the mental health of older adults of colour?

The UK's Black Caribbean population

The UK's Black Caribbean population (Figure 13.2), one of the largest and longest-established ethnic minority groups, has made a significant impact on British culture and society. Yet, when it comes to mental health, they face unique challenges deeply rooted in their cultural and migratory history. Many Black Caribbean individuals migrated to the United Kingdom in the mid-20th century. This generation, now ageing, carries with it the dual experiences of adapting to a new society, and preserving their cultural identity (Bailey & Tribe, 2021; Williams et al., 2015).

The Black Caribbean community in the United Kingdom is observed to underutilise formal mental health services. This trend is influenced by factors such as cultural perceptions of mental health and the stigma associated with seeking professional help. Instead, there is a distinct

Figure 13.2 UK's Black Caribbean population

preference within this community for community-based support (Majors et al., 2020; Sainsbury Centre for Mental Health, 2002). This type of support often includes informal networks such as family, friends, and religious or community groups, which provide emotional and psychological support in more familiar and culturally resonant settings, as opposed to the structured environment of formal healthcare services.

Additionally, within the UK's Black Caribbean community, there is a prevalent 'coping' approach to mental health, characterised by individuals managing emotional and psychological challenges independently. Often, this results in delaying the seeking of professional help until a crisis situation arises. The reasons for this coping strategy are multifaceted, encompassing cultural norms that emphasise strength and self-reliance, historical mistrust towards formal healthcare systems, and a lack of awareness or understanding of mental health issues and available services (Majors et al., 2020; Sainsbury Centre for Mental Health, 2002).

For practitioners working with this population, identifying this coping approach necessitates a deep understanding of the cultural and historical context. It involves actively listening for cues during consultations that suggest a tendency to minimise or internalise struggles. Practitioners should also be cognisant of the reluctance to discuss mental health openly, which can be a significant barrier to early intervention. Building trust and rapport, employing culturally sensitive communication, and fostering an environment where discussing mental health is normalised and de-stigmatised are essential steps in effectively supporting this population.

The insights gained from understanding the mental health landscape of the UK's Black Caribbean population highlight the need for culturally attuned mental health services. These services must acknowledge the unique challenges faced by this community, including their coping strategies and preferences for community-based support. Recognising these factors is crucial in designing and delivering mental health care that is not only effective but also respectful of the community's cultural heritage and personal experiences. It's within this context that the story of George, a 76-year-old Black Caribbean man, becomes especially poignant. George's narrative exemplifies the resilience, coping mechanisms, and often unspoken struggles that are characteristic of his generation's experience in the United Kingdom. His journey sheds light on the complex interplay between cultural identity, ageing, and mental health within the Black Caribbean community.

George's story: Silent resilience and the unspoken struggles of the Black Caribbean community in the United Kingdom

George aged 76 (Figure 13.3), typifies this generation's experiences. Having migrated to the United Kingdom from the Caribbean in his youth, he recalls,

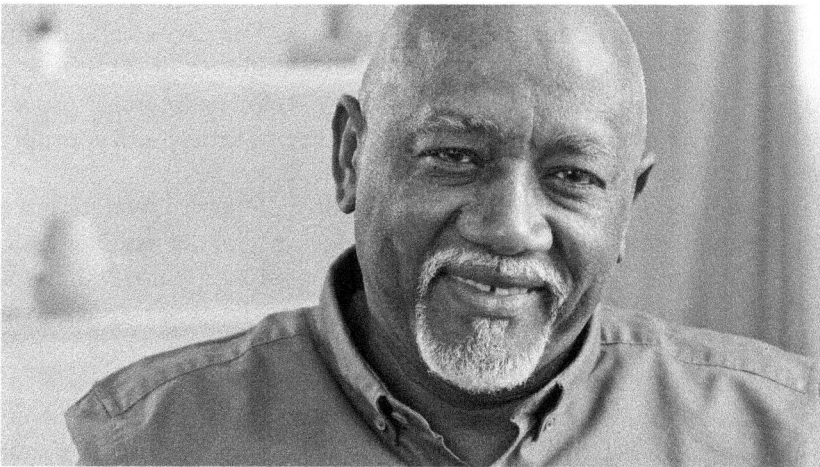

Figure 13.3 "George"

"We were taught to be strong, to keep our struggles to ourselves and to just get on with it." "Mental health was never a topic for open discussion in our community; it was a private affair."

George's reluctance to seek mental health support until a significant crisis is a pattern commonly observed among his peers. He notes, "We often turn to our church and community for support, rather than seeking formal mental health services." This statement underscores the community's reliance on faith and informal networks for emotional support.

In light of this, the role of the community and church becomes crucial in addressing mental health needs. These entities can play a pivotal role through co-production and collaboration with mental health services. Co-production involves the community and church actively participating in the design, implementation, and evaluation of mental health services. This collaboration ensures that the services are culturally sensitive and aligned with the community's needs and values.

Churches, often central to the community's life, can be instrumental in breaking down stigma associated with mental health. They can offer platforms for mental health awareness campaigns, facilitate conversations around mental health, and provide a supportive environment for those struggling with mental health issues.

Additionally, collaboration between mental health professionals and community leaders can lead to the development of tailored interventions. These interventions can integrate traditional support mechanisms with professional mental health services, offering a more holistic approach to mental health care.

Community-based workshops, support groups, and mental health literacy programmes, conducted in partnership with churches and community centres, can significantly enhance the community's understanding of mental health. They can also serve as a bridge to formal mental health services, ensuring that individuals like George receive timely and appropriate support.

Therefore, the church and community, through co-production and collaboration with mental health professionals, can play an essential role in enhancing mental health support for older adults of colour. This partnership ensures that their unique cultural and social needs are effectively addressed.

In summarising George's story and its broader implications, it becomes evident that addressing the mental health needs of older adults of colour, particularly within the Black Caribbean community, requires a nuanced and culturally aware approach. This approach should focus on reducing stigma, encouraging early intervention, and understanding the complex interplay of ageing, cultural identity, and mental health. Through collaboration with community and religious organisations, mental health professionals can develop strategies that are both effective and respectful of the community's unique cultural context. Thus, a commitment to cultural awareness and sensitivity becomes crucial in fostering a mental healthcare system that is both inclusive and responsive to the diverse needs of its users.

Questions to provoke thoughts:

1. What strategies can be implemented to reduce stigma and encourage early help-seeking behaviour within the Black Caribbean community?
2. What approaches can mental health professionals take to understand and address the intersecting challenges of ageing, cultural identity, and mental health among diverse older adults of colour?

Ageing in a new era: Understanding the rapid rise of an older diverse population

The global demographic landscape is witnessing a remarkable transformation: The population of older adults is expanding at an unprecedented rate. The United Nations' World Population Prospects (2019) project that by 2050, one in six people worldwide will be over the age of 65 (Figure 13.4). This shift is more pronounced in developed regions like Europe and North America, where one in four people could be in this age group. This demographic change is reshaping societal structures, necessitating adaptation in health care and mental health services to address the needs of this growing population.

In the United Kingdom, this demographic evolution is particularly noticeable. The Office for National Statistics (2019) documents a substantial increase in the number of older adults since the 1970s. As the number of individuals aged 65 and older surpasses that of younger age groups, the impact on health services, including mental health care, becomes increasingly significant. Among these older adults, individuals of colour, such as the Black Caribbean community, face unique challenges. Their experiences, often shaped by migration histories and cultural adjustments, add layers of complexity to their mental health needs.

Figure 13.4 Ageing in a new era

Winston's story: Navigating cultural identity and ageing

Winston, a 69-year-old Black Caribbean man (Figure 13.5), sits contemplatively, his eyes reflecting a lifetime of experience. "Aging in a foreign land," he begins, "is a journey marked by introspection and a deeper understanding

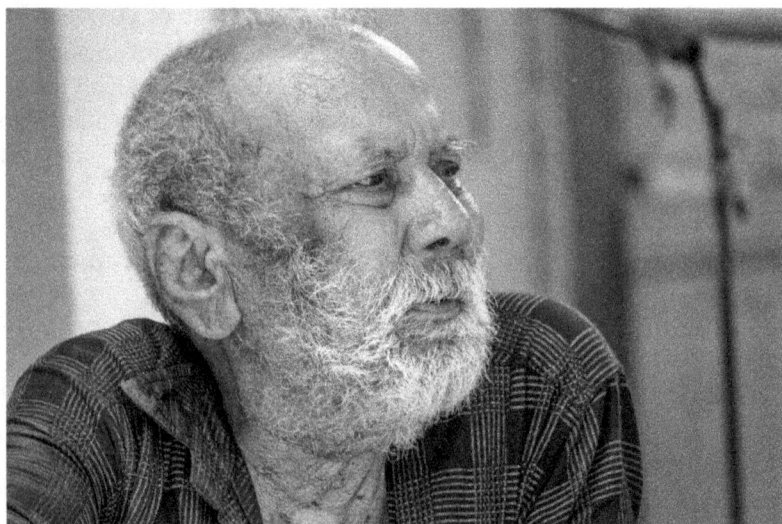

Figure 13.5 "Winston"

of one's identity." He shares how moving to the United Kingdom in his early 20s presented challenges that have evolved as he's grown older. "Back then, it was about building a life, finding my place. Now, it's about understanding who I am in the autumn of my years, bridging two worlds."

Winston speaks of the physical changes and health challenges that have come with age, and how these are interwoven with the cultural nuances of being a Black Caribbean man in the United Kingdom. "Getting older brings its own set of challenges, but for those of us from the diaspora, these are compounded by our struggle to maintain our cultural identity in a land that still feels somewhat foreign," he reflects.

He recounts stories from his past, contrasting them with his current experiences. "The vibrancy of youth in the Caribbean, the struggles of adapting to life here in the UK, and now, the contemplative nature of my older years – each phase has its unique challenges." Winston's insights underline the intricacies of ageing as an older adult of colour in a multicultural society, a demographic increasingly represented yet often overlooked in mental health research (Williams et al., 2015).

"As you age, the longing for your cultural roots grows stronger, even as you become more ingrained in this society," Winston notes. "There's a sense of looking back more often, reflecting on the journey, the losses, and the gains." His words resonate with the experiences of many older adults of colour, who often face a duality of existence – living in the present while maintaining a deep connection to their cultural past (Bailey & Tribe, 2021).

This duality of existence – living in the present while maintaining a deep connection to their cultural past – is a common experience for many older adults of colour. Winston's words highlight the psychological complexity inherent in this experience. Counselling Psychologists and other mental health professionals must be sensitive to this blend of nostalgia, loss, and cultural dissonance. It is crucial for mental health professionals to validate these feelings and understand how the intensification of cultural longing can impact their mental well-being, particularly in the context of therapy and support for older adults of colour.

Winston's narrative highlights the crucial need for mental health services that are finely attuned to the unique life experiences of ageing adults of colour. "Our mental wellbeing in these later years is shaped by our lifelong experiences, our culture, and our reflections on what we've left behind and what we've gained," he emphasises. This emphasises the necessity for culturally sensitive care that genuinely acknowledges the diverse backgrounds and life stories of this population (Fernando, 2014; Tribe & Morrissey, 2020).

His story, set against the backdrop of an ageing global population, highlights the urgent need for comprehensive mental healthcare approaches.

These approaches must incorporate an understanding of the cultural and personal histories of older adults of colour to ensure services are not only accessible but also culturally relevant and responsive.

Questions to provoke thoughts:

1. In light of Winston's experiences, how can mental health services be adapted to better meet the needs of an ageing, culturally diverse population?
2. What insights can Winston's reflections on ageing and cultural identity provide for enhancing mental health support for older adults of colour?

Older adults of colour accessing mental health services

Access to mental health services for older adults of colour is a complex issue fraught with various barriers. These barriers are not merely logistical but are deeply rooted in cultural, social, and systemic factors. As the Mental Health Foundation (2016) highlights, the underrepresentation of older adults of colour in mental health service use is a significant concern. This underrepresentation stems from a multitude of factors, including cultural stigma, lack of culturally sensitive services, and historical mistrust in the healthcare system.

One of the primary barriers is cultural stigma surrounding mental health. In many communities of colour, mental health issues are often stigmatised or misunderstood, leading to reluctance in seeking help. As Fernando (2014) notes, this stigma can be particularly pronounced among older generations, who may view mental health struggles as personal weaknesses or failings. This perception can prevent them from accessing necessary care.

Another significant barrier is the absence of mental health services that exhibit cultural humility and sensitivity. These concepts involve a continuous process of learning about and respecting the diverse cultural differences and unique needs of various populations. As Bhui and Bhugra (2002) highlight, a notable number of mental health services fail to demonstrate this level of cultural awareness, consequently becoming less accessible to older adults of colour.

The deficiency in cultural humility and sensitivity within these services can result in misdiagnosis, inappropriate treatment, and a pervasive sense of alienation among these populations. Emphasising cultural humility acknowledges the fluid and evolving nature of culture and highlights the importance of mental health professionals' commitment to ongoing learning and adaptation in their practice.

Historical mistrust in the healthcare system also plays a role in hindering access to mental health services. Past experiences of racism, discrimination, and inadequate care can lead to a deep-seated mistrust among older adults of colour, as discussed by Carr (2014). This mistrust can dissuade them from seeking help even when they recognise the need for it.

The concept of 'mental health literacy,' as highlighted by the Sainsbury Centre for Mental Health (2002), plays a pivotal role in shaping access to services for older adults of colour. To tackle this issue, mental health professionals should actively engage in community outreach, enhancing the understanding and awareness of mental health issues, and the services available to these groups. This could involve organising educational sessions in community centres and places of worship, tailored to meet the cultural and linguistic needs of these communities.

Additionally, the development of accessible, culturally relevant information materials, and the effective use of digital platforms can extend the reach and impact of these initiatives. Health care providers should also incorporate mental health literacy into their patient interactions, ensuring clarity in communication, and a thorough understanding of mental health concepts. Such measures can help close the knowledge gap, facilitating timely access to mental health care, and fostering a more inclusive healthcare environment.

Questions to provoke thoughts:

1. How can mental health services be restructured to overcome the barriers faced by older adults of colour in accessing care?
2. What role can community outreach and education play in enhancing mental health literacy among older adults of colour?

The impact of culture on mental health service use

Culture profoundly shapes the landscape of mental health service use. It influences how mental health issues are perceived, articulated, and addressed, particularly among older adults of colour. These individuals often navigate the complexities of mental health within the context of their unique cultural backgrounds and experiences. As Asnaani and Hofmann (2012) elucidate, culture is a shared system of viewpoints, values, and beliefs, deeply influencing individuals' approaches to mental health. Harper (2013) further adds that the perceptions and manifestations of mental health conditions can be heavily influenced by cultural factors. This cultural influence can result in variations in how mental health issues are understood, experienced, and expressed, thereby impacting the effectiveness of mental health service delivery and utilisation.

Crossing cultural bridges: Pearl's encounter with mental health services

Pearl, a 70-year-old woman from the Black Caribbean community (Figure 13.6), eloquently describes her journey with mental health services: "In my interactions with mental health services, I often felt a disconnect. It was akin to speaking different languages, not just linguistically, but in terms of cultural understanding." Pearl's experience underscores the challenges faced by many older adults of colour in engaging with mental health services. This disconnection can lead to feelings of being misunderstood and not fully heard, as echoed in the findings of Lawrence et al. (2006).

Pearl continues, "Explaining my feelings without referencing my culture felt like omitting a part of my identity. It's not just about the words,

Figure 13.6 "Pearl"

it's about the shared cultural experiences that shape them." Her narrative resonates with the findings of Fernando (2014), highlighting the need for mental health services that are culturally sensitive and acknowledge the role of cultural identity in shaping mental health experiences.

The cultural impact on mental health services significantly influences symptom expression and perception. Harper (2013) highlights that psychological distress may manifest as physical symptoms like headaches or fatigue in some cultures, rather than typical expressions of sadness or anxiety. Tribe (2017) adds that in certain cultures, mental health symptoms might be conveyed through metaphors or spiritual terms. This cultural variation affects both diagnosis and treatment. For instance, a practitioner who understands these nuances may interpret physical symptoms as indicators of psychological distress in cultures where openly expressing mental health issues is not customary.

Similarly, in societies where mental health is intertwined with spiritual beliefs, clinicians must integrate these beliefs into their therapeutic approach. Such culturally informed practice ensures that treatment is not just clinically effective but also culturally appropriate. It enhances patient engagement and improves therapeutic outcomes by acknowledging and respecting the cultural context of symptom expression.

Questions to provoke thoughts:

1. How can mental health practitioners enhance their understanding of cultural influences on the expression and management of mental health issues among older adults of colour?
2. What steps can be taken to ensure that mental health services are not just accessible but also culturally responsive to the needs of older adults like Pearl?

The discussion of culture's impact on mental health service use is incomplete without considering the role of 'mental health literacy,' a concept that encompasses awareness and understanding of mental health issues. Older adults with migratory histories, like many in the Black Caribbean community, may face challenges in navigating mental health services due to varying levels of mental health literacy (Sainsbury Centre for Mental Health, 2002).

Cultural beliefs and perceptions regarding mental health significantly influence service utilisation among ethnic minority communities. Fernando (2004) highlights that available services are often seen as culturally insensitive, inadequate, or inappropriate by people of colour. This perception can lead to underutilisation of services, misdiagnosis, and a general reluctance to seek help, as indicated in the work of Bhugra et al. (2004).

Additionally, a scoping review by Apers et al. (2023) on interventions to improve mental health among migrants and ethnic minority groups in Europe further reinforces the importance of mental health interventions attuned to cultural sensitivities. This review emphasises the need for mental health services that are effectively tailored to meet the unique needs and cultural contexts of Black and minority ethnic communities in high-income countries. It highlights the critical role of services infused with cultural awareness in ensuring accessibility and responsiveness to these diverse populations.

In summarising, the role of culture in shaping mental health service use among older adults of colour is complex and layered. This reality demands a comprehensive and culturally attuned approach to mental health care. Mental health professionals must go beyond mere recognition of cultural differences, integrating these perspectives, and experiences into their practice. Such an approach paves the way for a more inclusive, understanding, and effective mental healthcare environment that genuinely supports older adults of colour.

Enhancing health care for older adults of colour: Bridging cultural perspectives and clinical practice

Understanding and connection

In working with older adults of colour, especially those from the UK's Black Caribbean community, health professionals must delve into a profound understanding of their unique cultural backgrounds and life experiences. As the demographic landscape becomes increasingly diverse, it is crucial

Figure 13.7 "Bridging Cultural Perspectives"

for these professionals to enhance their cross-cultural communication skills (Figure 13.7) and develop a keen sensitivity to the cultural nuances that may influence mental health care.

Empathy and respect for worldviews

Empathy goes beyond awareness of cultural differences; it involves genuinely understanding and respecting the patient's worldview. Meryl's words resonate here: "It's not just about language; it's about connecting with our hearts and our stories." Health professionals must seek to understand the cultural background and personal history of their patients, as highlighted by Sewell (2009). This understanding significantly enhances the therapeutic relationship and the healthcare environment's effectiveness.

Communication and engagement

Clear and empathetic communication is key. Winston reminds us, "It's about building trust, showing true care for our health, beliefs, values, and stories." Active listening and validating patient experiences, as emphasised by Mulvaney-Day et al. (2011), are essential for improving patient outcomes.

Incorporating cultural perspectives into care

Integrating cultural perspectives into mental health care is vital for holistic treatment. Understanding how cultural beliefs and values might influence a patient's perception of illness and treatment is crucial. George's experience highlights the importance of considering community and faith in mental health support.

Ongoing training and supervision in cultural sensitivity

It is essential for health professionals to engage in continuous training and supervision in cultural sensitivity to understand various cultural norms, health beliefs, and practices. This includes theoretical knowledge and experiential learning, addressing potential biases. Achieving a holistic understanding of cultural, historical, and personal narratives is key to shaping effective mental health care for older adults of colour. This knowledge is crucial for navigating cultural barriers in health care, as noted by Patel et al. (2000) and Tribe (2017).

Adapting therapeutic strategies with indigenous approaches

Tailoring clinical strategies to incorporate the cultural and spiritual beliefs of older adults of colour is crucial. Indigenous therapeutic approaches, rooted in the patient's cultural heritage, can resonate deeply with patients, offering a familiar context for healing. Incorporating narrative therapy, community involvement, mindfulness, or spiritual practices in therapy sessions aligns treatment with the patient's lived experience and cultural identity.

Collaboration with community leaders and groups

Partnerships with community leaders and groups are instrumental in enhancing understanding of the health needs of communities of colour. These collaborations can guide the development of targeted outreach programmes and mental health services.

Inclusive health assessments

Health assessments should consider the broader cultural and social contexts of patients' lives. Going beyond standardised questionnaires to include culturally relevant questions can provide deeper insights into the patient's cultural background, family dynamics, and community ties.

Policy advocacy and research

Clinicians should engage in policy advocacy and research to improve mental health services for older adults of colour, identifying service gaps, and amplifying community voices and experiences.

Community engagement

Active engagement with communities of colour is vital for understanding their health needs. This engagement is foundational in developing targeted interventions and services.

Integrating these strategies into clinical practice transcends improving therapeutic outcomes; it involves creating an equitable and responsive healthcare system for older adults of colour. This approach leads to improved health outcomes and a more inclusive healthcare system that values patient diversity.

Remember, adapting clinical practice to meet the unique needs of older adults of colour is crucial for providing effective and culturally sensitive health care. This approach not only benefits patients but also enriches healthcare professionals' practice by broadening their understanding and skill sets.

Grounded in Counselling Psychology, this chapter has explored the complex mental health experiences of older Black Caribbean adults in the United Kingdom. Through the powerful narratives of Meryl, George, Winston, and Pearl, we gain insight into the resilience, challenges, and often hidden struggles faced by this demographic. These stories not only shed light on individual experiences but also collectively highlights some of the common challenges encountered by older adults of colour.

References

Apers, H., Van Praag, L., Nöstlinger, C., & Agyemang, C. (2023). *Interventions to improve the mental health or mental well-being of migrants and ethnic minority groups in Europe: A scoping review. Cambridge Prisms: Global Mental Health, 10*, e23.

Asnaani, A., & Hofmann, S. G. (2012). Collaboration in multicultural therapy: Establishing strong therapeutic alliance across cultural lines. *Journal of Clinical Psychology, 68*, 187–197.

Bailey, N. V., & Tribe, R. (2020). A qualitative study to explore the help-seeking views relating to depression among older Black Caribbean adults living in the UK. *International Journal of Social Psychiatry.* https://doi.org/10.1080/09540261.2020.1761138

Bailey, N. V., & Tribe, R. (2021). Help seeking views relating to depression among older Black Caribbean adults living in the UK. In: D. Moussaoui, D. Bhugra, R. Tribe, & A. Ventriglio (Eds.), *Mental health, mental illness and migration. Mental health and illness* worldwide. Springer, Singapore.

Bhugra, D., Harding, C., & Lippett, R. (2004). Pathways into care and satisfaction with primary care for Black patients in South London. *Journal of Mental Health, 13*(2), 171–183.

Bhui, K., & Bhugra, D. (2002). Mental illness in Black and Asian ethnic minorities: Pathways to care and outcomes. *Advances in Psychiatric Treatment, 8*(1), 26–33.

Carr, S. (2014). *Social care for marginalised communities: Balancing self-organisation, micro-provision and mainstream support. Policy Paper 18.* Health Services Management.

Fernando, S. (2004). *Cultural diversity, mental health and psychiatry: The struggle against racism.* Routledge.

Fernando, S. (2014). *Mental health worldwide: Culture, globalization and development.* Springer.

Harper, D. J. (2013). On the persistence of psychiatric diagnosis: Moving beyond a zombie classification system. *Feminism & Psychology, 23*(1), 78–85.

Lawrence, V., Banerjee, S., Bhugra, D., Sangha, K., Turner, S., & Murray, J. (2006). Coping with depression in later life: A qualitative study of help-seeking in three ethnic groups. *Psychological Medicine, 36*(10), 1375–1383.

Majors, R., Carberry, K., & Ransaw, T. S. (Eds.). (2020). *The international handbook of Black community mental health.* Emerald Publishing Limited.

Mental Health Foundation. (2016). *Fundamental facts about mental health.* https://www.mentalhealth.org.uk/publications/fundamental-facts-about-mental-health-2016

Mulvaney-Day, N. E., Earl, T. R., Diaz-Linhart, Y., & Alegría, M. (2011). Preferences for relational style with mental health clinicians: A qualitative comparison of African American, Latino and non-Latino White patients. *Journal of Clinical Psychology, 67*(1), 31–44.

Office for National Statistics. (2019). *Overview of the UK population.* August 2019.

Patel, N., Bennett, E., Dennis, M., Dosanjh, N., Miller, A., Mahtani, A., & Nadirshaw, Z. (Eds.). (2000). *Clinical psychology, 'race' and culture: A training manual.* Chichester.

Sainsbury Centre for Mental Health. (2002). *Breaking the circles of fear: A review of the relationship between mental health services and African and Caribbean communities.* Sainsbury Centre for Mental Health.

Sewell, H. (2009). *Working with ethnicity, race and culture in mental health: A handbook for practitioners.* Jessica Kingsley Publishers.

Smith, J. A., Flowers, P., & Larkin, M. (2009). *Interpretative phenomenological analysis: Theory, method and research.* Sage.

Tribe, R. (2017). Ageing, ethnicity and mental health. In P. Lane, & R. Tribe (Eds.), *Anti-discriminatory practice in mental health care for older people* (pp. 69–101). Jessica Kingsley Publishers.

Tribe, R., & Morrissey, J. (2020). *The handbook of professional, ethical and research practice for psychologists, psychotherapists, counsellors, psychiatrists and social workers.* Brunner-Routledge.

United Nations, Department of Economic and Social Affairs, Population Division. (2019). *World population prospects 2019: Highlights.* ST/ESA/SER.A/423.

Williams, E. D., Tillin, T., Richards, M., Tuson, C., Chaturvedi, N., Hughes, A. D. & Stewart, R. (2015). Depressive symptoms are doubled in older British South Asian and Black Caribbean people compared with Europeans: Associations with excess co-morbidity and socioeconomic disadvantage. *Psychological Medicine, 45*(9), 1861–1871.

Social hierarchies and societal values

14

Implications for Black queer men in the UK

Andrew Stockhausen

Overview

Whilst there is an increasing evolvement in the way the media are examining the lived experiences of Queer, Trans, Black, Indigenous People of Colour (QTBIPOC) lives, there is a paucity of research on the intersectional experiences of Black Queer men (BQM). The identities of BQM are sexualised, racialised and subject to the intersecting themes of homophobia, racism and hegemonic masculinity. Using extracts from in-depth interviews with six BQM living in Britain, this chapter will look at how the principles and norms of societal structures fundamentally shape the lived experiences of being both Black and queer. The chronicling of the participants accounts reveals a multifaceted phenomenon in which institutional beliefs and societal values combine to shape the Black queer experience explicitly and implicitly. The effect of these interconnecting systems is seen in their identity negotiation, whilst they simultaneously process the subjugation that comes from holding these unique minority positions.

Introduction

"The Black homosexual is hard pressed to gain audience among his heterosexual brothers; even if he is more talented, he is inhibited by his silence or his admissions. This is what the race has depended on in being able to erase

DOI: 10.4324/9781003415244-17

homosexuality from our recorded history. The 'chosen' history. But the sacred constructions of silence are futile exercises in denial. We will not go away with our issues of sexuality. We are coming home" (Hemphill, 1992, p. 70). In his book Ceremonies, Hemphill describes the omission of BQM in the dominant discourse in the Black community, and the threat queer sexuality poses to hegemonic and heterosexist constructions of Black society.

One could argue that recent cultural shifts have led to the strongest focus ever on the lived experiences of communities who have historically been marginalised. BQM are increasingly appearing in the mediums of film and TV. Prominent portrayals like Pray Tell in the series 'Pose' and Chiron in the film 'Moonlight' have been nuanced character studies, exploring the impact on individuals living at the intersection of minority racial and sexual identities. Societal research has identified that race and sexual orientation have historically been shaped by dominant ideologies and discourse, alongside societal principles that are oppressive in nature. For this reason, BQM are a unique population, as they exist at the meeting-point of socially constructed and historically stigmatised identities.

In the United Kingdom, there is a paucity of research exploring the lived experiences of BQM. The challenges faced by this distinct group are important to understand, given the impact of the socio-psychological complexities connected to their combined identities. In this chapter, I will use extracts from interviews with six BQM, to elucidate how these individuals actively explore, and negotiate their multiply marginalised identities, whilst simultaneously processing the subjugation that comes from holding to these unique positions. By chronicling their accounts, I will show a multifaceted phenomenon in which institutional beliefs and societal values combine to shape the Black queer experience explicitly and implicitly. This is of significance to the fields of Counselling Psychology, social justice and to the Lesbian, Gay, Bisexual, Transgender, Queer + (LGBTQ+) community, as such work is rare and can contribute to an understanding of the psychosocial needs of BQM.

The misnomer of Black queer representation and the mapping of sexual identity against heterosexism

The significance of authentic representation during the currently evolving cultural and societal understanding of QTBIPOC lives is enormously important. Positive and realistic Black queer representation is a highly salient factor in the stories of the men interviewed, as it signals normalcy and acceptance of Black queer lives. When speaking about representation in their formative life-experiences, those interviewed referenced the absence of any depictions in the media that aligned with their own identities.

'Peter'

"So, there was no one on the TV that was like me. There was a lot of R&B artists and Black men that I connected to somewhat, because they were very emotional and I'm a very emotional person. But I didn't connect with them because they were not queer. I connected with their masculinity and their blackness, but I didn't connect to a queerness. So, I always felt misplaced."

Black queer representation is a misnomer in a society that communicates Black is inferior to White; that Black queerness is unnatural as it is not heteronormative and where the acquisition of social status for Black men involves heeding scripts of masculinity that run counter to Black queerness (Martin, 2021; Riggs, 1991). In consequence to this, representations of Black queerness have often been reductive and stereotypical, confining queer men to images that do not permit room to express other identities. Peter's retrospection draws attention to a discourse, which has historically drawn a boundary between two communities, one Black and male, and the other Black, male and queer. Here, male Blackness can be aligned to heteronormativity and the performance of masculinity, but not to the expression of queerness. As a result, Peter experiences what Purdue-Vaughns and Eibach (2008) call intersectional invisibility. As a person with intersectional identities, he is not fully recognised in his racial group where queerness is in opposition to heterosexism.

'Stephen' also experiences intersectional invisibility as his intersecting identities render him atypical to his constituent population. He expresses that whilst White gay men were visible, they were aligned to campness during his upbringing and were more acceptable to the masses. He understood this acceptability was not available to him:

There were no gay people on television - I mean, that's a lie, there were gay people on television, but they were camp White men who made their fortunes on being laughed at because they were gay White and camp, and I think I knew I wasn't that. I knew for certain I wasn't White, and I knew me being and acting that way certainly wouldn't be acceptable socially by other people because I was not White.

For Stephen, the depiction of homosexuality performed as effeminate Whiteness has no relationship to his own identity. Effeminate expression has not traditionally been available to Black men as a communication of their queer identity. This is because the overt form of masculinity aligned with the Black male aesthetic is founded in hegemonic masculinity. Stephen's resistance to, and rejection of effeminate expression makes sense in this context. The performativity of effeminate homosexuality is not only inapposite with a prototypical understanding of Black male identity performance, but it also carries risks of social ostracism from the Black community. To this end, racial performativity is privileged over queer performativity. Whilst they are both subjugated social identities, Black, male, racial performativity is aligned with assumptions of heteronormativity.

Johnson (2004) explains that for Black individuals who must continuously fight racial oppression, any representation of effeminate homosexuality is not only considered sabotaging but is pivotal to the politics of hegemonic Blackness. Johnson declares, "In so far as ineffectiveness is problematically sutured to femininity and homosexuality within a Black cultural politic, that privileges race over other categories of oppression, it follows that subjects accorded these attributes would be marginalised and excluded from the boundaries of Blackness" (Johnson, 2004, p. 51). This blindness to intersectionality not only prevents a population recognising forms of racial and gendered privilege, but it also stops them from appreciating the subjugation of LGBTQ+ individuals as oppressive as that faced by Black people. This can prevent Black communities from seeing BQM as members of their larger community, and from seeing the community shares interests with BQM who are multiply oppressed.

Queering Blackness and disrupting hegemonic constructions of masculinity

Whilst decreasing levels of religious commitment are consistently reported in the United Kingdom, the church retains an important role in the Black community. This is illustrated by an exponential growth in Black majority churches in the United Kingdom (Codjoe et al., 2021). This means that religious principles can strongly influence the values that Black citizens hold. Undoubtedly, there are religious spaces that are LGBTQ+ affirming.

Reverend Jide Macaulay's House of Rainbow in London provides support specifically to the queer community and people of colour. Historically, however, the Christian church has been rejective of those who are not clearly heterosexual, which is exacerbated if these queer individuals are also Black

(Robinson-Brown, 2021). Societal values relating to homosexuality and the family structure are powerfully connected to religiosity. Given that hetero-sexism is a pillar of hegemonic constructions of masculinity, this means the church can powerfully reinforce homophobia, traditional gender roles and hegemonic masculinity in Black families who strongly align with religion (Barnes & Meyer, 2012). The contributors describe their negotiation of these values within their families.

'Jackson'

"I think my mum's always been, like, you know, amazing, and I think that even though she's, obviously, got the religious kind of belief about homosexuality, she's always kind of been there for me regardless."

Jackson acknowledges his mother's remarkableness, as she powerfully disrupts her religion's heteronormative notion of sexuality, by unequivo-cally supporting her queer son. In doing so, Jackson can embody and self-identify as queer, which may liberate his mother from the institution of heteronormativity and the Christian dogmatic idea of gay as sin.

Where contributors spoke about their process of identity exploration through the context of paternal relationships, several expressed that their fathers had been overwhelmingly supportive and accepting of their gay iden-tity. In Jerome's account, his mother, who has raised him as a single parent, refuses his admission of queer identity, as if the words were never spoken. There's an argument that heteronormative ideology obliges Black individ-uals to embrace conventional ideas of sexuality, family and gender ideology, even when evidence shows the many strengths and adaptive behaviour patterns of non-traditional Black families (Balaji et al., 2012). Coming out as queer within traditional and religious families from the Black diaspora can often be seen, as Lemelle (2012) describes it, an attack on conventional gender roles and a subversion of masculine and feminine hegemonic roles. As Black gay men are already negotiating their identities to avoid margin-alisation, family support can be seen as crucial to their ontological security (Giddens, 1991). Disclosure and acceptance from the fathers of BQM are crucial. A Black queer identity by its very existence challenges Black hege-monic masculinity. As Richardson (2010) asserts, heterosexuality, homo-phobia, misogyny and the exclusion of non-White men are the foundations of hegemonic masculinity. The Black family, and specifically Black fathers' acceptance of their Black queer sons offers them more than ontological security. It is a rejection of a hegemonic masculinity paradigm that excludes non-White racial groups. Familial support and acceptance strengthen the reflexive positionalities of BQM. This allows a queering of masculinities that pushes the limitations of what is imaginable, whilst exposing the inadequacies of discursive categories of race and sexuality.

Implications for practice

Practitioners could adopt liberation psychology approaches (Martín-Baró, 1996) to support queer communities of colour. Liberation psychology uses an enfranchising approach to understanding and addressing the sociocultural structures producing oppression. Practitioners could support BQM to understand how institutional beliefs and systemic practices affect their mental health. Moreover, psychologists can provide therapeutic spaces that empower BQM to develop critical analysis skills about their oppression and engage in transformational activism (Comas-Díaz & Rivera, 2020).

Socio-structural power and the formation of identities

Whilst discussing their experience of stigma, the contributors revealed they are prone to racial and sexual stereotypes, which create complex and often contradictory expectations of how they should behave. Throughout their narratives, they detailed an unceasing and varying discourse on their racial and sexual identity. The content of these dialogues was acknowledged as contingent upon if minority groups, or hegemonic groups held the discourse. In response to being marginalised, contributors to the research made sense of their experiences either through their acceptance and internationalisation or their resistance to them or generalising from any conclusions they establish.

For example, Stephen shares his experiences of rejecting his sexuality to escape the burden of being both a sexual and racial minority:

> It was shame that I felt, because I think you know, the one thing that is a constant always in your life is you're Black. You know you're less than, you're other, you're not equal to - so you don't count. I do know that was the underlying tone in the theme of my experiences in my life, so, there was never any room for being gay. I didn't make room for that. I just - you know, I'm having a hard-enough time as it is. I can't just - not this too.

Stephen's narrative reveals an internal self-analysis, mapping how the combination of a racial and sexual identity leads to the experience of marginalisation. He expresses how a race-based society sees him as less than, elaborating how race-related stress is the theme of his life. His self-evaluations of being othered and unequal are expressions of the psychological and emotional stress from exposure to racism. Racism is a threat to Stephen's ontological security as he is routinely defined as not belonging and told he doesn't 'fit'. His identity is repetitively reshaped through language, thought, representation and interpretation. Stephen feels shame from the racist denunciations. He internalises this rejection, and in-turn rejects his own burgeoning sexuality.

Crenshaw's (1991) intersectionality theoretical framework is vital here. The theory appreciates that BQM hold multiple social identities, and that these identities interact with each other to create complex and interlocking forms of oppression. By mapping how the combination of racial and sexuality identities impact individuals, intersectionality focuses on communities like BQM, who are traditionally not studied.

As a research tool, intersectionality enables us to understand what these communities think about, by enabling groups to deeply think about how their disadvantage and/or privilege is connected to the interrelated social groups they are members of. More crucially, understanding how BQM think is essential to understanding how they make sense of themselves; how they comprehend their socio-cultural context and interpret its symbols through interaction, and how this interpretation can impact their identity negotiation. Whilst the negotiation of marginalisation derived from societal, racial and sexual stereotypes are referenced by all those interviewed, I acknowledge the men interviewed are not a monolithic representation of the Black queer community. There are unique experiences in the community, in addition to the similarities expressed herein.

Discussing his mixed ethnic heritage, David describes the separation of his racial identities as symbolically related to the separation of his parents, and how being 'raced' influences the construction of his social identity as a marginalised individual.

> Because I'm Black, gay and I'm half Hispanic, growing up, I was only ever really in tune with my Hispanic side because my parents were divorced … so, being Black always felt and seemed like a foreign part of my identity. I knew that I was Black, and I knew that being Black because it's the cover of a book, essentially people would judge me based off that cover alone. So, I knew the kind of challenges as a result and struggles I might go through.

Reflecting on a racial identity he feels remote from, with experiences of rejection from the Black community, David is asked how this distinctiveness relates to his gay identity. He describes an internal negotiation in which his identity is apprehended as three constituents, but separate parts. Acknowledging that intersectionality was an unknown concept during his formative years, he expresses having to choose and commit to either being Black, Hispanic or queer. David describes an internal journey of identity exploration and a deeper self-awareness that is informed by the gay and Black discourse communities he belongs to. What becomes clear is that he constructs an intersectional identity that is simultaneously raced and sexed, and which is shaped by his perception of the influencing circumstances of his life (Han et al., 2017).

When considering the implications of being Black and queer, contributors responses demonstrate that they are actively exploring their multiple marginalised identities, whilst simultaneously processing the subjugation that comes from holding to these identities. Stephen speaks about his process of identity exploration, through the context of the Black community's expectations of him. His account shows how he is socialised to conform to hegemonic masculinity, and the heteronormative expectations of Black manhood.

> Clearly, you know, be a man. That was never clearly defined. One, don't be gay. Being gay is weak. Being gay is feminine. You're not strong. Yeah, I think it is limiting, if I'm honest, very limiting.

Moreover, his family's shaming response to his flamboyant cousin also cemented how his queer identity could not be performed. Despite the presence of such prescriptive social norms and anti-gay stigma, Stephen eventually becomes a dancer. His identity development ensues through developing deviating attitudes and opinions from his family, which inform his life choices. He also evaluates the Black community's social norms against his own artistic ambitions and navigates repressive responses to queer identity.

As contributors of the research reflect on their identities across the contexts of their families, their racial communities and their peer groups, it becomes evident that any intentional exploration of self, across these contexts, actualises their process of self-acceptance.

'Peter' says:

"I like to go to places where I'm surrounded by other Black queer men like me, that accept me for who I am. They don't try to diminish my identity, they embrace me, uplift me, and make me feel good about myself … I associate being Black as being powerful, as being strong, as being resilient, as coming from a wealth of history … Being gay for me … it's about resistance. I guess, I'm maybe more assigned up with queerness overall, where it's about being outside of the norm, understanding that you're different and then using those differences as strengths."

'Jerome' states:

"To me personally it involves a lot of struggle as well as a lot of accomplishment and happiness. To me it means a journey and it means - I think it means growth. There's definitely this idea of transition and growing and moving and I feel quite lucky. I found myself in a place where I feel quite lucky, this thing, this burden, has become quite a wonderful part of me."

Peter and Jerome show the development of a critical consciousness about their experiences of subjugation. For Peter, this creates self-reflection on principles of queerness, and seeking his Black queer peers. This moves him closer to liberation from oppressive ideas about Blackness and queerness. Arguably, both contributors are transforming and transcending the challenges of holding a Black queer identity. Their reflections show a continuing process of integrating their multiply marginalised identities, which are embedded in social perspectives and interpersonal relationships. Jerome defines this as a transition process, where personal development is the outcome. Their emergence of a critical thinking style about oppression leads to their emancipation from ascribed ideas about the phenomena of being BQM. Their personal growth gives rise to a graspable, a knowable and an acceptable self.

Implications for practice

Practitioners could integrate the liberation psychology tenets of critical consciousness, empowerment and social justice into their work to teach resilience strategies to Black queer individuals and communities (Singh et al., 2020). Such an approach would need to consider how systemic oppression impacts queer communities. The development of self-acceptance strategies and critical consciousness would enable BQM to explore levels of oppression and identify mechanisms towards their liberation (Comas-Díaz & Rivera, 2020).

Racialised sexual ascriptions, erotic imaginings and the lens of Whiteness

Descriptions of overt and subtle forms of racialised sexual ascriptions were recounted by contributors as they navigate sexual encounters in queer social communities. Experiences of fetishisation, racial discrimination masquerading as preference and unconscious biases in attraction are recounted. Nagel (2003) suggests that these forms of racist sexual ascriptions mimic a long history of the sexual racialisation of the ethnic other, where the actual or symbolic enactment of colonial supremacy over the racial body was performed. David speaks about the impact of his positioning as a Black man on the sexual hierarchy in the gay community:

> I started to get more depressed because I was a Black man, and then that whole preferential dating piece became this cornerstone of my identity. It was like, "Oh, well, maybe I'm not going to find a boyfriend again because I keep going for White men, but those White men don't want me because I'm Black" .... All of them in one way, shape or form have all, you know, in their devaluing, you know, consciously or unconsciously, you know, were trying to have sex with us, you know, and they never date us, but they certainly fuck us, and so I found that interesting.

Recounting the emotional impact of this form of preferential dating, David describes his self-loathing and depression from racial stress, and his internalisation of the fetishisation and racism he experiences. David's experience of racial discrimination disguised as preference exemplifies McBride's (2005) assertion that race is the biggest contributing factor to sexual attraction in the 'gay marketplace of desire', establishing one's place on the sexual hierarchy. Whether this interplay occurs consciously or unconsciously, Orne (2017) declares it as a system of racial oppression that shapes partner choice to privilege White individuals and harm people of colour. Orne names this as sexual racism, which manifests itself structurally, culturally and interactionally. Sexual racism masquerading as preference has been raised by queer men of colour in many public forums, and in several studies (Robinson, 2015). These substantiations suggest racial hierarchies in the queer community are comparable to, but ultimately different to those in heterosexual societies.

With continuous exposure to discrimination, David's negotiation of the sexual hierarchy and sexual racism is complex. An internalisation of his rejection prompts a desire to wholly accept himself as a Black man with intersecting identities. This emboldens him to actively confront sexual racism by evidencing that the queer community is a micro of the larger macro society. Hence, the queer community will exhibit equally discriminatory behaviours and attitudes. Peter offers his own experiences of sexual racism in the queer community:

> I've also been met with racism in those spaces. Direct racism, as in it's either I'm ostracised by White men in these spaces, or I've been groped in these spaces. I guess I've had people just assuming that I'm going to sleep with them, just because they find me attractive. And then it becomes more about their White privilege and believing that they have access to everything and everyone and Black bodies.

Peter understands the racialised landscape of the gay marketplace of desire. He is 'raced' in these sexual encounters, evidencing that race is the principal contributor to sexual attraction, which constitutes value in the queer arena of desire. The sexual advances and ostracisation he experiences can be seen as the symbolic performance of the invasion, conquest and control over the body of the racial other. Xavi offers his response to his racialisation in the gay marketplace of desire:

> 'Xavi'
>
> "I was in a house party and then this guy was chatting me up. And he says, "Oh, Black is beautiful." And I just thought, Oh! And I said, who said it isn't? Wait, no… I said, no, relax. I'm not picking a fight. Like I said before, how would you feel if I was telling you White is beautiful?"

Each exchange is negotiated either through contributors defining themselves in respect to Whiteness; in response to the normality of Whiteness as the most desired group; or understanding that White-with-White relationships are constructed as the archetype in the queer community (McBride, 2005). What these narratives illustrate is the centrality of Whiteness in the queer community. The implications of this are that not only is queer conflated with White, but race plays a critical role in the construction of desirability (Nagel, 2003). When Whiteness is the governing concept in queer life, it constructs an environment where Whiteness is prized per se in sexual exchange (McBride, 2005). Where desirability is connected to race, and Whiteness is indorsed with high sexual capital, Blackness is ascribed as an inferior erotic capital. Reasonably, BQM will experience the wounding of racial discrimination, and the humiliation, depression and low self-esteem associated with race-related stress and sexual racism (Carter, 2007).

Sexual racism in the queer community involves not only excluding Black men as possible partners, but also choosing them as sexual companions based on racial fetishisation. When describing the expectations placed on him by queer men, Jackson notes the expectancy that he will be well endowed with a 'massive black cock'. This is a reference to the fetishistic nature of Black male sexuality and the sexual language used in reference to the Black penis. McBride (2005) reminds us of the taxonomy of size is so integrated with Blackness to describe the penis, that it's impossible to separate the two. The fetishised nature of Black male sexuality is connected to hegemonic masculinity and the construction of the problematic masculinity of the Black man, fused as it is with ideas of aggressiveness and uncontrolled hypersexuality (Ferber, 2007). Such stereotypes can lead BQM to be pigeon-holed, reducing the options available to them in the queer marketplace to a limited number of tropes. Jackson talks about how expectations of his sexual behaviour lead to its performativity:

> I suppose there was always an expectation I would be, like, you know, top, whatever, and that kind of – that was an issue, I suppose, but I kind of - I think that probably maybe that became, like, a self-fulfilling prophecy, as it were, because it was just - that was an expectation that led me down that path, I suppose.

The sexual performativity described by Jackson can be understood through Simon and Gagnon's (1986) sexual scripting theory, which clarifies the link between the construction of sexuality in respect of race. The sexuality of Black men has been created through historical racial narratives, along with shared belief systems that dictate the sexual behaviours of the racial other in opposition to the appropriate sexual behaviours of Whiteness. Jackson's negotiation of sexual stereotypes and expectations draws upon historical and racialised discourses from both Black and queer communities. In sexual encounters, Jackson must engage in role-taking and intersubjectivity, seeing the world from the other persons perspective and himself from another's perspective. He is ascribed and internalises the position of the 'top' penetrating partner, the performance of which is 'raced' along the axis of masculinity and dominance.

Implications for practice

The centrality of race in queer desire means that racialisation forms the lens through which everyone is seen. Racial preferences in sexual attraction are clearly organised around practices of devaluing or glorifying raced individuals for characteristics they don't actually have. Psychologists then could undertake valuable work on intrapsychic sexual scripting with queer communities. This would support White and queer men of colour to understand when their own scripting ties their expression of sexual desire to a societal understanding of race.

Chapter questions to provoke thoughts:

1. How might this chapter encourage reflection on your current attitudes to race and sexuality and the way you approach work with queer clients of colour?
2. How might an enhanced understanding of intersectionality theory expand your practice in any current, or future work with QTBIPOC?
3. In what ways has this chapter aided your understanding of the societal forces impacting the lives of BQM?
4. In what ways could you increase your understanding of liberation psychology approaches?
5. How might you incorporate principles from liberation psychology into any current, or future work with queer communities of colour?

References

Balaji, A. B., Oster, A. M., Viall, A. H., Heffelfinger, J. D., Mena, L. A., & Toledo, C. A. (2012). Role flexing: How community, religion, and family shape the experiences of young Black men who have sex with men. *AIDS Patient Care and STDs, 26*(12), 730–737. https://doi.org/10.1089/apc.2012.0177

Barnes, D. M., & Meyer, I. H. (2012). Religious affiliation, internalized homophobia, and mental health in lesbians, gay men, and bisexuals. *American Journal of Orthopsychiatry, 82*(4), 505–515. https://doi.org/10.1111/j.1939-0025.2012.01185.x

Carter, R. T. (2007). Racism and psychological and emotional injury. *The Counselling Psychologist, 35*(1), 13–105. https://doi.org/10.1177/0011000006292033

Codjoe, L., Barber, S., Ahuja, S., Thornicroft, G., Henderson, C., Lempp, H., & N'Danga-Koroma, J. (2021). Evidence for interventions to promote mental health and reduce stigma in Black faith communities: Systematic review. *Social Psychiatry and Psychiatric Epidemiology, 56*(6), 895–911. https://doi.org/10.1007/s00127-021-02068-y

Comas-Díaz, L., & Rivera, E. T. (2020). *Liberation psychology: Theory, method, practice, and social justice.* American Psychological Association.

Crenshaw, K. (1991). Mapping the margins: Intersectionality, identity politics, and violence against women of colour. *Stanford Law Review, 43*(6), 1241–1299. https://doi.org/10.2307/1229039

Ferber, A. L. (2007). The construction of Black masculinity: White supremacy now and then. *Journal of Sport and Social Issues, 31*(1), 11–24. https://doi.org/10.1177/0193723506296829

Giddens, A. (1991). *Modernity and self-identity: Self and society in the late modern age.* Blackwell Publishing Ltd.

Han, C., Ayala, G., Paul, J. P., & Choi, K. H. (2017). West Hollywood is not that big on anything but White people: Constructing "Gay men of colour". *The Sociological Quarterly, 58*(4), 721–737. https://doi.org/10.1080/00380253.2017.1354734

Hemphill, E. (1992). *Ceremonies: Prose and poetry.* Penguin.

Johnson, E. P. (2004). *Appropriating Blackness: Performance and the politics of authenticity* (1st ed.). Duke University Press.

Lemelle, A. J. (2012). *Black masculinity and sexual politics.* Routledge, Taylor & Francis Group.

Martin, A. L. (2021). *The generic closet: Black gayness and the black-cast sitcom.* Indiana University Press.

Martín-Baró, I. (1996). *Toward a liberation psychology.* In A. Aron & S. Corne (Eds.). *Writings for a liberation psychology essay.* Harvard University Press.

McBride, D. (2005). *Why I hate Abercrombie & Fitch: Essays on race and sexuality.* New York University Press.

Nagel, J. (2003). *Race, ethnicity, and sexuality: Intimate intersections, forbidden frontiers.* Oxford University Press.

Orne, J. (2017). *Boystown – Sex and community in Chicago.* The University of Chicago Press.

Purdue-Vaughns, V., & Eibach, R. P. (2008). Intersectional invisibility: The distinctive advantages and disadvantages of multiple subordinate-group identities. *Sex Roles, 59*(5–6), 377–391. https://doi.org/10.1007/s11199-008-9424-4

Richardson, D. (2010). Youth masculinities: Compelling male heterosexuality. *The British Journal of Sociology, 61*(4), 737–756. https://doi.org/10.1111/j.1468-4446.2010.01339.x

Riggs, M. T. (1991). Black macho revisited: Reflections of a snap! Queen. *Black American Literature Forum, 25*(2), 294–389. https://doi.org/10.2307/3041695

Robinson, B. A. (2015). Personal preference as the new racism: Gay desire and racial cleansing in cyberspace. *Sociology of Race and Ethnicity, 1*(2), 317–330. https://doi.org/10.1177/2332649214546870

Robinson-Brown, J. (2021). *Black, gay, British, Christian, queer: The church and the famine of grace.* SCM Press.

Simon, W., & Gagnon, J. H. (1986). Sexual scripts: Permanence and change. *Archives of Sexual Behaviour, 15*(2), 97–120. https://doi.org/10.1007/bf01542219

Singh, A. A., Brean'a, B., Aqil, A. R., & Thacker, F. (2020). Liberation psychology and LGBTQ+ communities: Naming colonization, uplifting resilience, and reclaiming ancient his-stories, her-stories, and t-stories. In L. Comas-Díaz & E. Torres Rivera (Eds.), *Liberation psychology: Theory, method, practice, and social justice* (pp. 207–224). Essay, American Psychological Association.

PART 4
APPROACHES IN PRACTICE

Why I developed mindfulness calligraphy enhance therapy?

15

Juan Du

Overview

This brief chapter does not focus on presenting the mindfulness calligraphy enhance therapy (MCET)[1] theories and practical techniques in depth. It is, in fact, a more sensitive personal matter, a process of evolving that has shaped me as a human being and a Counselling Psychologist. In this chapter, I share my journey of research and practice, developing the MCET approach, navigating this culturally deep and nuanced therapy approach, and working with the Chinese communities in the United Kingdom and beyond.

During my eight years of doctorate Counselling Psychology and psychotherapy training in the United Kingdom, I never had training on the therapeutic approaches that deeply reflect on culturally sensitive aspects within the community. Whether this is because the training modalities and the well-known theorists are often White, I am not sure, but I could not help wondering why that is still the case. After all, we live in a diverse society. At the early stage of developing the MCET approach, as a trainee, I experienced treading a thin line between 'artful' rebellion and fear of not complying with the establishment's theorists and modalities; that authentic thin line is the very reason I hope to convey here and to inspire the readers to unlock your own inspirations and creativities.

DOI: 10.4324/9781003415244-19

Why I developed mindfulness calligraphy enhance therapy

I feel very fortunate to have the opportunity to contribute a chapter to this important book, especially as I have been encouraged to express my opinions professionally and personally freely. Such changes always take me to a position of feeling extremely privileged.

As a child who grew up in rural China in the 1980s, I did not go through a typical education trajectory mainly because the local culture, including family, believed it was not worth investing in girls' education from high school to university. So, I left school at just 16 years old with few qualifications. Although I have since pridefully collected a few higher education certificates in my drawer a few decades later, deep down, I still feel humbled and sometimes wake up wondering how this all happened and what a journey it has been. I am grateful for that young person's strength and stubbornness when I had very few resources and social support. The life experience has also shaped me to understand that experiential learning and humility have always been wise teachers in my life, as they have shaped me immensely in my development as a person and as a therapist, including developing the process of the MCET.

My experience in the psychological services in the United Kingdom

I have long been interested in improving the psychological well-being of ethnic communities. Initially, it was due to my own experience with long-term depression. I had various therapies, including cognitive behavioural therapy (CBT), person-centred therapy, psychodynamic and integrative therapy. Although it was tremendously helpful, I have not encountered any approach with consideration of cultural sensitivity, race and diversity, or empowering traditional healing. Similarly, throughout all my professional training in psychology and psychotherapy, almost all the teaching materials came from Westernised Eurocentric models. I encountered various therapeutic modalities in theoretical learning, often focussed on Western interventions and evidence-based practice research, where most studies were also done primarily with Caucasian participants. The Asian Chinese, for example, make up almost no participants in psychotherapy theory studies, and yet we use these modalities in our practice with them.

During my five years of clinical training within three clinical placements in the National Health Service (NHS), both in primary and secondary care services, I noticed that people from ethnic communities were significantly under-represented, especially Chinese clients. I rarely saw any Chinese clients on the waiting list or accessing any of the treatments. My curiosity began with the informal investigation with other psychologists and therapists from different NHS trusts in the United Kingdom, including regions with a high-density Chinese population. Feedback from the professionals was very similar; Chinese clients are underrepresented in accessing public mental health services. This response is also consistent with research of more than 30 years indicating that Chinese people are underrepresented in primary and secondary care NHS mental health services (Li & Logan, 1999; Wong & Cochrane, 1989). As I became more aware of this phenomenon, I tried a top-down approach, such as talking to senior leaders in the NHS about this. At the time, one senior Improving Access to Psychological Therapies (IAPT) manager said to me very calmly that the service was free for everyone; if the Chinese community did not engage, it was not the services/system's problem. Although I was disappointed by this response, it also ignited my early desire to be innovative and to consider somehow culturally informed interventions for reducing race inequality in the mental health field.

At this point, the stubbornness developed in my youth pushed me to feel that there was no point in waiting for lightning to strike and that just shouting about the problems would not suffice. Instead, I wanted to work on how to fill the gap of this clinical problem. I drew my inspiration from my clinical experience as a client, my understanding of Eastern philosophy and culture, my training in mindfulness and psychotherapy, and my clinical work with Chinese clients in practice. I felt a need to use more creative approaches to improve well-being and mental health so that the community would feel a cultural familiarity that would allow them to engage with treatment.

By focussing on a cultural and historical route with knowledge of traditional healing, integrating Chinese Calligraphy made sense, as it is a well-known body and mind well-being practice in Asian and Chinese-speaking communities. I also hoped that this process might, in some way, deconstruct the Western-centric paradigms and inspire more therapists from ethnic backgrounds to think about providing culturally appropriate mental health care that suits the community's needs.

Research on the 'invisible' population

Research over the last 20 years has strongly indicated that ethnic minorities in the United Kingdom are less likely to access and receive appropriate mental health interventions and psychological talking therapy (Kovandžić et al., 2011; Memon et al., 2016; Suresh & Bhui, 2006). In particular, according to data from the National Institute for Mental Health in England (2003), Chinese clients underutilise public psychological services and have been described as an 'invisible population' in talking therapy who tend not to seek support from available psychological services (Li & Logan, 2000; Li et al., 1999).

However, this does not mean Chinese people in the United Kingdom do not experience psychological struggles. A mixed-method study of Chinese immigrants in Birmingham found that over 60% of the 113 survey participants reported symptoms of poor mental health and that 23 interviewees experienced psychological distress but did not have access to suitable psychological services (Huang & Spurgeon, 2006). Cowan (2001) also suggested that Chinese clients would benefit from linguistically and culturally competent practitioners. There are obvious obstacles to accessing services, including therapists' training and services that need help to meet clients' social, cultural, and linguistic needs (Dowrick et al., 2009; McLean et al., 2003). Some people from ethnic communities also experience discrimination from professionals (Suresh & Bhui, 2006).

It is also acknowledged that Chinese culture views psychological and physical states as closely intertwined, and in therapy, they might talk about emotions using somatic terms (Ots, 1990). Linguistically, in Chinese, there is also a strong association between body parts and emotions (Ma-Kellams, 2014). Anger (生气), for example, can be translated as 'to create' (生) energy (气), which refers to deriving energy from within the body. Therefore, a need for culturally sensitive therapies responsive to Chinese clients has been recognised (Cowan, 2001).

Decolonising in mental health research

Psychology is a discipline continuously shaped by Western cultural traditions (Marsella & Yamada, 2010). Therefore, it seems legitimate to question the appropriateness and effectiveness of Western psychotherapy models for people from different cultures, such as China (Koç & Kafa, 2019).

The psychological research landscape shows that among six American Psychological Association (APA) journals, 95% of the research published had been conducted on Americans or Europeans (Arnett, 2008). As a Counselling Psychologist, I do not view all Chinese clients as homogenous. I believe in embracing a pluralistic view, considering how diverse Chinese culture is, with 56 official ethnic groups (Hu & Zhang, 2009). I am therefore conscious that it would be problematic to adopt a mindful calligraphy-enhanced approach for all Chinese clients in the United Kingdom just because they have a Chinese background.

Drawing on surveys in the Care Quality Commission's report (2010), Yeung et al. (2012) reported that Chinese people in the United Kingdom are less likely to seek help from primary care psychological services but are more likely to face compulsory admission (67%) than the national average (47%). This is indicative of their psychologically unmet needs. In a qualitative study, Yeung et al. (2017) studied people from Chinese backgrounds with severe mental health problems, and they pointed out that due to different conceptualisations of mental health distress and the stigma attached to it, clients could apply both Western medication and traditional healing to cope with their mental health struggles. They noted family also plays a significant role in caring for relatives with mental health problems.

In another study that compared Chinese and British university students, Tang et al. (2012) found no significant difference in awareness of mental health stigma, confidence in practitioners, or seeking professional psychological help. Chinese students did, however, report significantly less interpersonal openness, especially when disclosing emotional difficulties. They suggested, therefore, that it may be appropriate to incorporate and draw on Eastern philosophy because that is something Chinese students are more familiar with (Tang et al., 2012).

Therefore, as in cross-cultural therapeutic work, we need to understand cultural humility and collaboration to offer an approach that integrates psychology and cultural elements with traditional healing that may encompass culturally familiar ways of conveying thoughts and expressions embedded in clients' historical roots.

Why Chinese calligraphy writing?

Chinese calligraphy is an ancient national art heritage and one of the vital components of Chinese culture, as well as embodied mindful practice. It can be traced from the Shang (商) and Zhou (周) periods around the 16th to 10th century BC (Kwo, 1981). Calligraphy handwriting traditionally uses a natural ink stone with water added to generate ink, which is then applied on rice paper in strokes, using a soft-tipped brush to create Chinese characters (Kao, 2010) - see Figure 15.1. Compared to regular hard-tipped pens, the Chinese calligraphy brush demands greater attention to motor control (i.e., adjustment of the movement of shoulders, the arm, the wrist and so on) and manoeuvring of the brush. It is, therefore, considered a brush meditation that can achieve relaxation and harmony of the body and the mind, which are essential for physical and psychological functioning (Davey, 1999). Chinese people's calligraphy practice often begins at school age as part of the school curriculum; calligraphy practice is also recognised as a way of

Figure 15.1 An example of a traditional four-treasure set used in MCET

achieving relaxation and harmony of the body and the mind, which is essential for physical and psychological functioning (Davey, 1999; Kao et al., 2021; Qian & Fang, 2007). Therefore, the characteristics of calligraphy writing have semiotic properties and represent Chinese culture and history in the therapy room, which was influential in the therapeutic space.

Current research on calligraphy practice for Chinese communities

As a potential psychological intervention, calligraphy practice and well-being has been studied in Asia, particularly in the neuropsychiatric and psychological fields. A prominent scholar in this field is Professor Kao from Hong Kong, whose studies have shown that practising Calligraphy can enhance cognitive abilities in older adults with Alzheimer's (Kao et al., 2000). A randomised controlled trial (RCT) in Hong Kong found that calligraphy practice had similar effects on cognitive enhancement in older adults (Kwok et al., 2011). Calligraphy practice can also improve symptoms of psychosomatic diseases (e.g., hypertension and tachycardia: Yang et al., 2010). Among stroke patients undergoing rehabilitation, calligraphy treatment can increase the strength of fine motor coordination in the affected hand (Chiu et al., 2002). Long-term calligraphic practice has been associated with better executive function and working memory in adults (Chen et al., 2017). Research on children in China with ADHD has found that calligraphy training can improve attention span and social communication (Kao et al., 1997).

These studies provide insights that indicate that Chinese calligraphy practice can increase cognitive perception and perceptual sharpening and has a physiologically relaxing effect. However, many of these studies also use conveniently administered samples, for example, university students and school pupils. The heterogeneity of participants' backgrounds and their presenting psychological issues received very little focus. Equally, no consideration was given to other variables such as participants' mental health history, how long they practised per day, or the content of their calligraphy practice.

More than 20 years of research findings follow a similar trend: practising calligraphy can improve people's cognitive, physiological and emotional well-being and therefore have a healing quality in the sense that it enhances well-being and mental capacity. However, little attention has been paid to the experiences of calligraphy practice as a meaning bridge to trace psychological engagement and changes. There is also a need for consistent protocols and designs for these studies and a complete sense of how the integrated Chinese Calligraphy practice is done within a clinical practice framework.

Mindfulness calligraphy enhanced therapy (MCET)

I developed the MCET during my eight years of doctorate training in Counselling Psychology and psychotherapy (Du, 2020). It is a four-phase model designed for between 8 and 12 sessions or more; the session and calligraphy writings can be conducted in Chinese or English, or any other language to suit the client's needs. The four phases include Encouraging and Engaging, Allowing and Containing, Relationship with Self and Others, and Review and Reflections. The therapist and client might adopt a different sequence or change the length of the therapy to suit the client's needs. The different phases may vary, with respect to the client's work on other presentations and therapeutic journeys. The model also includes breathing and grounding techniques, with mindful calligraphy practice in the client's own time. This helps to enhance their awareness, self-reflection, and intrapersonal skills, and encourages their capacity to cultivate concentration, self-growth, and compassion within themselves.

MCET also has distinctive features compared to talking therapy, such as grinding ink and mindful preparations for the calligraphy writing process. At the start of the session, both the client and therapist prepare their calligraphy set spontaneously. The therapist also uses calligraphy writing to take notes and promote equality through shared practice experience in the room. The clients can also keep their calligraphy writings.

In MCET, the therapist encourages the client to use free association and attune to embodied experiences. The calligraphy characters are explored and reflected upon, so the clients' problematic experiences are expressed not only verbally, but also through calligraphy drawings. This enhances the intrapersonal reflection and helps clients to build meaningful bridges in understanding their problems whilst allowing them to integrate their previously painful experiences, with acceptance and growth (Brinegar et al., 2006).

Gaps in the culturally sensitive intervention

As a culturally sensitive therapeutic intervention, MCET is a novel concept in Western psychology and psychotherapy. There is a volume of empirical and theoretical data which focuses on the issues of adverse outcomes of people from ethnic minority backgrounds, for example, the lack of inclusive services and equality of access to psychological care (Dowrick et al., 2009; Kovandžić et al., 2011; Memon et al., 2016; Suresh & Bhui, 2006). Despite this, very few interventions directly offer potentially culturally familiar, pragmatic, and innovative interventions to engage ethnic communities. As a diverse society, we must stimulate new thinking and creativity as an ethical imperative and continue developing theories that involve tailoring psychotherapy to specific cultural contexts (Hall, 2001).

Collaboration beyond the United Kingdom

I am honoured to contribute my research and clinical practice to support Chinese-speaking communities internationally and there is an ongoing fostering of greater collaboration between disciplines across different countries where the therapists, researchers and people within the community continue to develop and test culturally sensitive approaches to serve the Chinese community globally.

At the time of writing (November 2023), I have just finished training on MCET for the therapists from the Chinatown Services Centre (CSC) in Los Angeles, United States. The conversation was started in the early summer of 2023, when the clinical leads from CSC contacted me as they hoped to have a more culturally familiar intervention programme to train their staff and to support their local Chinese communities, especially after the tragic mass shooting in Monterey Park in January 2023, where the majority of the victims were elderly adults.

CSC found that many people in the community were diagnosed with post-traumatic stress disorder after the horrific traffic shooting and whilst they provide free, unlimited psychological services to the local community, they soon found that very few people were willing to engage in typical talking therapy. Therefore, although the trauma was visible, it was invisible in access to mental health services. CSC felt that MCET, as a culturally sensitive approach, had enormous potential to work with their community and improve their access to therapy.

The training with CSC practitioners has now been completed. We are looking forward to further research and collaboration opportunity to improve the Chinese community's well-being in the United States. I hope such collaboration will contribute to a better understanding of the cultural factors that influence the mental health field, dismantling the barriers to equity in psychological care.

Clinical recommendations and training

I wanted to show MCET examples from two clients, 'A' (Figure 15.2) and 'B' (Figure 15.3). Both were in their first MCET session. In the session with 'A', the therapy was conducted in Chinese. 'A' had never experienced therapy before; 'A' was born and grew up in China and had years of experience in practising calligraphy since they were in school. Client B's therapy was conducted in English; 'B' is British-Chinese and had had a few years of therapy with a White therapist; it was 'B's' first time engaging with calligraphy practice. The therapist who conducted this session was a bilingual Counselling Psychologist, and the two calligraphy samples were extracted from my doctorate research (Du, 2024).

Chinese characters translation for Figure 15.2:

1. Peace (therapeutic goal)
2. Don't know what to do
3. Helpless
4. Need help
5. Drawing (her mind)
6. Heavy
7. Love and protection
8. Acceptance
9. Everything will be ok
10. The moon glimmers through the pine forest (Chinese verse)
11. The spring gently jingles on the stone (Chinese verse)
12. Tolerance
13. Do not fear
14. Discovery

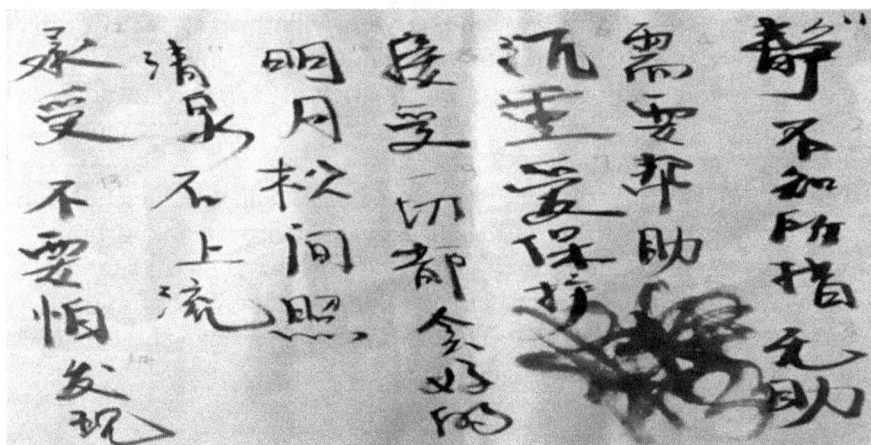

Figure 15.2 Client 'A'

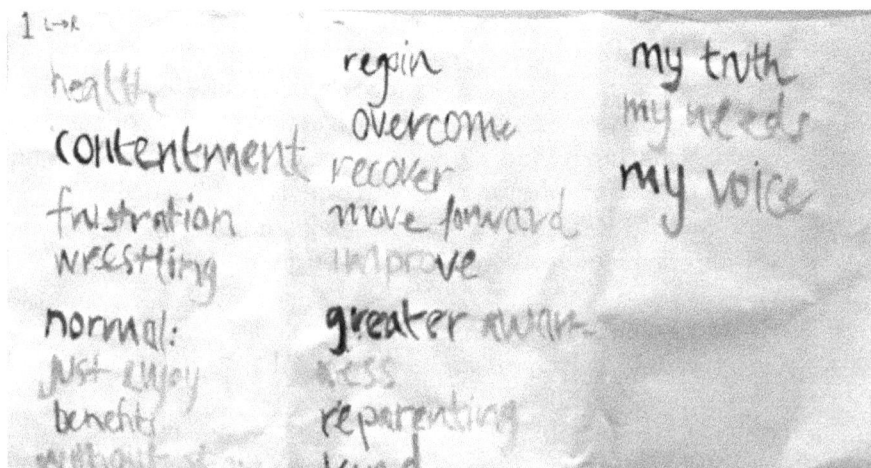

Figure 15.3 Client 'B'

For practitioners who are interested in applying MCET but whose cultural norms do not include using calligraphy practice, you can see from both samples above the experimental mindfulness calligraphy practice can be used in writing in Chinese or English, or any other language; in fact, it is best to use the language both the client and therapists are most comfortable with.

For practitioners who also want to practice and train, I would encourage them to reflect deeply on what has drawn them to this approach first. The MCET training process will take trainees on a journey from understanding the theory of the wisdom of zen brush meditation and practising the traditional Chinese calligraphy handwriting to understanding the embodied energy flow and how it can enhance the deep intrapersonal relationship in practice and therapy.

Conclusion

I am aware that the MCET approach is different from traditional talking therapy in Western psychotherapeutic tradition. Therefore, whether you are a qualified therapist or are on a training journey, I appreciate your open-mindedness to embrace the concept. I hope you have also felt the connection in the development of the MCET approach to be aligned with my Chinese cultural heritage, personal history, clinical practice, and professional training.

Developing the original MCET model has taken considerable effort and is a result of my experiential learning as well as my stubbornness and personality, which refuse to give up. I have met many inspirational people from many different cultures and races, who not only helped me through difficult times but who have also inspired me to continue working on finding my purpose in developing culturally sensitive psychological therapy and research. They continue to inspire me to shape this approach, enhance its adaptability, and give energy to my belief that the Western world needs to understand why creativity as defined within the parameters of non-Western perspectives in therapeutic interventions is essential to ensure client diversity is appropriately supported in our field.

As our world is facing so many challenges, I have those people who helped me in my mind and encourage people who could be struggling to find their path in troubled times. Whether you are a trainee, psychologist, therapist, or someone who just happened to read this chapter, we have the power and creativity to channel the collective energy in our communities. I hope we can truly embrace the complexity of race, diversity and cultural differences with authenticity in psychology. And I hope you can find the elements of inspiration that emerged in your process.

Chapter questions to provoke thoughts:

1. What is your view on the MCET approach, and what are its implications and potential impact on the Applied Psychology field?
2. As Counselling Psychologists, what can we contribute to culturally nuanced therapy approaches for our communities?

3. What are your hopes and challenges for the training and career development institutions that will support your creativity and passion for working for your diverse communities?
4. What are you seeking in your identity, cultural history and racial background to make sense as an Applied Psychologist working in contemporary society?

Note

1. Mindfulness Calligraphy Enhanced Therapy (MCET) has been a registered trademark to replace the original name Chinese Calligraphy Enhanced Therapy (CCET).

References

Arnett, J. J. (2008). The neglected 95%: Why American psychology needs to become less American. *American Psychologist*, *63*, 602–614. https://doi.org/10.1037/0003-066X.63.7.602

Brinegar, M. G., Salvi, L. M., Stiles, W. B., & Greenberg, L. S. (2006). Building a meaning bridge: Therapeutic progress from problem formulation to understanding. *Journal of Counseling Psychology*, *53*, 165–180.

Care Quality Commission. (2010). *Count me in 2009: Results of the 2009 national census of inpatients and patients on supervised community treatment in mental health and learning disability services in England and Wales*. Care Quality Commission.

Chen, W., He, Y., Gao, Y., Zhang, C., Chen, C., Bi, S., Yang, P., Wang, Y., & Wang, W. (2017). Long-term experience of Chinese calligraphic handwriting is associated with better executive functions and stronger resting-state functional connectivity in related brain regions. *PLoS ONE*, *12*(1), e0170660. https://doi.org/10.1371/journal.pone.0170660

Chiu, M. L., Kao, H. S. R., & Ho, M. Y. (2002). The efficacy of Chinese calligraphic handwriting on stroke patients: A multiple cases study. *Proceedings of the Second International Congress on Vascular Dementia, Salzburg, Austria* (pp. 207–212). Retrieved April 3, 2018, from: http://hub.hku.hk/handle/10722/109884

Cowan, C. (2001). The mental health of Chinese people in Britain: An update on current literature. *Journal of Mental Health*, *10*(5), 501–511. https://doi.org/10.1080/09638230120041263

Davey, H. E. (1999). *Brush meditation*. Stone Bridge Press.

Dowrick, C., Gask, L., & Edwards, S. (2009). Researching the mental health needs of hard-to-reach groups: Managing multiple sources of evidence. *BMC Health Services Research*, *9*, 226.

Du, J. (2020). Exploring integrating mindfulness Chinese calligraphy enhanced therapy (CCET) as a complementary psychotherapy to bridge underrepresented Chinese clients in the UK. *The British Psychological Society, Psychotherapy Section Review*, Winter (65), 84–85.

Du, J. (2024). *Chinese calligraphy enhanced therapy (CCET) as a culturally sensitive psychotherapy approach for Chinese clients in the UK – A qualitative theory building dual case study research* [Doctorate thesis]. Middlesex University & Metanoia Institute.

Hall, G. C. N. (2001). Psychotherapy research with ethnic minorities: Empirical, ethical, and conceptual issues. *Journal of Consulting and Clinical Psychology*, *69*(3), 502–510.

Huang, S. L., & Spurgeon, A. (2006). The mental health of Chinese immigrants in Birmingham, UK. *Ethnicity & Health*, *11*(4), 365–387. https://doi.org/10.1080/13557850600824161

Hu, H. B., & Zhang, L. M. (2009). Changes in ethnic identification principles and ethnic Population. Southwest University for Nationalities University Press (in Chinese).

Kao, H. S. R. (2010). 'Calligraphy therapy: A complementary approach to psychotherapy. *Asia Pacific Journal of Counselling and Psychotherapy*, *1*(1), 55–66.

Kao, H. S. R., Chen, C. C., & Chang, T. M. (1997) The effect of calligraphy practice on character recognition reaction time among children with ADHD disorder. In *Proceedings of the 55th Annual Convention of the Council of Psychologists* (pp. 45–49). Gfaz, 14–18, July, l997.

Kao, H. S. R., Gao, D. G., Wang, M. Q., Cheung, H. Y., & Chiu, J. (2000). Chinese Calligraphic handwriting: Treatment of cognitive deficiencies of Alzheimer's disease patients. *Alzheimer's Reports*, *3*(5/6), 281–287.

Kao, H. S. R., Xu, M., & Kao, T. T. (2021). Calligraphy, psychology and the Confucian literati personality. *Psychology and Developing Societies*, *33*(1), 54–72. https://doi.org/10.1177/0971333621990449

Koç, V., & Kafa, G. (2019). Cross-cultural research on psychotherapy: The need for a change. *Journal of Cross-Cultural Psychology*, *50*(1), 100–115.

Kovandžić, M., Chew-Graham, C., & Reeve, J. (2011). Access to primary mental health care for hard-to-reach groups: From 'silent suffering' to 'making it work'. *Social Science & Medicine*, *72*, 763–772.

Kwok, T.C.Y., Bai, X., Kao, H.S.R., Li, C.Y. & Ho, F.K. (2011). Cognitive effects of calligraphy therapy for older people: a randomized controlled trial in Hong Kong. *Clinical Interventions in Aging*, *6*, 269–273. https://doi.org/10.2147/CIA.S25395

Kwo, D. (1981). *Chinese Brushwork: Its history, aesthetics, and techniques*. Allanheld & Schram.

Li, P., & Logan, S. (2000). *The mental health needs of Chinese people in England: A report of a national survey*. Chinese National Healthy Living Centre.

Li, P. L., & Logan, S. (1999). *The mental health needs of Chinese people in England: A report of a national survey*. Chinese National Healthy Living Centre.

Li, P., Logan, S., Yee, L., & Ng, S. (1999). Barriers to meeting the mental health needs of the Chinese community. *Journal of Public Health Medicine*, *21*, 74–80.

Ma-Kellams, C. (2014). Cross-cultural differences in somatic awareness and interoceptive accuracy: A review of the literature and directions for future research. *Frontiers in Psychology*, *5*, 1379. https://doi.org/10.3389/fpsyg.2014.01379

Marsella, A. J., & Yamada, A. M. (2010). Culture and psychopathology: Foundations, issues, directions. *Journal of Pacific Rim Psychology*, *4*, 103–115.

McLean, C., Campbell, C., & Cornish, F. (2003). African-Caribbean Interactions with mental health services in the UK: Experiences and expectations of exclusion as (re)productive of health inequalities. *Social Science & Medicine*, *56*, 657–669.

Memon, A., Taylor, K., & Mohebati, L. M. (2016). Perceived barriers to accessing mental health services among Black and minority ethnic (BME) communities: A qualitative study in southeast England. *BMJ Open*, *6*, e012337. https://doi.org/10.1136/bmjopen-2016012337

National Institute for Mental Health in England. (2003). *Inside outside: Improving mental health services for Black and minority ethnic communities in England*. HMSO.

Ots, T. (1990). The angry liver, the anxious heart, and the melancholy spleen. *Culture Medicine and Psychiatry*, *14*, 22–58. https://doi.org/10.1007/BF00046703

Qian, Z. Z., & Fang, D. S. (2007). Towards Chinese calligraphy. *Macalester International*, *18*(1), 100–125. http://digitalcommons.macalester.edu/macintl/vol18/iss1/12

Suresh, K., & Bhui, K. (2006). Ethnic minority patients' access to mental health services. *Psychiatry, 5*, 413–416.

Tang, T., Reilly, J., & Dickson, J. M. (2012). Attitudes toward seeking professional psychological help among Chinese students at a UK university. *Counselling and Psychotherapy Research, 12*(4), 287–293.

Wong, G., & Cochrane, R. (1989). Generation and assimilation as predictors of psychological wellbeing in British Chinese. *Social Behaviour, 4*, 1–14.

Yang, X. L., Li, H. H., Hong, M. H., & Kao, H. S. R. (2010). The effects of Chinese calligraphy handwriting and relaxation training in Chinese nasopharyngeal carcinoma patients: A randomized controlled trial. *International Journal of Nursing Studies, 47*, 550–559.

Yeung, E. Y. W., Irvine, F., Ng, S. & Tsang, S. K. M. (2012). Role of social networks in the help-seeking experiences among Chinese suffering from severe mental illness in England: a qualitative study. *British Journal of Social Work, 43*(3), 486–503. https://doi.org/10.1093/bjsw/bcr199

Yeung, E. Y. W., Irvine, F., Ng, S. M., & Tsang, K. M. S. (2017). How people from Chinese backgrounds make sense of and respond to the experiences of mental distress: Thematic analysis. *Journal of Psychiatric Mental Health Nursing, 24*(8), 589–599. https://doi.org/10.1111/jpm.12406

Race and neurodiversity **16**

Understanding intersectionality and privilege – My story

Tumi Sotire

Overview

This chapter delves into the intricate intersection of race and neurodiversity, exploring the unique challenges faced by individuals navigating these intersecting identities. It begins by examining the concept of neurodiversity, emphasising the celebration of cognitive diversity and challenging stereotypes of neurodivergence as deficits. The intersection of race and neurodiversity is then explored, highlighting disparities in diagnosis, access to support services, and societal perceptions. Through personal narratives and empirical evidence, the chapter illustrates how systemic inequalities compound the challenges faced by neurodivergent individuals from marginalised racial backgrounds. The implications of these intersecting identities are examined across various sectors, including education, employment, mental health, and criminal justice, revealing a cycle of poverty, limited social mobility, and increased susceptibility to mental health challenges.

The chapter concludes by emphasising the importance of a multifaceted approach to address systemic barriers, promote inclusivity, and amplify marginalised voices. By prioritising intersectional perspectives and advocating for systemic reform, we can strive towards a more equitable and supportive environment for neurodivergent individuals across diverse racial backgrounds.

DOI: 10.4324/9781003415244-20

Introduction

"Before I even knew I was Black; I knew I had dyspraxia" is a quote I often share during my public speaking engagements. Diagnosed with dyspraxia at the age of 4, my early years were marked by challenges that set me apart from my peers. Perceiving simple tasks like participating in playground games, riding a bike, or excelling in sports seemed insurmountable due to my dyspraxia. My struggles with handwriting and reading persisted into adolescence, fuelling feelings of inadequacy and isolation. Till this day, I still find reading books difficult, thank God for audible. The stigma attached to my neurodivergence, compounded by derogatory labels like "spastic" and "retard", deeply impacted my self-esteem and mental well-being. As a teenager, I yearned to fit in and be like other Black boys I saw on TV who were athletic and had rhythm, but dyspraxia seemed to erect barriers to that aspiration. Looking back, I can see that having dyspraxia was a blessing as it forced me not to live up to the stereotypes of prominent Black men I saw in the media growing up and instead caused me to put more effort into my education. I have always taken my education very seriously.

In response to my experiences, I launched The Black Dyspraxic social media page in 2019 to raise awareness about the intersectionality of dyspraxia and other neurodivergent conditions like dyslexia, ADHD, and autism. Little did I anticipate the incredible opportunities that would arise from sharing my lived experiences. I have the honour of working with some of the world's largest companies, such as IBM and Universal Music, and charities close to my heart, like the Dyspraxia Foundation. My journey is dedicated to ensuring that individuals from similar backgrounds and with similar cognitive profiles receive the support needed to maximise their potential. In this chapter, I aim to explore the complexities of navigating the intersection of race and neurodiversity, drawing from personal experiences and empirical evidence to underscore the importance of addressing this intersection in various aspects of society.

Neurodiversity

The term "neurodiversity" is increasingly gaining traction in society and the global neurodiverse community. It represents a subset of biodiversity, emphasising the unique composition of every individual's brain. Each person possesses a distinct cognitive profile, with varying strengths and weaknesses. Neurodiversity aims to recognise inherent variation without pathologising neurodevelopmental conditions. Commonly known to be coined by sociologist Judy Singer in the late 1990s, neurodiversity seeks to categorise the population based on this natural diversity in brain function. Embracing neurodiversity enriches society by harnessing the diverse talents and perspectives stemming from these differences (Singer, 1999).

Terms like "neurodivergent" and "neurodistinct" highlight individuals whose brain functions significantly differ from society's notion of "normal". Those diagnosed with conditions such as ADHD, autism, dyslexia, or dyspraxia often identify as neurodivergent or neurodistinct (Doyle, 2020). However, the language surrounding neurodiversity is continually evolving, prompting reflection on what constitutes "normalcy". The discourse surrounding disability oscillates between the medical model, which pathologises individuals, and the social model, which highlights societal barriers as the root cause of disability. Neurodivergent individuals have a variety of strengths, famous neurodivergent individuals include Sir Richard Branson, Simone Biles, Mohammed Ali, Will Smith, Daniel Radcliffe, Whoopi Golberg, and Will I Am.

Intersectionality

Traditionally, discussions about neurodiversity have centred on White, middle-class men. However, recent years have seen a shift in awareness, acknowledging that women and minorities experience neurodivergent conditions at similar rates. Yet, the available data remains skewed due to its historical reliance on White male samples. This bias extends to diagnostic criteria, predominantly reflecting Western clinical perspectives and norms.

Moreover, societal norms frequently overlook the needs of neurodivergent individuals, resulting in misinterpretations and misunderstandings. For example, I often struggle with regulating the volume of my voice, which can lead others to perceive me as excessively loud or even aggressive. Cultural differences add another layer of complexity to this issue, as acceptable behavioural norms vary significantly across different communities. As a British-born Yoruba individual, I come from a culture known for its expressive and vocal nature.

This intersection of race and neurodiversity underscores the concept of intersectionality, coined by scholar Kimberlé Crenshaw (2017). Recognising that individuals experience multiple forms of discrimination simultaneously; Crenshaw highlights the unique challenges faced by individuals at the intersections of different social categories. While Crenshaw initially focussed on the experiences of Black women, intersectionality now encompasses a broader spectrum of identities and experiences.

Intersectionality emphasises that an individual's identity is shaped by various factors, including ethnicity, gender, geography, socioeconomic status, education, and disability. By acknowledging these intersecting identities, we gain a deeper understanding of the complex experiences' individuals navigate. Applying an intersectional lens to neurodiversity and race allows for a more nuanced examination of structural barriers and the formulation of inclusive policies and solutions.

My story

Being diagnosed with dyspraxia at a young age significantly influenced the course of my education. Upon learning about my condition, doctors informed my parents that I possessed above-average intelligence and would benefit from attending a sympathetic school. Armed with this knowledge, my parents were determined to provide me with an environment where I could thrive academically. They opted to enrol me in private schools to ensure smaller class sizes and more personalised attention. This decision was driven by their desire to avoid stigmatisation associated with special needs schools or to be statemented. These concerns are quite common with Black parents of neurodivergent individuals (Wheeler et al., 2024).

For my family, relocating from Southeast London to areas like Romford and Brentwood, Essex, was not just about finding better educational opportunities but also about ensuring adequate support for my needs. Attending schools in these environments exposed me to peers with aspirations for academic excellence, setting high standards for achievement. However, being both Nigerian and dyspraxic posed unique challenges. I struggled to excel in extracurricular activities like sports or music, where coordination played a significant role. Despite this, I discovered a talent for public speaking, though opportunities to develop this skill were limited within the school's offerings.

As a result of my dyspraxia, my handwriting was often illegible, and I struggled with literary tasks such as reading quickly and comprehending literature. Organising my workload and ensuring neat presentation of my work posed significant challenges for me. These difficulties were reflected in my school reports, where comments often highlighted my efforts but noted issues with readability and completeness. Despite my perseverance, achieving academic success was a struggle, especially considering the high expectations set by my peers and the school environment.

In my secondary school years, I faced severe bullying, which further exacerbated my self-esteem issues. The relentless pressure to excel academically, coupled with the emotional toll of being bullied, eventually took its toll on my mental well-being. In the first year of sixth form, I experienced a mental breakdown, prompting me to take time off from school. Uncertainty surrounded my future academic pursuits, and despite initial doubts, I eventually embarked on vocational training as a bookkeeper while trying to figure out what I need to do next.

During this challenging period, my parents recognised the importance of prioritising my mental health care. Concerned about the racial disparities in mental health treatment within the UK, they made the thoughtful decision to fly me to Nigeria for medical support. There, I received the necessary care and support that significantly contributed to my recovery journey. With time and divine intervention, I recovered and resumed my academic pursuits.

Recognising the intersectionality of race and neurodiversity, I acknowledge the privilege that has shaped my experiences. However, I am acutely aware of the structural barriers faced by individuals with similar backgrounds. In the following sections of this chapter, I will explore these barriers in various facets of society, including education, employment, criminal justice, and mental health. My journey serves as a testament to resilience in the face of adversity, but it also underscores the urgent need for systemic change to ensure equity and inclusion for all.

Despite facing doubts from others, I remained steadfast in my pursuit of a career in medicine, determined to defy expectations. However, my loved ones expressed concerns about my ability to pursue medicine due to the challenges posed by dyspraxia. Despite these doubts, I ultimately chose a different path, embarking on a career in health economics and applied health research.

Every neurodivergent individual needs to have that moment where they come to understand their strengths. This realisation is not only empowering but also essential for navigating the challenges posed by neurodiversity. It allows individuals to embrace their unique abilities and talents, recognising that they have much to offer despite the obstacles they may face.

For me, this moment of realisation came during my undergraduate studies. As I grappled with the challenges of dyspraxia, I began to recognise the inherent strengths that it had instilled in me. Through perseverance and determination, I discovered that I possessed resilience, visionary leadership, problem-solving skills, and strong interpersonal abilities. This understanding was transformative. It gave me the confidence to pursue my goals and chart my own path, even in the face of scepticism and doubt from others. It taught me to value myself for who I am and to embrace the unique perspective that neurodiversity affords me. I believe that every neurodivergent individual deserves to experience this moment of self-discovery and empowerment. It is a crucial step in their journey towards self-acceptance and fulfilment. By recognising and embracing their strengths, neurodivergent individuals can unlock their full potential and make meaningful contributions to the world around them.

In the following sections, I will delve into why it is imperative to address neurodiversity through an intersectional lens, particularly concerning race. By the chapter's conclusion, I aim to elucidate the importance of dismantling structural barriers using an intersectional approach, ensuring no one is left behind in our pursuit of a more inclusive society.

The intersectionality of race and neurodiversity in the education system

Reflecting on my educational journey, attending private schools undoubtedly provided me with opportunities to excel and reach my potential. However, it's essential to acknowledge that my success was not solely attributed to the school environment. Growing up in a community where academic achievement was the norm and where family members set high expectations also played a significant role. Unfortunately, this level of support and expectation is not universal for neurodivergent individuals, particularly those from marginalised communities.

A retrospective longitudinal cohort design study, drawing data from the national people database, examined 1,015,730 children residing in England who commenced state school education either in the academic years 2011–2012 or 2012–2013. These students would have undertaken their GCSE examinations during the years 2015/2016 and 2016/2017. The findings revealed significant disparities in school exclusion rates, particularly among children with special educational needs (SEN). Those with SEN were nearly three times as likely to face school exclusion, with rates soaring to 21.3%, in contrast to their peers without SEN, whose exclusion rate stood at 8.5% (Jay et al., 2023). Additionally, Black children were disproportionately affected, with an exclusion rate of 22.2%, surpassing that of White counterparts at 12.5% and Asian and mixed heritage students at 12.5% and 18.8%, respectively.

Further analysis demonstrated that students receiving SEN support were six times more prone to permanent exclusions compared to their counterparts. Similar trends were observed among pupils with SEN reports (Carroll et al., 2017). However, exclusion rates do not singularly depict educational outcomes.

A literature review conducted by the Department of Education highlighted the academic disparities among students with special needs and disabilities. In the academic year 2021/2022, only 22.5% of pupils requiring SEN support achieved grades 5 or above in English and Mathematics GCSEs, significantly lower than the 55.8% attainment rate among those without SEN support. Moreover, pupils with education, health, and care (EHC) plans fared even worse, with a mere 7.0% achieving similar grades. By age 19, only 22.5% of SEN students progressed to higher education, while a staggering 48.6% of their peers without SEN provisions did so (Department of Education, 2023).

Several factors contribute to these disparities. Firstly, there's a pervasive lack of awareness regarding neurodiversity, leading to inadequate support and accommodations for neurodivergent students within the education system. Additionally, the structural design of educational institutions often fails to cater to the diverse needs of neurodivergent individuals, hindering their ability to thrive academically. Moreover, years of austerity measures have resulted in significant underinvestment in the educational system, further exacerbating the challenges faced by neurodivergent students.

The intersection of race and neurodiversity introduces another layer of complexity to the already intricate landscape of the educational system. Disturbingly, perceptions regarding barriers to academic success reveal alarming disparities. A significant portion of young Black individuals identified racism (49%) and negative perceptions (50%) as primary obstacles hindering their educational achievements (Long et al., 2023). Reflecting on my personal experiences and the injustices in society I'm compelled to consider the compounded marginalisation experienced by Black students within our educational system.

The Black Child SEN report sheds crucial light on the hurdles faced by parents of Black or mixed Black heritage children. Concerns about stigma and the fear of labelling hinder access to SEN support, perpetuating misconceptions and biases within both communities and educational institutions. In addition to institutional barriers, implicit biases from teachers and school staff contribute significantly to the marginalisation of neurodivergent students. Misinterpretations of behaviour and unwarranted accusations of misconduct further compound the challenges faced by these individuals in accessing appropriate support and accommodations (Wheeler et al., 2024).

Access to quality education stands as a cornerstone for individual success and societal well-being, influencing employment opportunities, mental health, and social mobility. However, the evidence indicates that the current educational system falls short in adequately serving neurodivergent children, particularly those from Black and marginalised communities. By examining the experiences of Black neurodivergent individuals through an intersectional lens, we can identify systemic inequities and work towards implementing inclusive policies and practices that address the unique needs of these students.

Addressing these systemic inequities requires a multifaceted approach. Adequate funding and support for SEN provision are essential to ensure that all children receive the support they need to thrive academically. Moreover, efforts to combat implicit biases and dismantle stereotypes within educational institutions are imperative to create inclusive environments where neurodivergent students can flourish.

Ultimately, achieving educational equity for neurodivergent children necessitates a concerted effort from policymakers, educators, parents, and communities. Only through collaborative action can we create a more inclusive and supportive educational landscape where every child could succeed.

The intersectionality of race and neurodiversity employment

Employment plays a significant role in an individual's quality of life, affecting various aspects such as income, social status, mental well-being, and community contribution. However, statistics reveal that neurodivergent individuals often face challenges in the workplace compared to their non-neurodivergent counterparts.

The Buckland review (2024) illustrates this disparity, indicating that only 30% of autistic people of working age are employed, in contrast to 50% of disabled individuals and 80% of non-disabled people. Furthermore, individuals with autism experience the largest pay gap among all disability groups, earning a third less on average than their non-disabled counterparts. Research also suggests that within the first 15 months after graduation, autistic graduates are twice as likely to be unemployed compared to their non-disabled peers. Similarly, studies by Christiansen et al. (2021) and Gordon and Fabiano (2019) highlight a negative association between ADHD symptoms and educational outcomes, further contributing to employment challenges for neurodivergent individuals. The disparity in employment outcomes extends to the Black community, as evidenced by the Office of National Statistics. On average, Black employees earn £13.35 less than their White counterparts, despite possessing similar skills (Froud et al., 2023). The combination of these statistics imply that intersectional challenges faced by Black neurodivergent individuals in the workplace are due to multiple layers of marginalisation.

The Homecoming project conducted by The Diverse Creative CIC provides valuable insights into the experiences of Black neurodivergent individuals in the workforce. Through semi-structured interviews with 13 participants in the London borough of Lambeth, the project shed light on internal and external pressures faced by Black neurodivergent individuals. Many interviewees highlighted the need to work harder than their peers to achieve equivalent results, indicating the additional challenges they encounter. Moreover, participants expressed difficulties in distinguishing between the impact of their Blackness and their neurodivergence in the workplace.

These findings highlight the need for greater attention to the intersectionality of race and neurodivergence in employment research. While existing literature addresses the challenges faced by individuals with either race or neurodivergence, there is a notable lack of data on the experiences of those living at the intersection of these identities. Future research must prioritise exploring these complex dynamics to develop more inclusive workplace policies and practices.

In conclusion, the statistics and insights presented highlight the systemic barriers faced by neurodivergent individuals, particularly those belonging to marginalised communities. Addressing these disparities requires a multi-faceted approach that acknowledges and addresses the intersectional nature of discrimination and inequality in the workplace. By prioritising diversity, equity, and inclusion initiatives, organisations can create environments where all individuals, regardless of neurodivergence or race, can thrive and contribute their unique talents and perspectives.

Benefits of having an intersectional approach

The ramifications of poor education and employment outcomes extend far beyond individual lives, impacting societal well-being and exacerbating existing inequalities. Individuals who experience inadequate education and struggle to secure employment face heightened risks of poverty, limited social mobility, and mental health challenges. Research indicates that neurodivergent individuals are particularly susceptible to mental illnesses such as anxiety and depression, with a staggering 77.6% reporting struggles in maintaining mental well-being compared to their neurotypical counterparts (Houghton et al., 2018). Moreover, ethnic disparities in mental healthcare further compound the challenges faced by Black neurodivergent individuals, highlighting systemic inequities in access to essential services (Bansal et al., 2022).

Furthermore, poor educational and employment outcomes can contribute to involvement in criminal activity, perpetuating cycles of incarceration and exacerbating societal inequalities. Evidence as shown that least a third of the prison's population is thought to be neurodivergent, despite only approximately 1 in 6 individuals in the UK being neurodivergent (Commons Library UK). Factors such as lack of engagement in healthcare and educational services, particularly among those from lower socio-economic backgrounds, contribute to misdiagnoses and disproportionate representation in the criminal justice system.

These interconnected issues underscore the importance of adopting an intersectional approach to address systemic barriers faced by Black neurodivergent individuals. Positive outcomes in education serve as a catalyst for improvements in other sectors, highlighting the need for comprehensive policies that promote equity and inclusion. However, existing institutions are ill-equipped to accommodate neurodivergent individuals, necessitating a societal shift towards neuro-inclusivity.

The evidence laid out in this chapter stresses the pressing need for further research and policy interventions aimed at addressing the systemic inequities experienced by Black neurodivergent individuals. While the Black SEND Child report and the Homecoming Project report offer invaluable insights, both studies were based in south London. It is crucial to acknowledge that Black neurodivergent individuals are not a homogenous group. Therefore, our research efforts must be expansive and inclusive, capturing a diverse range of experiences across the UK and beyond.

To achieve this, we must embrace a variety of study designs, including longitudinal and cohort studies, alongside semi-structured interviews. By adopting this multifaceted approach, we can gain a more comprehensive understanding of the challenges faced by Black neurodivergent individuals and develop targeted interventions to promote equity and inclusion. This approach also allows us to quantify the realities of their experiences over time, as well as explore the interplay between different aspects of their lives and the potential impact on outcomes.

By bolstering the evidence base in this manner, we will enhance our capacity to devise effective solutions tailored to the needs of Black neurodivergent individuals. Ultimately, by expanding our understanding and addressing the unique challenges they face, we can work towards a more just and inclusive society for all.

The effect of my privilege

The disparities between the statistics presented in this chapter and my personal experience are striking, and I attribute much of it to the privileges I have been fortunate to have. I recognise that I am truly blessed and humbled by the grace of God, as my upbringing afforded me certain advantages that many individuals in society do not have.

One significant aspect of my privilege was attending a private school from primary school to Year 11. While it wasn't an elite institution like Harrow or Eton, it was still a considerable advantage. The school, owned by my local church, provided a unique environment with small class sizes and access to dedicated tutors. Academic excellence was the norm, with many of my peers achieving top grades and going on to attend prestigious universities. Witnessing the academic achievements of my cousins further normalised the pursuit of higher education for me.

Moreover, having healthcare professionals in my family, including my mother who was a pharmacist, facilitated my access to mental health services when needed. This familial support system eased my navigation of healthcare resources, ensuring timely assistance when coping with challenges. Additionally, the decision of my parents to relocate from Southeast London to Essex in the late 90s potentially had a profound impact on my life trajectory. This move may have provided access to better educational opportunities and support services, ultimately shaping my developmental journey.

Furthermore, being diagnosed with dyspraxia at the age of 4 and benefiting from early intervention services further underscored the importance of early diagnosis and support. Growing up surrounded by resources, including books about dyspraxia by experts like Professor Amanda Kirby, laid the foundation for understanding and managing my neurodivergent condition.

Reflecting on my privileges, it becomes evident that socio-economic status plays a pivotal role in determining outcomes for neurodivergent individuals, regardless of race. However, it is essential to acknowledge that my experiences may not be representative of all neurodivergent individuals, particularly those from marginalised backgrounds. While I am grateful for the privileges bestowed upon me, I recognise the need for more research to explore the intersectionality of socio-economic status and neurodivergence. Understanding the nuanced factors at play can inform targeted interventions to mitigate disparities and ensure equitable opportunities for all individuals, regardless of their neurodivergent status or socio-economic background.

In the context of intersectionality, the term was coined to elucidate the reality of experiencing multiple forms of marginalisation or discrimination simultaneously. For instance, it could entail being a Black woman or, in my case, a Black man with dyspraxia. However, the existence of this intersectionality does not negate the presence of personal privilege. Our society often tends to view privilege and barriers in binary terms, but

I believe the truth is much more nuanced than this simplistic dichotomy suggests. Everyone possesses a unique combination of lived experiences, privileges, biases, and barriers that collectively shape who they are.

Prioritising intersectionality is crucial because it ensures that no one's experiences or needs are overlooked or marginalised. By acknowledging and addressing the complexities of intersecting identities, we can work towards a more inclusive society where everyone has equitable opportunities to thrive.

Conclusion

In examining the intersection of race and neurodiversity, it becomes clear that individuals navigating these intersecting identities face unique challenges shaped by societal perceptions, systemic inequalities, and personal experiences. Throughout this chapter, we have delved into the nuanced complexities of living at the intersection of race and neurodivergence, drawing from personal narratives, empirical evidence, and scholarly research to shed light on the multifaceted nature of this intersectionality.

Firstly, we explored the concept of neurodiversity, emphasising the diversity of cognitive profiles and challenging the notion of neurodivergence as a deficit. Instead, neurodiversity celebrates the unique strengths and perspectives of individuals with neurodevelopmental differences, advocating for a more inclusive society that embraces cognitive diversity.

Next, we examined the intersectionality of race and neurodiversity, highlighting the disparities faced by individuals who navigate both identities. From disparities in diagnosis and access to support services to cultural stigmatisation and societal marginalisation, the intersection of race and neurodiversity amplifies systemic inequalities and compounds the challenges faced by neurodivergent individuals from racial minority backgrounds.

My personal narrative provided a glimpse into the lived experience of a Black neurodivergent male individual, illustrating the impact of societal perceptions, familial support systems, and access to resources on one's developmental journey. From early intervention services and educational opportunities to navigating mental health support, my story reflects the influence of privilege in shaping outcomes for neurodivergent individuals.

Moreover, we explored the implications of these intersecting identities across various sectors of society, including education, employment, mental health, and criminal justice. Poor educational and employment outcomes, exacerbated by systemic inequalities, contribute to a cycle of poverty, limited social mobility, and increased susceptibility to mental health challenges among neurodivergent individuals, particularly those from marginalised racial backgrounds. Additionally, the overrepresentation of neurodivergent individuals in the criminal justice system underscores the need for targeted interventions to address systemic barriers and ensure equitable access to support services.

Addressing the intersection of race and neurodiversity demands a comprehensive approach involving systemic reform, cultural sensitivity, and individual empowerment. It requires us to challenge entrenched societal norms, advocate for inclusive policies, and amplify the voices of marginalised communities to create a truly equitable and supportive environment for neurodivergent individuals from diverse racial backgrounds.

Critical to this endeavour is ensuring that our data collection efforts accurately reflect the rich tapestry of human experience. However, barriers to diversity in our evidence base persist. Whether due to reluctance from certain communities to engage with research or a lack of diversity within research teams and funding bodies, these factors shape the research landscape, influencing the types of studies conducted and the narratives they produce.

Therefore, we must incorporate intersectionality and equality, diversity, and inclusion from the outset of our research endeavours. This means moving beyond token gestures and superficial diversity initiatives, and instead embedding these principles into the very fabric of our research plans. Only then can we hope to uncover the full spectrum of human experience and pave the way for a more inclusive and equitable future.

Moving forward, it is imperative to prioritise intersectional perspectives in research, policymaking, and advocacy efforts to ensure that the needs of neurodivergent individuals are adequately addressed. This includes expanding access to culturally sensitive competent support services, promoting diversity and inclusion in educational and workplace settings, and combating stigma and discrimination associated with neurodivergence and race.

Ultimately, by recognising and embracing the diversity of human cognition and experience, we can create a society that values and celebrates the unique contributions of all individuals, irrespective of their neurodivergent status or racial background. Through collective action and solidarity, we can strive towards a more inclusive and equitable future for neurodivergent individuals across the globe.

Useful resources

If you would like to find out more about the experiences of Black individuals, please see the list in Table 16.1.

Table 16.1 List of useful books authored by Black neurodivergent individuals

Title	Author
Autism and Black	Kala Allen Omeiza
Black Brilliant and Dyslexia	Marcia Brissett-Bailey
Dyslexia and Me	Onyinye Udokporo
Black and Neurodiverse	Oluseyitan Ojedokun
Empowering Dyslexics	Keisha Adair
Neurotypicality and White Supremacy	R Renee

List of organisations supporting Black neurodivergent individuals:

- The Diverse Creatives CIC
- ADHD BABES
- Black SEN Mamas
- Africa Dyslexia
- One Word Africa
- The Black Dyspraxic

Call to action and chapter questions to provoke thoughts:

1. Prioritise intersectional research: How can we ensure that research on neurodiversity and race includes diverse perspectives and experiences, particularly those of marginalised communities, to inform more effective interventions and policies?
2. Promote inclusive education: What steps can educational institutions take to create more inclusive learning environments that accommodate the diverse needs of neurodivergent students from racial minority backgrounds, while addressing systemic barriers to academic success?
3. Combat stigma and discrimination: How can we challenge societal stereotypes and combat stigma and discrimination against neurodivergent individuals, particularly those from racial minority backgrounds, to foster greater acceptance and inclusion in all aspects of society?
4. Enhance access to support services: What measures can be implemented to improve access to culturally competent support services, including early intervention programs, mental health care, and employment assistance, for neurodivergent individuals from diverse racial backgrounds?

5. Empower marginalised voices: How can we amplify the voices and experiences of neurodivergent individuals from racial minority backgrounds, ensuring that their perspectives are central to decision-making processes and advocacy efforts aimed at promoting greater equity and inclusion in society?

References

Bansal, N., Karlsen, S., Sashidharan, S. P., Cohen, R., Chew-Graham, C. A., & Malpass, A. (2022). Understanding ethnic inequalities in mental healthcare in the UK: A meta-ethnography. *PLoS Medicine, 19*(12), e1004139.

Buckland, R. (2024). *The Buckland review of autism employment: Report and recommendations.* Retrieved April 3, 2024, from https://www.gov.uk/government/publications/the-buckland-review-of-autism-employment-report-and-recommendations/the-buckland-review-of-autism-employment-report-and-recommendations#foreword-by-sir-robert-buckland

Carroll, J., Bradley, L., Crawford, H., Hannant, P., Johnson, H., & Thompson, A. (2017). *SEN support: A rapid evidence assessment. Research report.* Department of Education.

Christiansen, M. S., Labriola, M., Kirkeskov, L., & Lund, T. (2021). The impact of childhood diagnosed ADHD versus controls without ADHD diagnoses on later labour market attachment—A systematic review of longitudinal studies. *Child and Adolescent Psychiatry and Mental Health, 15*(1), 34.

Crenshaw, K.W. (2017). Race, reform, and retrenchment: transformation and legitimation in antidiscrimination law. In *Law and social movements* (pp. 475–531). Routledge.

Department of Education. (2023). *Special educational needs and disability: An analysis and summary of data sources.* Retrieved April 2, 2024, from https://assets.publishing.service.gov.uk/media/64930eef103ca6001303a3a6/Special_educational_needs_and_disability_an_analysis_and_summary_of_data_sources.pdf

Doyle, N. (2020). Neurodiversity at work: A biopsychosocial model and the impact on working adults. *British Medical Bulletin, 135*(1), 108.

Froud, E., Becker, M., Mayhew, M., Amoaku, U. & Lewis, B. (2023). *Ethnicity pay gaps, UK: 2012 to 2022.* Office of National Statistics, Census 2021. https://www.ons.gov.uk/employmentandlabourmarket/peopleinwork/earningsandworkinghours/articles/ethnicitypaygapsingreatbritain/2012to2022

Gordon, C. T., & Fabiano, G. A. (2019). The transition of youth with ADHD into the workforce: Review and future directions. *Clinical Child and Family Psychology Review, 22,* 316–347.

Houghton, R., Liu, C., & Bolognani, F. (2018). Psychiatric comorbidities and psychotropic medication use in autism: A matched cohort study with ADHD and general population comparator groups in the United Kingdom. *Autism Research, 11*(12), 1690–1700.

Jay, M. A., Mc Grath-Lone, L., De Stavola, B., & Gilbert, R. (2023). Risk of school exclusion among adolescents receiving social care or special educational needs services: A whole-population administrative data cohort study. *Child Abuse & Neglect, 144,* 106325.

Long, R., Roberts, N.N., & Lewis, A.A. (2023). *Racial discrimination in schools.* House of Commons Library.

Singer, J. (1999). Why can't you be normal for once in your life? From a 'problem with no name' to a new category of disability. In M. Corker & S. French (Eds.), *Disability discourse* (pp. 59–67). Open University Press.

Wheeler, R., Agyepong, A., Benhura, C., Martin, M., & Peter, M. (2024). *Accessing special educational needs and disabilities (SEND) provision for Black and mixed Black heritage children: Lived experiences from parents and professionals living in South London.* Global Black Maternal Health. https://www.blackchildsend.com/_files/ugd/6e0914_096b4feb22b84593bf7db08f3c23ef26.pdf

Faith, religion and spirituality

17

Asuka Yamashina

Asperges me hyssopo, et mundabor:
Lavabis me, et super nivem dealbabor.

Thou shalt purge me with hyssop, and I shall be clean:
Thou shalt wash me, and I shall be whiter than snow.
Psalm 50:7. 'Miserere Mei, Deus'

Overview

The question of how race intersects with faith, religion and spirituality requires cross-cultural perspectives and conceptual exploration of historical and current divergence between Christianity and non-monotheistic spiritual traditions, as it coincides with the divide between colonial and indigenous, Western and non-Western, White and non-White, monotheistic and poly-theistic. In challenging Western bias in psychology and psychotherapy towards individual autonomy and morality dictated by Judeo-Christian God rather than human community and collective of multiple Gods, this chapter first discusses the history of racist oppression and transgression among differing religions, and secondly polytheistic psychology as a connection to mythology and its archetypes as ancestral wisdom, and principle of holistic co-existence. Thirdly, it explores the religious pluralism as integration of monotheistic and polytheistic psychical structures.

DOI: 10.4324/9781003415244-21

Introduction

It is said that the Roman Emperor Constantine, the first emperor to legalise Christianity, saw a miraculous vision before the crucial battle to take Rome in 312. A vision of a cross of light in the sky bore the Greek inscription "Εν τούτῳ νίκα" "By this sign shalt thou conquer". Conquer did Christianity since then, over the people of foreign lands under the cross, rather than to 'unite' by their choice. But what if the inscription meant to conquer the internal tyranny in one's own soul, rather than the external tyranny of a political enemy? It is my belief that every culture and every religion has a positive contribution to make to humanity, as well as a negative contribution should it try to forcefully replace another. And so are their contributions to the question of how to achieve freedom and sovereignty from the intrusion of oppressive non-self, externally and internally.

The subjective position I inhabit in exploring such a question is far from the norm in Western society, for I was born and raised in Japan, which in my view is the only country of the Global North where the monotheistic religion did not replace the pantheistic and polytheistic native religions, retaining unique religious pluralism of Shintoism, Buddhism and secularism. Japanese Jungian analyst Hayao Kawai shared words of American theologist David Miller to him: "Us Christians need to desperately know the merit of polytheism and you believers of polytheism need to desperately know the merit of monotheism" (Kawai, 2003, p. 330, my translation from Japanese). The question of what monotheism and polytheism are to learn from each other is a crucial one which demarcates the ideological and historical orientation between the global North and South, and between East and West. For historically, the universal evangelical claim of Christianity and its geopolitical competition with Islam played a significant role in its expansive drive into colonialism and racialised exploitation, oppression, slavery, massacre and conversion of non-White people who traditionally practiced earth-based polytheistic, shamanic or pantheistic religions. Historically, racial hierarchy was accompanied with religious intolerance in colonialism.

Racist underpinning and Western bias in the early psychoanalysis such as in Freud's (1913) Totem and Taboo is now widely criticised (Brickman, 2002; Morgan, 2021). However, in my view, from a cross-cultural perspective, current psychotherapeutic theory and practice still carry the bias towards individual autonomy and morality dictated by individual Abrahamic God, rather than community and religious pluralism. If so, what knowledge and awareness are needed for redressing such imbalance and practising anti-oppression and decolonisation, to truly honour the spiritual mooring of non-White minorities who have travelled to and settled in this land? And what are the majority Whites to learn from the minority other for their own spiritual belonging? Such considerations require understanding of historical, political, cultural and theological context beyond the usual purview of counselling psychology and psychotherapy.

The issues I discuss in this chapter are therefore interdisciplinary and also include highly subjective views based on my identity and experience as a person belonging to the cultural and spiritual tradition of Japan. Since minorities expressing their congruence and respect for their own minority backgrounds may be perceived as expressing their sense of superiority over the majority, I would like to preface that whenever I refer to the Japanese context of my views it is not my intention to ascribe superiority or universal value to it. I only share them as an equal fellow seeker of knowledge, neither superior nor inferior to others.

I will first discuss the history of racist oppression and transgression among differing religions and what awareness is needed to rebalance such power dynamics. Secondly, I will explore polytheistic psychology as a connection to the wisdom of mythological and archetypal ancestors as well as belonging to holism of all of Creation. Thirdly, I will explicate the possibility of religious pluralism as the integration of a monotheistic psyche and a polytheistic psyche.

Rebalancing the power and ontological differentials in religious locations

I would like to firstly introduce a concept of "religious location", a term introduced by American pastoral counsellor and Methodist minister Kathleen Greider (2019). It denotes a particular location each person inhabits relative to religion, the attitudes and positions that we embody, whether we call ourselves "religious", "not religious", "not religious but spiritual", "atheist", "humanist", "agnostic" or "disinterested" (Greider, 2019, p. 11).

> Religious location is akin to social location, our particular identities in social contexts, and personal location, the particularities of our individuality and our family and life history. Our religious is but one aspect of – and also always dynamically interacting with – our complex cultural identity as a whole, which includes all aspects of our identity, such as personality, age, sexuality, economic status, gender, ethnicity and race, nationality, and first language.

Because of this interplay of different aspects of identity, Greider argues, differences or similarities in religious locations between the therapist and the client are always at work in the therapeutic process, even when religious or spiritual issues are not explicitly mentioned. As such, therapists' religious locations may give rise to certain countertransference relative to clients' religious locations, and therapists' interventions may unconsciously promote certain values consistent with their religious locations.

I resonated with the term 'location' because it gives the sense of embodied space where not only one's different parts intersect but also the intersubjective reality that we need to co-exist and interact with others inhabiting their location around us. Whereas 'identity' is subjectively self-defined and doesn't ontologically require other's confirmation, location is associative of how one's identity changes depending on what environment we are in, as we travel through different places and different groups of people, in other words, how we are responsive to and reflective of our environment. It gives the sense of direction and distance among our web of interconnection with other people, phenomena and constructs. It also evokes the reality principle regarding the choices we make in life, that we cannot arrive at different places at the same time, entailing the gain and the loss involved in any movement.

Adding to such construct of religious location the vertical and hierarchical continuum of power and control between the polarity of superiority and inferiority, or "privilege and otherness" (Turner, 2021), the historical, sociological, economic and global domain of power difference associated with different religious identities emerges more clearly. Belief in transcendental good may accompany the belief in transcendental evil, and by attributing the transcendental evil or inferiority onto outsiders, religions and faith can turn into a destructive force and a tool of mind control, creating xenophobic and racialised hostility to outsider groups. For White and Western therapists, whether Christian or secular, history of violence and transgression in the name of Christian God needs to be considered for their own self-reflexivity. For historically, the assumed theological supremacy of Christianity equated racial supremacy of the White. It is important to be mindful that the 18th century racist ideology of biological reproduction of superiority or inferiority can be traced back to the 15th century Spanish politico-theological ideology of *limpieza de sangre*, 'purity of blood', which demarcated the privilege of 'Old Christians' from 'New Christians' whose ancestors were forced to convert from Judaism and Islam. The word *raza* ('race'), originally used for horse breeding, came to mean in mediaeval Spanish and Castilian, 'blemish' or 'defect,' and marked the New Christians of Jewish and Muslim ancestry to be discriminated, persecuted and killed during *Reconquesta* and Inquisition of the Iberian Peninsula, for heresy was assumed to be biologically hereditary (Martínez, 2008). The Inquisition in the New World extended the Spanish statue of *limpieza de sangre* as marking religious difference to include Portuguese invention of *systema de castas*, a hierarchical caste system based on skin colour gradation that discriminated and oppressed indigenous Americans, African slaves and the mixed-race (Martínez, 2008; Mörner, 1967). Such impact still affects racialised people in modernity, says Puerto Rican philosopher and decolonial theorist Nelson Maldonado-Torres, because they are seen as void of ontology, whose existence is deemed non-beings and sub-human 'Others' and therefore have been assigned "the darker side of being" (Maldonado-Torres, 2007, p. 254).

From my personal cross-cultural perspective, the use of the word "dark" in English language to describe non-White skin colour brings discomfort, since in my native Japanese the words "light" and "dark" are not used to describe skin colour. If the word "dark" is used in the description of people at all in Japanese, it rather describes internal attributes or state of pessimistic thinking, sadness and despair and has no connection to race. It appears to me a hugely problematic overlap of meaning in English, since historically to the White colonialists the racial difference conferred spiritual difference of the non-White, where light is associated with good and darkness is associated with evil, as American family therapist Kenneth V. Hardy refers as "deification of Whiteness and demonisation of Blackness" (Hardy, 2023, p. 37). In psychotherapeutic literature, the hidden or negative aspect of an attribute is often described as its "dark" or "darker" side. From a cross-cultural and cross-racial perspective, I personally prefer the use of the word "shadow" to describe such aspects.

For those who have been oppressed by the other belonging to different religions, religion and its scripture can be misused to internalise the justification of the oppression. One of the leaders of the American abolitionist movement Frederick Douglas, born enslaved and having escaped to the North around age 20 and subsequently became a preacher at African Methodist Church, argued against other abolitionists' effort to send the Bible to the slaves in the South (Callahan, 2008). His concern was that the slave-holding class used the Bible for proslavery propaganda, to justify to their slaves that enslavement was God's will, and read passages such as Ephesians 6:5: "Slaves, obey your earthly masters with respect and fear, and with sincerity of heart, just as you would obey Christ". Corruption of the religious tenets also reaches the clergy. History is replete with religious authority's silence or collusion with oppressive and genocidal governments, such as Vatican's alliance with fascist governments and its silence on holocaust (Kertzer & Benedetti, 2023). Also silent were the Shinto and Buddhist priests in Japan during World War II when Japanese military government separated hitherto syncretic Buddhism and Shintoism, and nationalised State Shintoism for war propaganda and for its "holy war" with which Japanese military committed violent oppression, massacre, rape, labour and sexual slavery in Japanese occupied Asian territories. How did this wrong turn happen for Japan leading up to and during World War II, where animistic Shinto holds everything to be sacred, and Buddhism teaches compassion and non-violence? Two atomic bombs and almost 80 years later, has Japan found its soul again? These are questions I need to be able to answer as a Japanese psychologist working with people of different races and cultures whose ancestors, or current generation, have been oppressed or are oppressors.

It has been my experience in my private practice that many East and South-East Asians, whether raised in Asia or are second or third generation of UK residents, seek my psychotherapeutic service because they expect me to understand their collectivist cultural identity, relational style, family dynamic and problems that they encounter in the Western individualistic culture. Tracing back their current difficulty to intergenerational trauma of their parents and grandparents, when issues such as familial violence and abuse, alcoholism and traumatised attachment history are mentioned, I ask such clients from former Japanese-occupied countries "Who was the oppressor outside of the home for that to have to happen in your lineage, was it the Japanese army?" If they had not named it, it is my collective responsibility as a Japanese abuser to enquire and hear the truth. Or it might be with the White American or British nationals whose ancestors were World War II prisoners of war held by the Japanese military. If it becomes apparent that the Japanese regime had a role in traumatisation of the lineage, the sense of unsafety, broken attachment bonds and dysfunctional coping strategies that they entailed, I first take a deep inbreath, then I apologise for the destruction and suffering caused by my ancestors and my nation. Then, I would ask the client about the experience and meaning of us talking about this in the current moment. It is my tradition and my personal belief that the sins of the ancestors that were not atoned must be rectified by the descendants. It is often the moment when both of us try to hold back tears and exhale a big outbreath, which marks the lightening of the traumatic burden.

Polytheism: Wisdom of mythological and archetypal ancestors belonging to the whole

Polytheistic and shamanic spirituality pervaded humanity before the birth of monotheistic religions, and typically consisted of localised worship of nature spirits, ancestor spirits, multiple major and minor deities masculine, feminine and non-gendered and practice of magic and divination. There is not enough space to give examples of different myths in this chapter, however I endeavour to summarise what I understand as main features of polytheism indicative of structures of the human psyche. In polytheism, Gods have their community, their own social relationships with each other and responsibility they share for humans through their particular specialisation. While scriptures of monotheistic religions teach human the boundaries between the God and the human, polytheistic myths mostly teach the boundaries between Gods. In polytheistic mythology, which is essentially a family drama of divine beings, the cycles of uniting and separating occur as they go through their journey of relationships and physical landscapes. In monotheism, there is one command system that goes back to the solitary Creator God who determines the difference between good and bad, and between salvation and damnation. In polytheism in contrast, the power structure and perspective are pluralistic. Many Gods have power to create, and possess capacity for their own moral judgements in their situational contexts while not claiming to be absolutely good. With such capacity of self-determination, Gods weave the story of birth, death and regeneration over many generations of divine offspring.

No one God exterminates all other Gods in polytheistic myths even when they experience conflicts. Egyptian pharaoh Akhenaten's introduction of more monotheistic Atenism, for example, did not last after his death and Egyptians reverted back to polytheistic worship of many Gods until the domination and prohibition by Christianity. Instead of supremacy and infallibility of one God, polytheistic myths rather teach the wisdom of compromise to foster co-existence. Polytheists not only venerated Gods but also Nature itself and all Creation, as well as ancestors' spirits. Collective healing rituals were led by shamans calling upon the spirits to resolve problems such as social disharmony, ill health and damage by natural disasters and brought the community cohesion as well as humility and gratitude for the interconnected web of all Creation to sustain each other. Holistic harmony of the community of the Gods was to be emulated by the community of humans, to manifest their harmony with all that is in this realm and in other realms.

What benefits does such polytheistic spiritual system have for health and organisation of human psyche? In polytheism the Divine is divided into multiple identities to reflect and distinguish certain attributes and capacity of the Divine, that in turn are encouraged to be internalised and expressed by the human, so that all of their different inherent capabilities are connected and developed. The ancestors who shaped the polytheistic pantheons by identifying and naming different Gods and their relationships taught their descendants, through their acknowledgement and praise of these Gods' function as part of the Whole, the capacity for symbolic thinking, and for accepting plurality and interconnection of truths and meaning. They also taught that life was a sequence of many encounters with the different faces of the Divine in this lifetime, not just after death in the Pure Land as told in monotheistic traditions. Moreover, many Gods and spirits can symbolise varieties of unconscious malevolent or morally ambiguous psychic contents that lie in the shadow of the conscious psyche. As such, the disavowed aspects of the Divine and of the self in such differentiated forms may be faced, transformed and integrated more easily than with more dense, unified and powerful shadow figure in monotheism as Satan or Devil, possibly allowing projection of the Shadow to others be less intense and more nuanced.

Bringing into therapeutic discussion a client's inspiration or omen from tales of their ancestors, divine, cultural or familial and identifying archetypal forces at play in them invigorates the potential of progress and breakthrough in seemingly immutable status quo of the present. Jung's Depth Psychology championed the importance of polytheistic myths for human psyche, connecting different protagonists of the myths and folklores such as Gods, heroes and monsters as multiple archetypes existent in each individual while they reflected collective archetypes shared with others. In Jung's words, "myths are first and foremost psychic phenomena that reveal the nature of the soul" (Jung, 1981, p. 6). From a 'cross-spiritual' perspective, it is important to be aware that those who belong to indigenous spirituality or shamanistic tradition would regard such archetypal energy as real beings independent of their psyche. For them, it is not imagination or metaphor but is a real ontological entity, whereas many therapists who work with archetypes regard them as mere projection of the internal psychic mechanism. Encountering and merging with ancestral spirits, power animals, elemental spirits, deities and spiritual guides for healing, guidance and charging of power, is possible in practices that accompany polytheism such as shamanic journeying, meditation and incantation of mantras where meditative altered state of consciousness allows entry into non-ordinary reality or spirit world. This might be considered in Western context as psychic ability of receiving paranormal information or psychotic symptoms, yet in such non-Western practices it is simply an activation of innate human capacity to be receptive to information beyond the five senses' confirmation. For clients who are accustomed to being aided by such disincarnate allies, the latter may accompany the psychotherapeutic work and protect such clients as they go inward and beyond.

Another significant presence which polytheistic tradition and its practice of ancestral healing can highlight is that of invisible familial ancestors who are with the client. Imagine them standing behind the client with immense attachment to their own stories of what life is about, and whispering to the client "Do as I did, and don't do what I didn't". One of the most problematic of such whispers is "You can heal only as far as I healed. You cannot leave me". Therapeutic change is possible if and when such wounded ancestors can stand aside and allow the client to hear the voice of a more resilient and healthy ancestor who says instead "I could heal despite the odds, and so can you. Start living". Such healing principle of connecting to ancestors as source of strength and wisdom is central to shamanism as well as in psychotherapeutic approaches such as systemic constellation developed by German systemic psychotherapist Bert Hellinger (Hellinger et al., 1998; Van Kampenhout, 2001). Stories of the mythical, archetypal and familial ancestors can be the source and nurturance for imaginative capacity of clients and therapists to co-create a new story of recovery, resolution and reconciliation.

Towards a union of monotheistic psyche and polytheistic psyche

Historically, monotheism and polytheism stood as irreconcilable opposites, inextricably linked to violation and even destruction of religious, political and economic sovereignty of the opposite side. For therapists and clients who explore the meaning and nature of religious pluralism, history of where their own nation, tribe, ancestors and family stood in the monotheism-polytheism dichotomy is significant. I would like to share my own exploration. Japan fostered peaceful religious pluralism since the 6th century as originally foreign Buddhism was assimilated alongside preexisting Shinto faith, which is the polytheistic and animistic tradition of worship of spirits of nature and ancestors, divine and human, expressed as Kami (神) so numerous that are often addressed collectively as "Yaorozu-no-Kami", "The eight hundred myriad Gods". With Buddhism came not only the worship of Gautama Buddha but also many Bodhisattvas (仏 Hotoke) that were heavily influenced by the Hindu pantheon as well as Chinese folk Gods. The early Japanese were practically and imaginatively tolerant of the initial inconsistency of the two groups of sacred beings. Identities of Kami and Hotoke became interrelated over time to the extent the question of superiority or inferiority didn't arise between the two in people's faith. Both religions were equally the instrument that promoted peace and order of the nation. The Japanese polytheistic psyche, then and now, simply regards that the more sacred beings who purify, consecrate and protect the nation and people there are the better.

Such pluralism was not possible however with Christianity which first arrived with the Jesuit missionaries in 1549. I quote statements of my cultural ancestor Hideyoshi Toyotomi, the 'unifier' ruler of Japan, to the Portuguese conquistadors after his 1587 edicts to expel Christian missionaries:

> *Kami* and *hotoke* are none other than the Lords of Japan, who, by their victories and exploits deserve to be worshipped as true *kami* by the people.—The law preached by the Fathers, being so opposed to *kami* and *hotoke* of Japan, is for this reason opposed to the Lords of Japan: although it may be good for other countries, it is not good for Japan.
> (Boscaro, 1973, p. 220)

Toyotomi's belief that Japan was the 'Land of the Gods' however did not dissuade Catholic conquistadors from claiming supremacy and universality of Christian God as they considered Shinto as motivated by the Devil. In 1969 Japan entered a period of national isolation by terminating all trades with foreign nations except China and non-evangelical Netherlands which lasted for approximately 200 years until the arrival of the US military ships. This drastic separation presumably enabled Japan to defend itself from Western imperial conquest, unlike the Philippines which was colonised by Spain and unlike China which was paralysed by the British opium trade. This is the history of my people, the history which also includes the hubris and fallibility of losing its polytheistic soul in the 20th century westernisation and invading other 'Land of Gods' as did Emperor Constantine. For those oppressed and massacred in the World War II, the Japanese military was devil incarnate indeed, as the conquistadors had regarded them to be.

My own view on religious pluralism given historical experience of my nation, my personal history and appreciation of different cultures and religions, is that I would eschew assumption of correctness of certain religion over the others, and also essentialist unified system such as the framework of universal integration or perennial philosophy. The religious pluralism that I prefer is not convergence of streams that loses the distinct quality of the water from different springs, but rather a tapestry in which different coloured threads are combined to create patterns and colours but not losing its own hue. Otherwise, I fear that the most strident and over-entitled of the majority views would overtake such a system in its quest after the 'purity of spiritual wisdom'. In my view, spiritual heritage of the land and ancestors, before and after any dislocation and conversion that happened in the lineage, and how different faiths are syncretised or remain distinct, all contribute to the unique location each individual stands in time and space. Spiritual and mystical experience can be both localised and universal, and my contention is that it is about time humankind experiences both monotheism and polytheism as metaphor of the human need for simultaneously belonging to an exclusive relationship with an individual and to collective relationships within a community.

Take for example, one of the most famous commandments in the Bible, Mark 12:31 "Love your neighbour as yourself". Even if everyone was unified in agreement that this is Truth, what it means for each of them would be different and therefore its meaning is pluralistic. And it is pluralistic internally also, in each individual's psyche, since such a statement divides oneself into parts that yearn to love oneself and other parts that are afraid to love oneself, and anything in between. Loving oneself is exactly what is so hard to do. What was the kind of love one ever received? What is the kind of love which one is able to give to oneself and the other? The divided parts of the self emerge to give different answers. In polytheistic metaphor, each of such divided parts is equally 'divine' in its potential capacity to create future action and lead other parts. It is worth exploring in psychotherapy therefore, what was said in the 'myths' and 'commandments' of the family, community, race, religion and nation and multiplicity of its meaning. In so doing, the aim is to uncover parts of the self that is in the shadow of conscious understanding, such as the pain of not having experienced the perfect love, one's capacity to do harm to others, so that there would be no confusion of one's decisions and choices with infallibility of the monotheistic God.

American theologian David Miller (1975) put forth the thesis that pluralistic psyche and societal structure still remained in the Western society, even after the long history of monotheism, and polytheistic views needed to be revived since:

> Polytheism is not a historical or an academic matter. It is a feeling for the deep, abiding, urgent, and exciting tension that arises when, with a radical experience of the plurality of both social and psychological life, one discovers that a single story, a monovalent logic, a rigid theology, and a confining morality are not adequate to help in understanding the nature of real meaning.
>
> (p. 11)

Let us ponder then, if the White British rediscovered the Celtic myths rather than Greco-Roman myths or Shakespeare as currently accustomed to, and the Black British rediscovered the myths of their African ancestors, what influence would it have to their understanding of themselves and the world? What would happen if more people participated in Paganism, Druidry and Wicca that have been revived in the United Kingdom, to reclaim the practices, healing arts and wisdom of this land dispossessed by Christianity? It is up to each individual to discover ancestral gifts and how to synthesise them with their current faith. Psychotherapeutic practitioners must be open to learning with and from the clients of different races and cultures their songs and tales of ancient times, and witness them reclaim the coherence, complexity and balance of the psyche, with dignity and sovereignty.

Conclusion

This chapter presented cross-cultural perspectives on intersectionality of race, faith, spirituality and religion to counter the Western bias in the dominant academic discourse, which is structured on the primacy of individual self and individual God as opposed to collective selves and collective Gods. It explored the division between monotheism and polytheism and how it manifested in the history of colonialism, war and racial oppression. It suggested the possible form of religious pluralism to bridge the two, and how it manifests in the human psyche and in therapeutic contexts, from my subjective position of a Japanese Counselling Psychologist practising in the United Kingdom. It discussed how the connection to ancestors – familial, cultural, mythological and archetypal – can be empowering and nurturing of one's essence, illuminating the path forward. Exploring the source of one's being as well as the ground where one currently stands, therapeutic encounter can be a soulful meeting beyond mere tolerance or appeasement of differences. I look forward to hearing and learning from other psychologists and psychotherapists, monotheistic, polytheistic or secular, of their unique discoveries of how that happens, with the hope of weaving together a new story of collective repair and healing.

Chapter questions to provoke thoughts:

1. How do you understand your own 'religious location', your views and attitudes that you have relative to religion and how does it interact with your racial identity?
2. What are your experiences of transference and countertransference with clients who have different racial, cultural, or religious background from you?
3. What is your view on religious pluralism, in particular, any conflict or complementarity between monotheistic religion and non-monotheistic religion?

4. What is your view on Christianity's role in transgression and violence of colonialism, and how does it stand at the current time?
5. What can be the psychological usefulness in discussing mythology?

References

Boscaro, A. (1973). Toyotomi Hideyoshi and the 1587 edicts against Christianity. *Orients Extremus, 20*(2), 219–241.

Brickman, C. (2002). Primitivity, race, and religion in psychoanalysis. *The Journal of Religion, 82*(1), 53–74.

Callahan, A. D. (2008). *The talking book: African Americans and the bible*. Yale University Press.

Freud, S. (1913/2001). *Totem and taboo: Some points of agreement between the mental lives of savages and neurotics*. Routledge.

Greider, K. J. (2019). Religious location and counseling: Engaging diversity and difference in views of religion. In J. L. Snodgrass (Ed.), *Navigating religious difference in spiritual care and counseling: Essays in honor of Kathleen J. Greider* (pp. 11–43). Claremont Press.

Hardy, K. (2023). *Racial trauma: Clinical strategies and techniques for healing invisible wounds*. WW Norton & Co.

Hellinger, B., Weber, B., & Beaumont, H. (1998). *Love's hidden symmetry: What makes love work in relationships*. Zeig, Tucker & Co.

Jung, C. G. (1969/1981). *The archetypes and the collective unconscious (Collected works of C.G. Jung vol.9 part 1)*. Princeton University Press.

Kawai, H. (2003). 神話と日本人の心。岩波書店

Kertzer, D. I., & Benedetti, R. (2023). Jews as non-Aryans: The Vatican's ambivalent embrace of fascist Italy's racialization of Jews. *Journal of Contemporary History, 58*(2), 247–266.

Maldonado-Torres, N. (2007). On the coloniality of being. *Cultural Studies, 21*(2), 240–270.

Martínez, M. E. (2008). *Genealogical fictions: Limpieza de Sangre, religion, and gender in colonial Mexico*. Stanford University Press.

Miller, D. (1975). *The new polytheism*. Harper and Row.

Morgan, H. (2021). *The work of Whiteness: A psychoanalytic perspective*. Routledge.

Mörner, M. (1967). *Race mixture in the history of Latin America*. Little, Brown and Company.

Turner, D. (2021). *Intersections of privilege and otherness in counselling and psychotherapy*. Routledge.

Van Kampenhout, D. (2001). *Images of the soul: The workings of the soul in Shamanic rituals and family constellations*. Carl-Auer-Systeme Verlag und Verlagsbuchhandlung GmbH.

Postscript

Word-work is sublime, because it is generative; it makes meaning that secures our difference, our human difference – the way in which we are like no other life.

We die. That may be the meaning of life. But we do language. That may be the measure of our lives.

–(Toni Morrison, Nobel Laureate speech)

Language, narratives, accounts, stories and knowledge afford us the opportunity to Reimagine. Re appraise. Deconstruct. Re-learn and express ideas which can be consumed from different standpoints and perspectives. As suggested by Toni Morrison's speech above, we have in our arsenal the choice to choose the words and knowledge we consume and the ones we do not. As far as is possible, we can also choose what we do with these words we absorb and internalise.

As this book was taking form, one pertinent hope was that whoever choses to engage with it might experience it as an ongoing resource, taking something different from it each time. As a practitioner, how can you reframe supervision as an anti-racist tool? As someone with lived experience, is there reframed meaning-making to be found in the musings within these chapters? As a student, how might your sense of your influence and impact shift as you engage with these narratives about race? As an interested reader, what positioning and lens are you bringing to this exploration of race, and how does this impact what you see?

In keeping with the ethos of the book, we pose some final reflective questions, to prompt (re)thinking and to re-emphasise the notion that the learning process is ongoing. Whilst one can harness acquired knowledge and experience concurrently, there can also be space to re-imagine our engagement with race and psychology.

- Some of the content may be familiar. If it is, can you engage with it from where you are now? Is there a different lens you might employ to challenge thinking and practice?
- Some of what you read might be new to you. What can you do with this novel information? Can you absorb, apply and share these insights?
- Parts of this book might resonate. In this regard, perhaps it allows you or others to feel seen.
- Different feelings might be triggered. What does this give rise to within you?
- What do race, racialised experiences, and racial positionings mean to you now?
- What meaningful action might you now take following your consumption of these chapters?
- We hope that the chapters in this book both raise and interrogate awareness, in addition to liberating us from engaging with race from a singular standpoint. Thank you for reading.

Index

Note: Italicized page references refer to the figures, **Bold** references refer to tables and page references with "n" refer to endnotes.

For Product Safety Concerns and Information please contact our EU
representative GPSR@taylorandfrancis.com
Taylor & Francis Verlag GmbH, Kaufingerstraße 24, 80331 München, Germany